Martin J. Buss
The Prophetic Word of Hosea

Martin J. Buss

The Prophetic Word of Hosea

A Morphological Study

Verlag Alfred Töpelmann

Berlin 1969

Beihefte zur Zeitschrift für die alttestamentliche Wissenschaft

Herausgegeben von Georg Fohrer

111

To
Millar Burrows

Preface

The present study grew out of a seminar on Hosea led by Millar Burrows. To him, as one inspiring scholarship, it is dedicated. In an earlier form, it was presented to Yale University in 1958 as a Ph. D. dissertation in religion. That form was microfilmed later by Dissertation Abstracts; it contains a history of form criticism, especially on the prophets, here omitted. Professors B. Davie Napier, Marvin Pope, and (by letter) Gerhard von Rad stimulated it with helpful suggestions.

The revision of the dissertation for publication was aided by a grant from the American Council of Learned Societies in 1964/65, as part of a more comprehensive study of literary analysis. It involved a stay at the Center for Advanced Studies of Wesleyan University, in Middletown, Conn.; during that time Professor Brevard S. Childs at nearby Yale graciously read and commented on part of the manuscript. The research fund of Emory University has covered expenses of typing and of some traveling. The major area of revision has been in the final chapter, since the data of Hosea, inherently and in a comparative view, appeared to force or facilitate a development in the writer's theological perspective. To aid a theological discussion, the needs of the general reader have been kept in mind in the presentation, even though the Old Testament specialist is primarily addressed.

I am grateful to Professor Dr. Georg Fohrer for the inclusion of the study in the Beihefte to ZAW. My wife deserves thanks for her careful editing.

Abbreviations

AfO	Archiv für Orientforschung
AJSL	American Journal of Semitic Languages and Literatures
ANET	Ancient Near Eastern Texts Relating to the Old Testament, ed. J. B. Pritchard, 1955²
AOT	Altorientalische Texte zum Alten Testament, ed. H. Gressmann, 1926²
BZ	Biblische Zeitschrift
CBQ	Catholic Biblical Quarterly
C. H.	Codex Hammurabi
DA	Dissertation Abstracts
EvTh	Evangelische Theologie
ExpT	Expository Times
HTR	Harvard Theological Review
HUCA	Hebrew Union College Annual
IDB	Interpreter's Dictionary of the Bible
JAOS	Journal of the American Oriental Society
JBL	Journal of Biblical Literature
JBR	Journal of Bible and Religion
JNES	Journal of Near Eastern Studies
JPOS	Journal of the Palestine Oriental Society
JQR	Jewish Quarterly Review
JTS	Journal of Theological Studies
KuD	Kerygma und Dogma
LXX	Septuagint
MGWJ	Monatsschrift für Geschichte und Wissenschaft des Judentums
MSS	Manuscripts
MT	Masoretic Text
NKZ	Neue kirchliche Zeitschrift
Norsk TT	Norsk Teologisk Tidsskrift
OS	Oudtestamentische Studiën
RB	Revue Biblique
RGG	Die Religion in Geschichte und Gegenwart
RHPR	Revue d'Histoire et de Philosophie Religieuses
SVT	Supplements to Vetus Testamentum
TL	Theologische Literaturzeitung
TR	Theologische Rundschau
TZ	Theologische Zeitschrift
TWNT	Theologisches Wörterbuch zum Neuen Testament, ed. G. Kittel
VT	Vetus Testamentum
WuD	Wort und Dienst

WZ, G.-s.	Wissenschaftliche Zeitschrift, Gesellschafts- und sprachwissenschaftliche Reihe
ZA	Zeitschrift für Assyriologie
ZAW	Zeitschrift für die alttestamentliche Wissenschaft
ZDMG	Zeitschrift der Deutschen Morgenländischen Gesellschaft
ZEE	Zeitschrift für evangelische Ethik
ZS	Zeitschrift für Semitistik
ZTK	Zeitschrift für Theologie und Kirche

Bibliography

The following commentaries and studies of Hosea are cited only by the author's last name without title; for other monographs by the same writer, regular data are given.

Brown, S. L., The Book of Hosea, 1932

Bruno, A., Das Buch der Zwölf, 1957

Deissler, A., Les petits prophètes, part I (La Sainte Bible, ed. L. Pirot and A. Clamer), 1961

Duhm, B., The Twelve Prophets, 1912 (German, 1910)

Good, E. M., The Composition of Hosea, Svensk Exegetisk Årsbok 31 (1966), 21—63

Gressmann, H., Die älteste Geschichtsschreibung und Prophetie Israels, 1921² (the first edition, 1910, is cited by title for its form-critical introduction)

Guthe, H., Der Prophet Hosea, in E. Kautzsch, Die Heilige Schrift des Alten Testaments, II 1923⁴, 1—23

Harper, W. R., A Critical and Exegetical Commentary on Amos and Hosea, 1905

Jacob, E. (with C. Keller and S. Amsler), Osée, Joël, Amos, Abdias, Jonas, 1965

Keil, C. F., Biblischer Commentar über die zwölf kleinen Propheten, 1866

Kraeling, E. G., Commentary on the Prophets, II 1966

Lindblom, J., Hosea literarisch untersucht, 1928

Lippl, J., Die zwölf kleinen Propheten, I 1937

Marti, K., Das Dodekapropheton, 1904

Mauchline, J., Hosea, The Interpreter's Bible, VI 1956, 553—725

Mowinckel, S. (with S. Michelet and N. Messel), Det Gamle Testamentet, III: De senere profeter, 1944

Nowack, W., Die kleinen Propheten, 1922³

Nyberg, H. S., Studien zum Hoseabuche, 1935

Procksch, O., Die kleinen prophetischen Schriften vor dem Exil, 1910

Rinaldi, P. G., I profeti minori, II 1960

Robinson, T. H., Die zwölf kleinen Propheten, I 1938 (1954²)

Rudolph, W., Hosea, 1966

Sellin, E., Das Zwölfprophetenbuch, 1929²

Smith, G. A., The Book of the Twelve Prophets, I 1928

Tur-Sinai, N. H., Die Heilige Schrift, 4 vols., with philological Beilage zum Schlußband, 1954 (cf. his The Book of Job, 1957, index)

Ward, James M., Hosea, A Theological Commentary, 1966

Weiser, A., Das Buch der zwölf kleinen Propheten, 1949

Wellhausen, J., Die kleinen Propheten, 1898³

Wolff, H. W., Hosea, 1965² (page numbers are virtually the same as in the first edition, 1957—61)

The following works by more than one author are cited simply with last names connected by hyphen:

Brown, F.; Driver, S. R.; Briggs, C., Hebrew and English Lexicon of the Old Testament, 1907 (reissued 1952)

Falkenstein, A.; Soden, W. von, Sumerische und Akkadische Hymnen und Gebete, 1953

Gesenius' Hebrew Grammar, ed. E. Kautzsch (English ed., A. E. Cowley), 1910

Gunkel, H., Einleitung in die Psalmen, completed by J. Begrich, 1928—33

Table of Contents

Chapter I: Introduction

I. FORM CRITICISM AND MORPHOLOGICAL METHOD

The present work stands simultaneously within the form-critical tradition stemming from H. Gunkel and within general anthropological studies. Gunkel summarized his method succinctly by stating the following thesis: A literary type or genre is characterized by 1) its "thoughts and moods," 2) its "form-language," including vocabulary, grammatical and expressive peculiarities, and other aspects of style, and 3) a "life-situation" *(Sitz im Leben)* out of which it grows[1].

The concept of a life-situation refers not to a historical occasion, but to a structural element in a society (an "institution"). In this respect, Gunkel's approach parallels a widespread interest since about the year 1900 in structure or function rather than in history. Thus, for instance, in anthropology, functional and structural approaches were developed in addition to the older historical ones.

A morphological approach, as here defined, differs somewhat from Gunkel's pattern by not limiting itself to an analysis of genres and by dealing freely with any form of verbal patterns and also with stylistic tendencies which may not be absolutely rigorous or may cut across other aspects of classification. It consciously relates the element of the sociological life-situation to a conception of human existence developed in cooperation with other disciplines — such as the social sciences, criticism (as in the humanities), systematic theology, and philosophy. It tends to take the concept of "institution" in the broad sense, now widely employed in sociology, for a structural aspect of culture which may receive varying concrete embodiments. It develops in reference to Gunkel's three aspects a fourth one, that of rationale *(raison d'être)*, interrelating the other three or any two of these with each other, to reach "insight" *(Verstehen)*. These points are not altogether new, but are deliberately embraced[1a].

While the English term "form-critical" can designate such an approach, that term has a historical, developmental connotation (de-

---

[1] ZAW 42 (1924), 182f.
[1a] Also the method of F. Zwicky, Morphological Astronomy, 1957 (followed now by others), emphasizes both multidimensional intersecting categories and correlations between coexisting phenomena.

rived from the German *Formgeschichte*) which the term "morphological" can avoid. A similar employment of the term "morphology" is
current in German anthropological studies, though often with a more
pronounced developmental overtone, without a clear distinction between synchronic and diachronic aspects. The diachronic dimension
can never be ignored, but for the most part its conclusions must be
reached by methods other than structural analysis.

Previous form-critical work in Hosea has been done especially,
though not exclusively, by Gressmann (1910, 1921), Lindblom (1928),
Mowinckel (1944), Weiser (1949), Wolff (1961, 1965), Frey (1957,
1961), Deissler (1961), Rudolph (1966), and Good (1966)[2]. Most of
these, however, are organized largely in the form of a commentary
rather than that of a systematic study, as is the present work; each
type of organization has its peculiar advantages. Especially important
for a difference in approach is the fact that not all of them are intimately related to secular disciplines. A theological approach, however, can hardly afford such an isolation. As a possible way of dealing
with expanding knowledge, one can follow the principle of applying
simultaneously a number of perspectives to a relatively narrow subject matter[3], as will be attempted here.

II. THE ANALYSIS OF LITERARY FORMS

"Literature" includes not only written matter, but all verbal
expressions of human life, especially as they are intended for transmission from one generation to another. The expression "oral literature," indeed, is widely used in scholarship bearing on this topic.
The value of having a single word, literature, for both oral and written products is indicated by the fact that the two groups have essentially the same role and character. Functional observations about the
one are true also for the other, differing only in degree. Furthermore,
in a culture before the invention of the printing press and the phenomenon of widespread literacy, especially during the beginning stages
of the use of writing and while collective feeling is still fairly strong,
it is difficult to separate oral and written products precisely. Written
works, for instance, can be modified by oral tradition; frequently
they represent the crystallization of oral literature. Indeed, silent reading is a modern invention; even letters were at one time only crystal-

---

[2] H. Frey, WuD NF 5 (1957), 9—103; Das Buch des Werbens Gottes um seine Kirche,
1961[2]; E. Good, JBL 85 (1966), 273—286; VT 16 (1966), 137—171; and works
listed under "Abbreviations," including one by Good.

[3] That is now done widely; see, for British science, P. B. Medawar, Encounter 25
(Aug. 1965), 53.

lizations of messages, to be read aloud. Written literature was thus "oral," even when it was read. Of course, differences between oral and written transmission do exist and must be kept in mind[4].

In their general presentations of Old Testament literature, J. Hempel and O. Eißfeldt divide literary genres into three groups: prose, short sayings, and songs[5]. A. Weiser and A. Bentzen classify some short sayings under poetry, others under prose[6]. Some inconsequences appear. Though Eißfeldt and Weiser list narratives as the main literary body in the division of prose, they then subdivide them into "poetic" and "prose" (or "historical") narratives.

A functional view may supply clarity. Narration, singing, or brevity — separately or together — characterize all oral literature designed for enjoyment or transmission. Special elements are needed to impress literature on one's memory and to lift it out of the ordinary humdrum of existence. Especially in the absence of writing — with its possibilities of copying, seeing, and individual meditation — literature avails itself usually of one or both of the two main known esthetic-mnemonic aids, rhythmic music and story-form[7], or else adopts brevity for succinctness. Often relative brevity also characterizes songs and narratives, while poetic features frequently appear in short sayings.

The two most important features of what is known as poetry are repetition[8] and vividness. Simple repetition, often with only minor variations, is very common in primitive literature; more subtle types of repetition are represented by alliteration, rhyme, and, especially for the Old Testament, parallelism. Rhythm, too, is a form of repetition, namely of a more or less regular pattern of pauses or beats. Pregnancy of expression and concreteness bring about visual images or striking formulations which enhance the liveliness of the experience and aid memory. The popularity of narratives lies largely in the fact that they portray their subject matter in terms of human life, producing easily-remembered pictures related to the listener's experience.

---

[4] See, e. g., S. Gandz, "The Dawn of Literature," Osiris 7 (1939), 261—522; R. Culley, VT 13 (1963), 113—125; Jan Vansina, Oral Tradition, 1965 (French, 1961).

[5] J. Hempel, Die althebräische Literatur und ihr hellenistisch-jüdisches Nachleben, 1930, 19—101. O. Eißfeldt, The Old Testament, 1965, 9—127.

[6] A. Weiser, The Old Testament, 1961, 21—68; A. Bentzen, Introduction to the Old Testament, I 1948, 118—251.

[7] E. D. Chapple and C. S. Coon, Principles of Anthropology, 1942, 601, consider "poetry" and "story telling" as the two "branches" of literature.

[8] The role of repetition is emphasized by F. Boas, Primitive Art, 1927; E. Staiger, Grundbegriffe der Poetik, 1951[2], 27; and others, both for pleasure and memory. A fine exhaustive study is furnished by J. Gonda, Stylistic Repetition in the Veda, 1959.

Another important factor in some forms of literature is the use of artificial modes of expression. It shows itself in the use of a special poetic vocabulary, re-enforcing the power of tradition to keep alive archaic words for poetic use. More importantly, it creates a stylization of literature. Stylization has tremendous charm and contributes to one's ability to focus attention on the essential rather than on the accidental; it is also itself a mnemonic aid and gives the participant a sense of identity with his community, past and present.

The artificiality, or special character, of poetical literature, including its graceful repetition and expressiveness — in short, its art — necessitates in the poet a heightening of the power of mental processes and a lowering of inhibitions against them. This is often accomplished under the stress of emotion or through the reduction of self-consciousness (or through both) — a fact important for the study of the prophets[9].

Not until the rise of writing and of individualism, the latter being partly a result of the former, does the need for poetic features decrease. They never die out completely, but their importance is broken down. Even in the Old Testament the distinction between prose and poetry is often only a relative one. It is wisest to recognize different degrees of poetic character.

Poetry, brevity, and narrative, then, form definite categories, not in the sense of exclusive classes, but rather as several (sometimes simultaneous) principles or forms, applicable in various degrees.

These categories cut across the major divisions of human life — cult, court (or civil administration), and common life. In the cult, narrative is represented by the credo, poetry by the psalms, and short sayings by apodictic law. In the life of the community or the nation, important roles are played by hero narratives or court records and by such elements as the victory song and judicial law. Popular types of literature are represented by amusing tales, wedding songs, and homespun proverbs. The short sayings are usually didactic; narratives — including popular stories — tend to define one's position in the world[10]; songs often give expression to deep emotion. But the tone of each sociological situation is different.

---

[9] Emotional and unselfconscious artistic powers are already available to at least some animals; D. Morris, The Biology of Art, 1962, 158. 161, found for certain apes the following principles of art: self-rewarding activation, compositional control (steadiness, symmetry, repetition, rhythm), calligraphic differentiation, thematic variation, optimum heterogeneity, and universal imagery. Non-assertive (even if trained) activity in man can include these.

[10] That includes wishful thinking in fairy-tales (F. Boas, General Anthropology, 1938, 610; A. A. Brill, Basic Principles of Psychoanalysis, 1949, 251—260), and more serious implications in historical narratives and myths.

Another element of classification, again cutting across those mentioned, is a division according to the positive or negative character of feeling, namely joy or sorrow. In religious poems one may, accordingly, distinguish between hymns and laments. This classification highlights differences in purpose; in a lament one hopes to move deity to come to one's aid, while the hymn expresses adoration and thanksgiving. These genres, then, reflect certain basic situations in human life.

Since the essential, or inner, situation may be similar under a variety of external conditions, it is possible that a genre is used outside its ordinary or original position. The prophet can burst forth in a lament. A psalm can be sung outside the temple. "Cultic" language takes place not only at the official place of worship, though it is regularly centered there. The literary structure of human speech in its relation to God is largely constant, whatever a person's physical circumstances may be.

The precise nature of stylization is determined in part by accidental features due to chance development. They receive meaning, however, as they move out of the realm of accident, are standardized, and make "sense" in a given structure. Standardization is a result of the power of tradition, which need not be a static one, over thought, feelings, and expressions. Not just an outward form-language is thereby affected, but the content of thought, the very nature of existence. While there are hardly universally valid symbol systems, and while borrowed symbols often change meaning, the recognition of stylized expression in a given literary production can point to its essential meaning in human life.

Chapter II: The Data in Translation

The book of Hosea presents numerous problems of text and interpretation; to deal with these adequately requires a full-length commentary, a task which is not the purpose of the present study[1]. Fortunately, the general drift of a passage is usually clear even if the details are not. Among the many individual possibilities, one often has to select almost blindly a given alternative; a different reading has in many cases an equal attractiveness.

For the consonantal text only a few unsupported conjectures have been accepted; other cases seem to require conjectural emendations, but none offered so far seem acceptable. In many of the difficult cases, the ancient versions, especially the Old Greek, supplied useful variants. Attention to other Semitic languages may seem to be especially appropriate in Hosea, since it represents a non-Judean writing and may thus exhibit linguistic usages not otherwise preserved in the Old Testament. Yet of the large number of new interpretations based on a comparison with cognate languages only a handful appear at all reasonable and even fewer of these are genuinely convincing[2]. Sometimes linguistic parallels within the Old Testament explain certain difficult readings and make emendations unnecessary.

Textual criticism is not always easily distinguished from "higher" criticism nor from tradition criticism. "Lower" (textual) criticism deals largely with mechanical errors, which, since they carry no meaning when they happen (though they may acquire a meaning later on) are best simply corrected. "Higher" criticism treats of consciously made expansions, which, since they are witnesses of a definite point of view, are best translated, though indicated as secondary. Such additions are enclosed in brackets. Tradition criticism attempts to evaluate factors which represent a tendency of the transmitting group but are largely unconscious and of such a subtle nature that it is usually impossible to represent them without further comment in such a translation as that which follows; they must simply be kept in mind at all times, here especially for the material of chs. 1—3.

---

[1] Most useful for an analysis of text and grammar are Harper, Robinson, Rinaldi, Wolff, and Rudolph. Material available there is ordinarily not repeated here. Masoretic vowels have sometimes been changed without notice.

[2] Arabic comparisons must guard against secondary meanings, e. g., against H. Hirschberg, VT 11 (1961), 378, on Hos 4 14.

The following translation is designed to exhibit the data and, to a degree, the conclusions for parts of the discussion which is to follow. Rhythmic structure and word-repetitions (italicized) are indicated for analysis in Chapter III. The sign ✳ at the end of a line indicates a change from divine to non-divine speech or vice versa, to be discussed in Chapter IV. Words tying oracles together are repeated in parentheses between sections. Double quotes indicate quotations or parodies; single quotes refer to proverbs or to proverbial and certain figurative expressions. It must be emphasized, however, that none of these data are sufficiently mechanical to be represented adequately in the translation.

A. Chs. 1—3: ISRAEL, THE WHORE

1 1   [The word of Yahweh which came to Hosea, the son of Beeri, in the days of Uzziah, Jotham, Ahaz, and Hezekiah, kings of Judah, and in the days of Jeroboam, the son of Joash, king of Israel.]

1. A Prostitute Wife

1 2   The beginning of Yahweh's speaking through Hosea. Yahweh said to Hosea: ✳
    "Go, take a wife of *whoredom*,
      and children of *whoredom*,
    For the land goes greatly *whoring*
      away from Yahweh." ✳

3   He went and took Gomer, the daughter of Diblaim; and she *conceived*
4   *and bore* him a son. And Yahweh said to him: ✳
    Call his name *Jezreel:*
    For in a little while I will visit
      the blood of *Jezreel*
      on the house of Jehu. —
    I will end the kingdom
      of the house of *Israel*. —

5   [And it will be in that day]
    I will break the bow of *Israel*
      in the valley of *Jezreel*. ✳

6   And she *conceived* again *and bore* a daughter. And he said to him: ✳
    Call her name *Not-pitied:*
    For I will *not pity* yet again
      the house of Israel,
    That I should forgive them. (?)

7   [But the house of Judah I will *pity*. I will *save* them through Yahweh their god. I will not *save* through *bow* and *sword* and *war*, through horses and riders.] ✳

8.9   She weaned *Not-pitied* and *conceived and bore* a son. And he said: ✳
    Call his name *Not-my-people:*
    For you are *not my people*,
      and I am not for you. (?) ✳

(Additions to 1:) The Curse Reversed.

2 1 [The number of the *children* of Israel will be as the sand of the sea, which cannot be measured or counted; in the place in which *it was said to them*, "You are not my people," *it will be said to them* (i. e., they will be called), "*Children* of the living God."

2 The *children* of Judah and the *children* of Israel will gather together; they will set for themselves a single head and come up (to the central sanctuary or to Jerusalem) out of the land. For great is the

3 day of *Jezreel;* say to your brothers, "*My-people*," and to your sisters, "*Pitied*."] ✳

(whoredom, pity)

2. Return Through Chastisement

2 4 *Plead* with your mother, *plead!* —
　　For she is *not* my wife,
　　　　and I am *not* her *husband* — (genuine?)
　That she remove her (signs of) *whoredom* from her face
　　and her adultery from between her breasts.

5 Lest I strip her *naked*
　　and set her as in the day of her birth,
　And make her like the desert
　　and turn her into dry land
　[and kill her through thirst].

6 Her children I will *not pity;*
　　for they are children of *whoredom.*

7 For their mother *whored*,
　　shamefully acted she who bore them.
　For *she said, "I will go* after my *lovers,*
　Who give me my bread and my water,
　　my *wool* and my *flax,*
　　my oil and my drink."

8 Therefore, behold, I will hedge in her[3] way with thorns,
　　and I will build up her wall,
　That she will not find her way.

9 She will pursue her *lovers,*
　　but will not overtake them;
　She will seek them and not find them.
　(Then) *she will say, "I will go*
　　and return to my former man *(husband);*
　For I was better off then than now."

10 She did not know
　That it was I who gave her
　　the *grain* and the *wine* and the *oil*

---

[3] With LXX.

And who multiplied silver for her and gold
    [which they made into *Baal*].
11 Therefore I will take back again my *grain* in its season
    and my *wine* in its time;
And I will remove my *wool* and my *flax*,
    which were to cover her *nakedness*.
12 Now I will uncover her private parts
    before the eyes of her *lovers*,
And no man will save her from my hand.

13 I will bring to *rest (šabăt)* all her joy,
    Her festival, her new moon, and her *sabbath*,
    and all her sacred gathering.[5]
14 And I will devastate her vines and fig trees,
    of which she said, "these are my (harlot's) hire,
    which my *lovers* have given me."
I will turn them into a thicket;
    the beasts of the field will eat them.
15 And I will visit upon her all the days of the *Baals*,
During which she sacrificed to them,
    put on her ring and her finery,
    and went after her *lovers*
    [and forgot me, says Yahweh].

16 Therefore, behold, I will allure her
    and take her into the desert,
And I will speak to her heart.
17 [I will give her from there her vineyards (?)
    and (make) the Valley of Achor a door of hope[4].]
She will answer me there as in the *days* of her youth,
    in the *day* when she came out of the land of Egypt.
18 [And it will be in that day, says Yahweh,]
She[5] will *say to me*, "my husband,"
    and will not *say to me* again, "my Baal."
19 [I will remove the *names* of the Baals from her mouth,
    and they will be mentioned by *name* no more.]
20 [I will make for them a covenant, in that day, with *the beasts of the field*, with the birds of the air, and with the ground animals. I will abolish *bow* and *sword* and *war* from the land, and they will dwell securely.]
21 And I will *betroth* you to me forever:
    I will *betroth* you to me in rightness and judgment,
        in loving-kindness and care *(pity);*
22   I will *betroth* you to me in faithfulness,
And you will know Yahweh.

---

4 נתן לְ means "to make . . . into . . ." (here awkward).
5 So, LXX; or read "you" with MT, but that is not euphonic.

23 [It will be in that day that I, says Yahweh, will answer the heavens;
24 and they will answer the earth; and the earth will answer the *grain*
and the *wine* and the *oil;* and they will answer *Jezreel*. I will *sow*
25 her for me in the land (Jezreel = "God sow[s]")[6]; I will have *pity*
on *Not-pitied;* and I will say to *Not-my-people,* "you are *my people,*"
and he will say, "my God."] ✳

(love, whore)

3. A Purchase on the Basis of Love

3 1 Yahweh said to me again, ✳
"Go, *love* a woman
loving (or, *loved* by) a friend and adulterous,
As Yahweh *loves* the *children of Israel,*
Though they turn to other gods
and *love* raisin cakes." ✳
2 So I bought her for me for fifteen pieces of silver and for a homer
3 and a lethek of barley. And I said to her:
"*Many days* you will *sit* (waiting?) for me[7]
and not *whore*
and not be for a man[8].
Also I (will be?) for you."
4 [For *many days* the *children of Israel* will *sit* without king and without prince, without sacrifice and without pillar, without ephod and
5 without teraphim. *After* that, the *children of Israel* will turn and
seek Yahweh their God and David their king and trembling come
to Yahweh and to his goodness in the *after*-days.]

B. Chs. 4—14: GOD AND ISRAEL AT ODDS
Cycle I. Cult Ruin ("Whoredom")

(whoredom)

4. "Like People Like Priest"

4 1 Hear the word of Yahweh,
children of Israel,
For Yahweh has a *controversy (rîb)*
with those *that dwell* in the *land* (earth).
For there is no truthfulness and no loving-kindness
and no *knowledge* of God in the *land.*
2 Cursing, lying, killing, stealing, adultery — *spread*[9];
and *blood* touches *blood.*

---

[6] Not "impregnate" (Jacob, Rudolph), for it is "in the land."
[7] יֹשֵׁב לְ, a rare idiom, means "waiting" in Ex 24 14.
[8] Perhaps read, or interpret, "another man," with LXX.
[9] Or read: וּפָרֹץ, "Rechtbrechen"? Cf. W. Zimmerli, Ezechiel, 1959, 409; C. Schedl,
BZ NF 6 (1962), 100—102. But the verb itself is not attested with this meaning.

3   For this reason the *land* mourns,
        and all *that dwell* in it wither —
    From the beast of the field to the birds of the air,
        and even the fish of the sea are gathered.
4   Let no one *denounce (rîb)*,
        Let no one reprove;
    For the *people*[10] are (only) like the *priests* who are
                denouncing (them)[11]. (?)
5   You (the priest) will *stumble* today,
        and the prophet will *stumble* with you at night. ✷
    I *destroy* the *people*[12]? (or: You *destroy* the *people*.)
6   *My people* are *destroyed* by lack of *knowledge!*
    Since you have *rejected* the '*knowledge*,'
        I will *reject* you from *being priest* to me.
    Since you have *forgotten* the torah of your God,
        I also will *forget* your children.
7   According to their multitude they have sinned against me —
        their glory I will change into ignominy!
8   They *eat* the sin of *my people*,
        and for their iniquity they lift their appetite[13].
9   It will be 'like *people*, like *priest*':
    I will visit his ways upon him
        and return his deeds to him. ✷

10 They will *eat* and not be satisfied,
        whore and not *increase (spread);*
    For they have forsaken Yahweh[14]
11   to follow *whoredom*. (?)

                    (Whoredom; my people)

5. Whoredom — Figurative and Literal

    'Wine and must take away the mind.' ✷
4 12 *My people* — it inquires of its wood,
        and its staff instructs it! ✷
    For the spirit of *whoredom* has misled them,
        and they have *whored* away from their God.
13 Upon the tops of the mountains they sacrifice,
        and upon the heights they make smoke —

---

[10] Perhaps עַמְּךָ is an expanded form of עָם; cf. S. Feigin, AJSL 42 (1925), 64—68. Otherwise translate, "your people."

[11] On מְרִיבֵי כֹהֵן as "denouncing priests," cf. Nyberg and C. Brockelmann, Hebräische Syntax, 1956, 70 (one should translate with the plural, however!). The same construction also occurs in Hos 6 9 and perhaps in 13 2 (sacrificers?).

[12] On the form אָמֵךּ, cf. Feigin loc. cit. R. Vuilleumier-Bessard, La tradition cultuelle, 1960, 54, reads וְדָמְתִי עַמְּךָ, to be considered.

[13] So. versions and some MSS.

[14] עזב is not used with an infinitive but often with Yahweh.

Under the oak and the poplar,
    and the terebinth, because its shade is good.
This is why your *daughters whore*
    and your *women* commit *adultery!* ✶
14 I will not visit upon your *daughters* their *whoring*
    and upon your *women* their *adultery.* ✶
For they (the men themselves?) go aside with *whores*
    and sacrifice with 'sacred ones,'
And a foolish *people* comes to fall with a *whore*[15]. (?)

(Whoredom)

6. Wanton Cult

4 15 You, Israel, do not become guilty[16]; (MT adds: Judah)
Do not go to Gilgal,
    do not get up to Beth-awen,
Do not swear, "Thus lives the Lord."
16 For as a *rebellious* calf,
    Israel is *rebellious.*
Now Yahweh will lead them
    as a lamb on a broad pasture! (Or: question)
17 A companion of idols is Ephraim —
    leave him!
18 *Rebellious* (?) is their drinking-party[17]. (?)
A-whoring they *whore,*
    lovingly[18] they love the ignominy of shamelessness[19]. (?)
19 The wind will wrap it (?) in its wings, (proph. perf.)
    and they will be ashamed of their altars[20]!

(Whoredom)

7. Spiritual Break Between God and Israel

5 1 Hear this, O priests!
    and listen, O house of Israel!
    Give ear, house of the king!

---

[15] Read עַם זֹנֶה with LXX?

[16] Read תֶּאְשַׁם with LXX?

[17] The Hebrew adjective סַר, derived from סרר (to be stubborn, rebellious), is attested elsewhere with the meaning "ill-willed." "Drinking-party" is the interpretation also of some versions and fits the theme of הבר in v. 17. A derivation from סור (cf. Keil) can easily yield a similar meaning; in that case, alliteration with סרר is present.

[18] A variation of the stem אהב (though *not* with Arabic), or: "passionately." See J. J. Glück, in: Die O. T. Werkgemeenskap in Suid-Afrika, Studies on the Books of Hosea and Amos, 1965, 57.

[19] From the root מגן (with G. R. Driver), but reading מָגְנָּה. Or: "mocking-song," מַגִּנָה מַגְנָה (מַגִּנָה)? An allusion to Ugaritic 51:III:15—22 (Gordon's numbers)?

[20] Read thus with versions.

For judgment is coming to you. ✳
As you have become a snare in Mispah
and a net spread out on Mt. Tabor
2   and a pit in Shittim, dug deep[21] —
Thus I will be a fetter to all of you[22].

3   *I know* Ephraim,
and Israel is not hid from me. ✳
For now Ephraim has *whored*[23],
Israel is defiled.
4   Their deeds do not allow them
to return to their God;
For the spirit of *whoredom* is in them,
and Yahweh they do not *know*.
5   [And the pride of Israel answers to his face.
Israel and Ephraim will *stumble* in their iniquity.
Judah also will *stumble* with them.]
6   With their flocks and their herds they go
to seek Yahweh —
But they do not find him;
he has withdrawn from them.
7   Toward Yahweh they have been unfaithful; (family break)
for they have borne foreign sons.
Now the destroyer[24] will eat their portions.

Cycle II. The disorder of Politics and Society ("Kings and Princes")

8. Fraternal Strife

5 8   Blow the horn in Gibeah,
the trumpet in Ramah.
Raise the war cry in Beth-awen,
"After you, Benjamin[25]!" (?)
9   Ephraim is destined to desolation
in the day of reproof.
Among the tribes of Israel
I announce the truth.
10   The *princes* of Israel have become (MT: Judah)
as boundary thieves — ✳

---

[21] Conjecturally assimilated to the context and freely translated.
[22] Read thus (partially with LXX) ?
[23] Read as 3rd person feminine; cf. v. 9. Some MSS actually have הזנתה (according to Harper), which is then probably also presupposed by the versions (rather than הזנה). The hiph. of זנה occurs also in 4 10. 18.
[24] Read perhaps יאכֵל מְחַדֵשׁ, following I. Eitan, HUCA 14 (1939), 2, comparing Arabic ḥadasa.
[25] Cf. Judg 5 14; is it ironical here?

On them I will pour out
     like water my wrath. ✳

          (princes; Judah?)

     9. Is There Healing — While There Are Social Sins?

5 11 Crushed is Ephraim,
          broken in judgment;
     For it has insisted on following after worthlessness. ✳
 12   I, indeed, am as a moth to Ephraim
          and as rottenness to the house of Israel. ✳ (MT: Judah)
 13   Ephraim has seen its malady,
          and Israel its wound;
     So Ephraim went to Assyria,
          and sent to the Great *King*.
     But he is not able to *heal* you,
          and cannot cure your wound; ✳
 14   For I am as a wild lion to Ephraim,
          and like a young lion to the house of Israel. (MT: Judah)
     I, yes I, *rend* and go,
          I seize and no one rescues.
 15   I will go and return to my place,
     Until they suffer in their guilt
          and seek my face
          and in their distress search after me. ✳
6 1   "Come, let us return to Yahweh —
     For he *rent* and will *heal* us,
          he has stricken and will bind us up.
 2   After two days he will make us *live* again,
     On the third day he will raise us
          so that we will *live* before him.
 3   Let us *know*, let us pursue to *know*, Yahweh.
          As the dawn is set his coming forth.
     He will come as a shower to us,
          as the spring rain waters the earth." ✳

 4   What can I do with you, Ephraim?
          what can I do with you, Israel? (MT: Judah)
     Your *devotion* is like a morning cloud,
          like the dew that goes early away.
 5   For this reason I have hewn (them) through the prophets,
          I have killed them through the words of my mouth,
     And my judgment came forth like light. (?)   (secondary?)
 6   For I desire *loving-kindness (devotion)* and not sacrifice,
          the *knowledge* of God rather than burnt-offerings.
 7   But they have in Adam[26] broken the covenant.
          there (then) they acted treacherously against me. ✳

_____

[26] Read thus? One must note, however, that in ancient Hebrew script *b* and *k* are
not similar.

8 Gilead is a city of evil-doers,
        tracked with blood.
9 Like ambushing robbers[27]
        is the band of priests;
  They kill on the road to Shechem,
        to commit villainy.
10 In the "house of God"[28] I have seen a horrible thing;
  There is the whoredom of Ephraim,
        Israel is defiled.
11 [Also for you, Judah, a harvest is appointed!] ✶

  When I would restore the fortunes of my people,
7 1   when I would *heal* Israel —
  There is revealed the iniquity of Ephraim,
        and the *evils* of Samaria. ✶
  For they do falsehood;
  The thief enters,
        the *robber* raids outside. ✶
2 They do not think in their hearts
        that I remember all their *evil*.
  Now their deeds have surrounded them —
        they have come before my face. ✶
3 With their *evil* they make the *king* rejoice,
        and with their lies the *princes*.
4 All of them commit adultery,
        they are like a burning *oven* . . . . (?)
5 On the day of our *king*,
        they made the *princes* weak with the heat of wine;
  His hand drew the deriders (?).
6 For their inward is like an *oven* in their ambush[29].
  All night long their anger sleeps —
        in the morning it burns like a fiery flame.
7 They all become hot like an *oven*
        and *devour* their rulers.
  All their *kings* have *fallen* — ✶ (Or: proph. perf.?)
        none of them call to me. ✶
                              (princes; baking?; *fall?; devour?)*

  10. Israel — Turning Elsewhere Than to Yahweh

7 8 Ephraim —
        he is 'blended' among the peoples[29a],

---

[27] Pointable as כְּחַכֵּי; cf. Hos 4 4.
[28] Read thus, instead of "In the house of Israel"? (Israel is mentioned shortly here-
    after). Cf. 10 15 8 1.
[29] See below.
[29a] Cf. the Akkadian; S. Paul, VT 18 (1968), 118.

Ephraim has become
    a cake unturned. *(baking figure)*
9   Strangers have *devoured* his strength —
    unknown to him.
He has become moldy[30] — (?)
    unknown to him.
10 The pride of Israel answers to its face,
    But they do not return to Yahweh their God,   (secondary?)
    and do not seek him for all this.
11 Ephraim has become like a dove,
    silly and without sense.
They call to Egypt
    and *go* to Assyria. ✳
12 As they *go* —
    I will spread over them my net.
Like birds of the air I will bring them down.
    I will chastise them when hearing of their appointment[31].
13 Woe to them, for they have wandered from me.
    destruction to them, for they have revolted against me.
I would redeem them —
    but they speak lies against me.
14 They do not *cry* to me out of their hearts,
    when they wail upon their beds
    and cut themselves for grain and must.
They rebel against me.
15 I trained them, I strengthened their arms —
    but they devise evil against me. ✳
16 They turn — not upward[32]; (?)
    they have become like a warped bow.
Their *princes* will *fall* by the sword
    through the cursing of their tongue —
This will be for derision in the land of Egypt.
                      (cry; princes)

11. God-less Kings and Images

8 1   To your mouth the trumpet,
    as an announcer[33] over the house of Yahweh, ✳
Because they have broken my covenant
    and have revolted against my law,
2   To me they *cry* —
    "(my) God, we, Israel, know thee!" ✳

---

[30] T. H. Gaster, VT 4 (1954), 79, compares the Hebrew phrase with the expression for the moldy cake in the Gilgamesh Epic (XI, 227). The traditional interpretation, however, can be bolstered by 2 Aqht:VI:36f.

[31] Or, "gathering" (on free qal inf., G. Bergsträsser II § 11f), and see 10 10.

[32] See Brown-Driver-Briggs, referring to II Sam 23 1, etc.

[33] Tur-Sinai compares Arabic *naṣṣar*, "herald."

3 Israel has *rejected* the good —
   the enemy will pursue him. ✶
4 They make *kings* but not from me,
   princes, without my knowledge. ✶
Their gold and their silver they turn for themselves
   into graven images — to be destroyed.

5 He has *rejected* your *calf, Samaria!* ✶
   my anger is hot against them. ✶
How long can they not become clean?
6 It is from Israel; (?)
   a workman made it —
   it is not God.
Verily, splinters will become the *calf* of *Samaria*.
7 'Since they sow the wind,
   they will reap the whirlwind.'
'No grain stalk for the shoot
   means it makes no flour.'   (Cf. ANET 425.)
If it should make some —
   strangers will *swallow* it!

                        (swallow; king; princes)

12. Israel Lost in the Gentile Empire

8 8 Israel is *swallowed* — (proph. perf.?)
   Now they have become *among the peoples* (proph. perf.?)
      like an undesirable vessel.
9 For they have gone to Assyria;
   A lonely wild ass,
      Ephraim has *hired* lovers. ✶
10 As they are hiring *among the peoples* —
      now I will gather them. ✶
   And they will rest[34] awhile (?) (proph. perf.?)
      from the burden of *a king* and *princes!*

Cycle III. Religious Chaos ("Return to Egypt")
                        (law: 8 1. 12 ?*)*

13. "No Pleasure"

8 11 As Ephraim *multiplied* altars for *sin-offerings* —
      they became to him *altars* for *sinning.* ✶
12 Though I write to him *multiples* of my law —
      they appear strange to him. ✶
13 *Sacrifices* they love[35], (?)
      they *sacrifice* meat and eat.

---

[34] Cf. G. R. Driver, JTS 39 (1938), 158.
[35] As in 4 18, some alternate formation to אהב ?

Yahweh has no pleasure in them!
*Now he will remember their iniquity
        and visit their sins.*
They will *return to Egypt.*   } (secondary here?)

14 [Israel has forgotten his maker
        and has built palaces,
And Judah has *multiplied* fortified cities. ✶
I will send a fire into his cities
        and it will devour his strongholds.] ✶
                    (Cf. 8 13 with 9 3. 4. 9)

14(a). Trouble for God's House

9 1 Do not rejoice, Israel,
        do not exult[36] like the peoples;
For you have whored away from your god,
        you have loved hire
        on every *threshing floor.*

2 The *threshing floor* and the wine press will not feed them,
        and the must will fail them[37].

3 They will not remain in the land of Yahweh —
        Ephraim will *return to Egypt*
        [and in Assyria they will eat unclean food].

4 They will not pour out wine to Yahweh,
        they will not bring him[38] *sacrifices;*
[As bread of mourners to them[39], (?)
        all who eat of it will be defiled.]
For their food will be for themselves,
        it will not come into the *house* of Yahweh.

5 What will you do on the appointed *day,*
        on the *day* of the feast of Yahweh?

6 For behold, as they will go from destruction — (?)
Egypt will gather them,
        Memphis will bury them!
The 'desired place'[40] of their booths[41] weeds will inherit; (?)
        thorns will be in their tents.

                        (day, house)

---

[36] This must be the meaning, however one may read the Hebrew.
[37] Read thus with some MSS and versions.
[38] Cf. South-Arabic (G. R. Driver op. cit. 158f.).
[39] The expander of the text seems to have divided the phrases in the manner reflected in the masoretic punctuation, misunderstanding יערבו. (A reading of לָחְמָם for לָהֶם yields rather poor repetition.)
[40] מַחְמַד has frequently a cultic reference; cf. Sellin, 1929.
[41] Read לְסֻכֹּתָם (with J. Fischer, Die Propheten Obadja, Joël, Amos, Hosea, 1909)? MT's "silver" may have been influenced by מַחְמַד.

14(b). Trouble in God's House

9 7 The *days* of *visitation* have come, (proph. perf.)
    the *days* of 'fulfilment' have come,
Israel will know it. (?)
"A fool is the *prophet*,
    a madman the man of the spirit" —
Because of the greatness of your *iniquity* —
    a great *enmity* !⁴²

8 The watchman of Ephraim with (my) God,
    the *prophet* —
A fowler's snare is on all his ways,
    there is *enmity* in the *house* of his god.

9 They have become deeply corrupted,
    as in the days of Gibeah —
He will remember their iniquity
    and visit their sins. ✶

Cycle IV. Israel's Sin in History

15. (Baal-Peor and Gilgal) Establishment in Palestine: A Failure

9 10 Like grapes in the wilderness
    I found Israel,
Like an early fig on a young tree
    I saw your fathers. ✶
They came to Baal-Peor
    and dedicated themselves to Shame (Baal),
And they became detestable like their *love.*

11 Ephraim — like a bird their glory flies away.
    No *birth*, no pregnancy ("*womb*"), no conception ! ✶
(Place here 16 b)

12 If they do raise *children* —
    I will *bereave* them, leaving none;
Verily woe to them,
    (with) their offspring⁴³ ! ✶

13 Ephraim, as far as I can see,
    'is planted on a rock as a (or: in the) meadow⁴⁴;'
Ephraim must bring forth his *children* to the slayer.

14 *Give* them, Yahweh —
    what will you *give?*

---

⁴² See L. Prijs, BZ NF 8 (1964), 106. 109 (with M. Pope). It is not clear, however, whether enmity refers to one or to both sides.

⁴³ Partly with LXX. Read וּבְשָׂר ?

⁴⁴ Recognize (without consonantal change?) a proverbial expression for unfruitful conditions, here applied to Israel's situation in Palestine. The resultant pun between "meadow" and "children" is better than LXX's repetition.

Give them miscarrying *("bereaving")* uterus
and shriveled breasts! ✶
15 All their *evil* is in Gilgal:
there (already) I hated them.
For the *evil* of their deeds
I will drive them out of my house.
I will not *love* them again — ✶
'All their princes are rebels.'
16 Stricken is Ephraim; (proph. perf.?)
Their root is dried up, (proph. perf.?)
fruit (p^erî) they do not produce. ✶
If they do give *birth* —   ⎫ (Place
I will kill the darlings of their *womb*. ✶ ⎭ after v. 11)
17 (My) God will reject them,
for they did not listen to him;
And they will be wanderers among the peoples.
(fruit)

16. (Bethel) In the Land: The Vanity of Constructions

10 1 A luxuriant vine is Israel,
fruit he produces.
According to the *multitude* of his *fruit* he *multiplies altars*,
according to the *goodness* of his earth he makes *good* his *pillars*.
2 Smooth (false) is their heart —
now they will suffer in their guilt.
He will break their *altars*
and destroy their *pillars*.
3 Yes, now they will say,
"We have no *king;*
For we did not fear Yahweh — (?)
and the '*king*,' what could he do for us?"
4 Speaking[45] words,
swearing vanity,
covenant making!
Judgment grows like poison weeds
on the furrows of the field.
5 For the calf[46] of Beth-*awæn*
the inhabitants of Samaria are frightened;
Its people will mourn over it, (proph. perf.)
and the priests wail over it —
over its glory, since it has passed from it.
6 Yes, it will be taken to Assyria
as an offering to the Great *King*.

---

[45] With LXX.
[46] Read with versions.

Shame will be Ephraim's lot[47],
  and Israel will be *ashamed* of its counsels.
7 *Undone* is Samaria's '*king*' — (proph. perf.)
  like a snapped twig on the water.
8 Destroyed will be the high places of *Awæn*,
  the sin of Israel.
Thistles and thorns will grow up on their *altars*,
And they will say to the mountains, "Cover us!"
  and to the *hills*, "Fall over us!"
  (Gibeah = "hill"; king undone?)

17. (Gibeah) War Overtakes Social Badness

10 9 From the days of *Gibeah*
  you, Israel, have sinned.
There already they stood (or: there they have remained).
  Will not[48] *war* overtake them in *Gibeah?* ✶
10 Upon the sons of *badness* I will come[49] (?) (proph. perf.?)
  and *chastise*[50] them.
Peoples will be gathered against them
  when I *chastise* them[51] for their double iniquity.

11 Ephraim was a trained calf,
  loving to thresh;
And I laid a yoke[52]
  on its fair neck.
I made Ephraim pull —
Israel plows, (MT: Judah)
  Jacob harrows for himself. ✶
12 "Sow in *righteousness*,
  reap according to loving-kindness.
Break fallow ground of knowledge[53]
  to seek Yahweh,
Until he come
  and rain *rightness* on you."
13 You have plowed wickedness,
  you will reap *badness;* (proph. perf.)

---

[47] Free translation. (Cf. Ez 36 30, partly with Wolff.)
[48] Cf. S. Grill, TZ 16 (1960), 134, following König.
[49] Cf. LXX. Or follow Rudolph (cf. Judg 6 31 for עמד על)?
[50] Or, "bind" (אסר and יסר form variants of one stem in Aramaic, according to G. R. Driver op. cit. 160; see further Deissler, 81, for such interchanging). Kings are "bound:" Ps 149 8.
[51] Masoretic pointing reads "when they are chastised;" if this is original, the sentence can be taken as non-divine speech.
[52] Insert עֹל ?
[53] Read thus with LXX?

You will eat the fruit of falsehood. (proph. perf.)

Since you have trusted in your strength[54],
  in the multitude of your warriors,
14 War tumult will arise among your people.
All your fortifications will be *destroyed*,
  as Shalman[55] *destroyed* Beth-Arbel.
In the day of *war*
  women will be dashed with their children[56]. (proph. perf.)
15 Thus will he[57] do to you, O "house of God[58]," (proph. perf.)
  because of the *evilness* of your *evil*.
At dawn will be utterly *undone* (proph. perf.)
  the *king* of Israel. ✳

18. Israel, the Unmindful Child

11 1 When Israel was a child I loved him,
  and from Egypt I *called* my son.
2 The more I *called* them,
  the more they went away from me[59]. ✳
To the Baals they sacrifice,
  and to the idols they raise smoke! ✳
3 I taught Ephraim to walk,
  I held them on my arms[60];
  And they did not know that I healed them.
4 With the cord of a man I led them,
  with bands of love,
And I became to them as one who *raises* a child to his cheek[61]
  and turns to him to feed him. (?) ✳
5 He will *return* to the land of *Egypt*,
  and *Assyria* will be his king.
For they have refused to *turn*.
6 The sword will whirl in their cities,
  and consume their bars[62]. (?)
It will devour — because of their counsels. ✳
7 My people is bent on *turning* away from me. ✳
They call upward, (?)
    but *(totally)* no one *raises* them. ✳

---

[54] Cf. Ugaritic *drkt*, "rule, power", as repeatedly suggested.
[55] Harper claims Arabic and Palmyrene parallels, without citing sources. Perhaps Salamanu of Moab is intended; or did a Shalmaneser destroy the sacred Arbela?
[56] The expression is proverbial (Gen 32 12 Dtn 22 6).
[57] Or, "I," with LXX, as an imperfect.
[58] Or read, with LXX, "house of Israel."
[59] Cf. LXX.
[60] Cf. versions.
[61] With G. R. Driver op. cit. 161f. See below, p. 110.
[62] Cf. Nah 3 13.

8 How can I hand you over, Ephraim,
  how can I deliver you up, Israel?
How can I make you like Admah,
  how can I make you like Zeboiim?
My heart is turned within me,
  my compassion becomes *totally* excited.
9 I will not execute the heat of my wrath,
  I will not wipe out I̶s̶r̶a̶e̶l̶ again. *Ephraim/*
For I am God — and not man,
  the holy one in your midst,
And I will not come in anger (?). ✳
10 [After Yahweh they will go;
  like a lion he roars.
For he will roar,
  and sons will come trembling from the west.
11 They will come like birds from *Egypt*
  and like doves from the land of *Assyria;* ✳
And I will make them dwell in their houses, ⟳
  says the Lord.] ✳

Final Collection: The Overthrow of Sacred Traditions
(Egypt, Assyria)

19. The Falsehood of Jacob's Descendents

12 1 With falsehood Ephraim has surrounded me,
  and with *deceit* the house of Israel. ✳
It[63] constantly roams in its relation to God, (?)
  but it is faithful toward the 'holy ones[64].'
2 Ephraim herds the wind,
  and pursues the east wind all day long.
[Lying and destruction it multiplies.][65]
They make a covenant with *Assyria*
  and carry oil to *Egypt*[66].

3 Yahweh has a controversy with *Israel* — (MT: Judah)
To visit on *Jacob (ya'aqob)* his ways
  and to *return him* his deeds.
4 "In the womb he *caught the heel ('aqăb)* of his brother,
  as an adult *('ôn)* he fought *(śarā)* with deity.
5 He *fought* with the angel and prevailed,
  he wept and besought him.

---

[63] Read הוא for "Judah" (with Sellin)? The present MT may praise Judah.
[64] According to T. H. Gaster, JTS 38 (1937), 163, קְדוֹשִׁים denotes "demons" in Aramaic texts, but no such specific reference may be intended here.
[65] Considered secondary by Duhm, Gressmann, and Wolff.
[66] Read יוֹבִלוּ at end, with ו from v. 3.

In Beth-*Awæn* (Beth-*'On*), he found him[67],
> and there he (God) spoke to him[68] —

6 Yahweh, God of hosts,
> Yahweh is his name —:

7 Be directed toward your God,
> Give heed to loving-kindness and judgment,
> and hope in your God continually."

8 A Canaanite trader — he uses *deceitful* balances,
> he loves to oppress.

9 Ephraim says, "Ah, I have become rich[69],
> I have *found* wealth *('ôn)* for myself."
> All his gain — will not be *found*,
> because of the guilt he has made in sinning[70]. ✶

10 *"I am Yahweh your God,*
> *from the land of Egypt.*
> I will once more make you dwell in tents,
> as in days of meeting.

11 I speak to[71] the *prophets*,
> I have multiplied visions,
> And through the *prophets* I will picture the future[72]." ✶

12 If in Gilead there is wickedness *('awæn)* (?)
> verily, nothingness they will be. (proph. perf.?)
> In Gilgal they sacrifice bulls, (?)
> their altars will be like stone heaps[73]
> on the furrows. (proph. perf.)

13 "Jacob fled to the fields of Aram,
> and Israel served *for a wife* —
> *for a wife* he *shepherded.*

14 Through a *prophet* Yahweh led Israel out of *Egypt;*
> through a *prophet* he was *shepherded.*"

15 Ephraim has offended bitterly;
> His Lord will abandon his blood on him,
> and will *return him* his reproaches. ✶
>> *("I am Yahweh, your God")* ✶

20. A Fall From Yahweh, the Only Savior

13 1 When Ephraim spoke, there was trembling, (?)
> he was great in Israel. (?)
> But he made himself *guilty* with Baal and *died.*

---

[67] See LXX. Or, "(The god) Bethel found him," with MT.

[68] Emend or interpret with versions. עַ (עִמָן ?) here means "to" as in Ugaritic (M. Dahood, Ugaritic-Hebrew Philology, 1965, 32).

[69] Cf. Zech 11 5; the expression appears to be a proverbial parody.

[70] Cf. LXX.

[71] Cf. A. Wünsche, Der Prophet Hosea, 1868.

[72] So, A. R. Johnson in S. H. Hooke, ed., The Labyrinth, 94.

[73] For the pun, related to a Jacob tradition, see p. 40.

2 Now they add to sin
    and make themselves molten images,
Idols out of their silver, according to their skill —
    the work of the artisan, all of it!
"Sacrifice[74] to them!" they say; (?)
    men kiss calves.

3 Therefore they will be as a morning cloud,
    as the dew that goes early away,
Like chaff blown from the threshing floor,
    like smoke out of the chimney. ✶

4 *"I am Yahweh, your God,*
    from the land of Egypt:
A God outside of me you do not *know,*
    and (there is) no *savior* beside me.

5 I *knew*[75] you in the wilderness,
    in the land of heat —"

6 As they were fed[76], they *became full,*
    they *became full* and lifted their hearts —
Therefore they forgot me.

7 *I will be ('æhî)* to them as a wild lion,
    like a leopard on the way, I will leap[77];

8 I will encounter them as a bereaved she-bear,
    I will tear open their breasts. ✶
Then the dogs will eat them[78],
    the beasts of the field will rend them.

9 He (or: it) will wipe you out, Israel — (proph. perf.)
    for who will be your help[79]? ✶

10 Where *('æhî)* is now your *king,* to *save* you,
    and your *princes,* to defend you[80] —
Of which you have said,
    "give me a *king* and *princes?*"

11 I give you a *king* in my anger,
    I take him in my wrath. ✶

('æhî; quotations; *guilt?, death?)*

21. Sheol (No Life From the Womb)

13 12 Ephraim's *iniquity* is bound up;
    his sin is stored.

13 'The pangs of birth have come for him —
    but *he* is an unwise son,

---

[74] Read thus with LXX?
[75] Or, "fed" (with LXX), repeated in 6.
[76] This is the meaning, however one may read in detail.
[77] Cf. Arabic and Aramaic (since Smith).
[78] Partly with LXX. Or: "I will devour them like a lion."
[79] With LXX and Ps 118 7.
[80] Emended, as by others.

> For he does not appear in time
> > at the mouth of the womb[81].' ✳

14   "From *sheol* I will ransom them,
> > from *death* I will redeem them:
> > *I will be ('æhî)* your plague, o *Death*[82],
> > *I will be* your sickness, o *Sheol*,
> > compassion is hid from my eyes." ✳

15   Though *he* flourish *(pr')* among the reeds[83] —
> The east wind, Yahweh's, will come,
> > arising out of the wilderness.
> His fountain will become dry,
> > his spring will dry up.
> *He* will be plundered of[84] the supply
> > of all desired (i. e., cultic?) items.

14 1   Samaria will suffer in her *guilt*,
> for she has been disobedient to her god.
> By the sword they will fall —
> Their sucklings will be dashed,
> > their pregnant women rent open.
> > > > *(iniquity ?; Yahweh your God* [cf. 12 10 13 4]*?)*

22. Turning

14 2   Turn, Israel, to *Yahweh your God,*
> for you have stumbled in your *iniquity.*

3   Take with you words
> and *return* to Yahweh.
> Say to him,
> > "Take away all our *iniquity;*
> > accept (us) kindly[85] —
> And we shall bring words of praise.

4   Assyria shall not save us,
> upon horses we will not ride.
> We will no longer say, 'Our God,'
> > to the product of our hand.
> For in thee the orphan finds mercy." ✳ (genuine?)

5   I will heal their *turning away* —
> Loving them out of my own decision,
> > for my anger has *turned* from them.

6   I will be as dew to Israel — ✳

---

[81] A similar image in II Kings 19 3 is clearly proverbial.

[82] Or "Where is," implying absence (Sellin). Similarly, T. Worden, VT 3 (1953), 296. Cf. Hab 3 5 and Ugaritic 127:1 (ANET 148).

[83] Are these reeds an allusion to the land or lake of reeds which play a role in Egyptian descriptions of death and rebirth ? (See J. Towers, JNES 18 [1959], 152f.).

[84] Point thus ? (Cf. niph. of שׁסס.)

[85] Or translate "bring good" (cf., e. g., II Kings 4 41) ?

He will blossom like a lily
    and strike (?) his roots like a poplar[86]   (Or: *Lebanon*-trees).
7 His shoots will go forth,
    He will have majesty like an olive
       and fragrance like *Lebanon*.
8 They will *return* and (i. e., again) dwell[87] in his shadow;
    they will (truly) live in the Garden[88]. (?)
    They will flourish like a vine[89]
       whose fame is like the wine of *Lebanon* (or: Helbon[90]). ✶
9 What does Ephraim still have to do with idols[91]? (?)
    I will answer and regard him. (?) (proph. perf.?)
  I am like a luxuriant tree,
    from me your fruit *(pᵉrî)* is found. (?) ✶
10 [Let him who is wise understand these things,
    let him who is discerning know them.
  For straight are the ways of Yahweh —
    the righteous walk in them,
    but the transgressors stumble in them.]

---

[86] Read כְּלִבְנֶה, alliterating with "Lebanon?"

[87] Read with LXX יֵשְׁבוּ in assonance with "return."

[88] Read בַּגַּ. In old Hebrew script, *b* and *d* were similar. The Garden (of God) stands for a flourishing state in Ez 28 13 31 8f. (cf. "Lebanon" in 31 3). See also, below.

[89] In its literal sense, פרת is applied especially to גֶּפֶן. V. 8 may be secondary and can be read as a description of agricultural growth, reading "grain" earlier with MT and emending here.

[90] So, Gressmann and others. (Cf. Ez 27 18.)

[91] With LXX.

Chapter III: The Word as Literature

All literature is "word," but not every spoken or written word is literature. As already indicated in Chapter I, one may speak of "literature" when the word is intended to rise above the ordinary incidental communication to express reality in an ecstatic (i. e., "outstanding") manner, usually with the intent that such expression be preserved and remembered. It has further been pointed out that such literature regularly adopts the form of poetry, narrative, or brevity (or of more than one of these), especially when oral transmission is presupposed.

The book of Hosea, by these standards, is literature. Its contents fall easily into two classes, rhythmic utterances and narratives. The category of brevity — or of the length of sayings or complexes — makes itself felt as a problem within both of these classes.

I. THE SIZE OF UNITS AND THE PROCESS OF TRANSMISSION

In his methodologically self-conscious study of Hos 2 1-3, H. W. Wolff[1] expresses an opinion widespread among form-critics that the first question to be raised concerns the demarcation of individual units[2]. It is very doubtful that such a priority is necessary. In fact, the present inquiry soft-pedaled this question in its earlier stages, treating the book largely as though it were an amorphous mass. Nevertheless, for the sake of convenience, one may begin with this topic.

The determination of the original units is especially difficult in Hosea. It is not easy to follow the "intuition picture" or the "inner structure," which, according to Mowinckel and Wolff, respectively[3], are the determinants for recognizing units. There is even an absence of prophetic formulas — like "thus says the Lord" — which have been regarded as useful aids for discovering divisions.

First, one may ask for the lower limit of possible length. How small are the units that can be understood independently, without

---

[1] EvTh 12 (1952/53), 78—104.

[2] Ibid. 82. Similarly, E. Balla, Die Droh- und Scheltworte des Amos, 1926, 7, and already H. Gunkel, Die Propheten, 1917, 116.

[3] S. Mowinckel, Prophecy and Tradition, 1946, 55 ff.; H. W. Wolff op. cit. 83.

the context in which they now stand? The immediate answer to such a question is that the book of Hosea is full of very small fragments, which are by no means necessarily or even strongly tied to what precedes or follows. Jerome already commented on this, in an oft-quoted sentence, "Hosea is concise and speaketh, as it were, in detached sayings"[4].

The pronouncements imbedded in the narrative of Hos 1 (especially the main statements in v. 2. 4[?]. 6 and 9) exhibit the length of a short unit-paragraph equivalent to a stanza to be discussed later. They further include what may be called one-word or one-phrase oracles, namely the names "Jezreel," "Not-pitied," and "Not-my-people". These resemble similar pregnant words or phrases appearing elsewhere in prophetic literature; even the "sibilant and gutteral sounds" which R. B. Y. Scott has noted in embryonic oracles[5] are present.

Next one may ask whether there are indications that the small expressions are parts of larger ones. One working hypothesis that can be set up is that individual utterances began in a full manner, i. e., mentioning Israel by name rather than opening with an expressed or unexpressed "they" without antecedent. Another possibility lies in noting the repetition of words. Such repetitions may be due to two somewhat different causes. Either the collector of the oracles arranged these in such a manner that catchword connection would aid the memory, or the prophet himself repeated within an oracle a significant word he had just uttered.

A major difficulty now lies in determining whether a repetition is original in the saying or secondary as part of the arrangement, if it is not simply accidental and to be ignored. Generally, one may postulate that a tight or rich connection indicates an originally intended continuity. A superficial, mechanical bridge probably reflects a later juxtaposition.

Is one justified in assuming the existence of both types of conscious verbal associations? Actually, though the existence of external connections is perhaps the better known and the more widely discussed of the two[6], it is precisely the phenomenon of stylistic repeti-

---

[4] As translated by E. B. Pusey, The Minor Prophets, I 1888, 16.

[5] T. H. Robinson-Festschrift, 1950, 186.

[6] Perhaps the first to have made use of this principle is E. König, NKZ 9 (1898), 933 (on Second Isaiah). In Hosea, this phenomenon has been discussed (not always convincingly) by Gressmann, Nyberg, Lindblom, Weiser, Wolff, Rudolph, Birkeland (Norsk TT 38 [1937], 302), B. W. Anderson (Interpretation 8 [1954], 290—303), and, most extensively, Good. To be regarded as accidental are, e. g., the repetitions of "ignominy," 4 7. 18, and "spirit," 4 12. 19.

tion which has been the more firmly established through a series of studies. Though not all analyses in the field are equally convincing (some fail to go far enough), word-repetition has been found in Isaiah, Jeremiah, and other prophets, in the Pentateuch, in the Psalms and other writings of the Old Testament, as well as in both neighboring and unrelated literatures[7]. Some of the repetitions noted are probably either coincidental or secondary; but the existence of deliberate original reiterations can hardly be denied. Though in practice a distinction is hard to draw, the division of word-repetitions into the three groups of accidental, primary, and secondary associations cannot be avoided. A differentiation among these groups is made especially difficult by the fact that ancient poets could employ mechanical associations already in the primary process of production. So A. Erman states for the Egyptian: "The (poet) is improvising, and accordingly any word which he has used in the last verse leads him on purely extraneous grounds to a new idea, which he immediately expresses[8]."

Whatever the explanation for their occurrence may be, a difference between external and internal associational repetitions may be observed. An especially clear example of the situation is presented by Hos 10 1-8. External mechanical connections are evident at the beginning and end of the section by the appearance of the words "fruit" and "hill" in different senses from those which these same words bear in the adjacent passages. Internal organic repetition is strong with the reiteration of "fruit," "multitude," "goodness," "altars," "pillars," "king," "Awen," and "shame."

---

[7] D. H. Müller, Die Propheten in ihrer ursprünglichen Form, I 1896 (R. Smend commented in TL 21 [1896], 227, that this phenomenon is "allbekannt," well-known); Biblische Studien, 5 vols., 1904—1908; Das Johannes-Evangelium, 1909; E. Kautzsch, Die Poesie und die poetischen Bücher des Alten Testaments, 1902, 4f.; A. Condamin, Le Livre d'Isaïe, 1905; Poèmes de la Bible, 1933²; Le Livre de Jérémie, 1936; J. Ziegler, on Isaiah, BZ 21 (1933), 131—149; U. Cassuto, La questione della Genesi, 1934, 278f. 365 (referring also to repetitions and allusions noted by Gunkel, Genesis, 1922, xlix, etc.); M. Buber (with F. Rosenzweig), Die Schrift und ihre Verdeutschung, 1936, 211—238. 262—275 (for the Pentateuch); J. Muilenburg, Congress Volume 1953 (SVT, I), 103—105 (quite widely); L. J. Liebreich, JQR NS 46 (1955/56), 259—277; 47 (1956/57), 114—138; HUCA 27 (1956), 181—192; N. Sarna, Ps 89, in: A. Altmann, Biblical and Other Studies, 1962, 29—46; N. H. Ridderbos, The Psalms, OS 13 (1963), 43—76; L. Alonso Schökel, Estudios de Poética Hebrea, 1963, 309—335. 363—381; H. Lubsczyk, Der Auszug aus Ägypten, 1963. Further studies, including some works in Hebrew, are listed by Liebreich, Sarna, and Ridderbos. In Near Eastern literature, certain types at least are common, as in adjacent lines; so, E. P. Dhorme, Le livre de Job, 1926, cxlvii. For repetition elsewhere, see above, p. 3.
[8] The Literature of the Ancient Egyptians, 1927, xxxiv.

The hypothesis of a full beginning and the criterion of catchword association support each other in the outlining and separation of sections; for non-stylistic, secondary repetitions always have between them a break marked by a strong opening. It is true, in certain cases a full grammatical beginning occurs at some point other than between external connectors, but such cases are not numerous and usually there are considerations of content that militate against making a separation at these points; a full expression may occur not only at the beginning of a section.

The resulting wholes exhibit a relatively homogeneous compositional structure, which would be violated by accepting divisions elsewhere. Each unit begins and ends in a characteristic manner. Openings consist of an address or call in the second person[9], an announcement of a *rîb* or day of judgment[10], or a historical reference which usually presents a lamenting or especially an ironical description of Israel's fall[11]. In most cases, the opening includes an accusation[12]. The closing note is always one of disaster, either as it has already happened or as it is expected, or else of hope. Five oracles end in a general word of judgment; four of these climactic words announce a "visitation" or "returning" of Israel's evil[13].

In a few cases there is no significant verbal connection between adjacent oracles. At such points, however, there is either a major shift in content between groups of oracles, to be called "cycles," or a transition to a hopeful oracle which has been assigned its place without regard to catchwords, in order to end a collection on a positive note. Precise details are given in the translation, above.

The oracles of Hos 4—11 form one large collection, subdivided into cycles. Cycle I — comprising 4 1-9 (10) 4 11-14 4 15-19 and 5 1-7 — deals with the cult. The constituent sections are bound together by the term "whoring;" one might even speak of arrangement by content rather than by catchword. Cycle II — which seems to comprise the groups 5 8-10 5 11-7 7 7 8-16 8 1-7 8 8-10 — deals with social and political evils; occasional cultic references had already been included in these oracles before they were joined to each other. The recurrent use of the words "king" and "princes" is as much a matter of content as of catchword associations; but distinctly external connections between oracles are also apparent. Cycle III — with 8 11-13 and 9 1-9 (composed of two separate oracles?) — deals with the cult and includes the motif

---

[9] Hos 2 4 4 1. 15 5 1. 8 8 1 9 1 14 2.
[10] Hos 2 4 4 1 9 7 (?) 12 3.
[11] Hos 4 11f. 5 11 7 8 8 8. 11 9 10 10 1. 9 11 1f. 13 1. 12.
[12] So also 1 2 3 1. Exceptions: 5 8 7 8 (?) 8 8 9 7 (?).
[13] The four: 4 9 8 13 9 9 12 15. The fifth: 5 10.

of a return to Egypt; it shows some external repetitions within the cycle. Cycle IV presents a series of historical reviews — namely 9 10-17 10 1-8 10 9-15 11 1-11. The mechanical connections between the first three of these oracles by means of the words "fruit" and "hill" have already been discussed; the final one is verbally unconnected with what precedes.

Thereafter probably a new collection begins[14]. It includes the oracles of 12 3-15 13 1-11 and 13 12-14 1, each of which contains at least one quotation from cultic tradition in its center[15]. These three oracles are attached to each other by catchwords. They are followed by a section of exhortation and hope (14 2-9), with perhaps only an accidental repetition of a preceding word. The two verses 12 1f. link the collection with earlier material, probably as a secondary editorial development.

It is clear that the book of Hosea contains a much sharper structure in content than has usually been thought. Some investigators have described the book of Hosea as planless[16]. Some previous attempts at finding an order have been problematic; neither the sequence of accusation, threat, and positive emphasis (Ewald and a few others[17]) nor a grouping of 4 1—7 7 and 7 8—10 15 as dealing respectively with moral and political decay (G. A. Smith, followed by some) is satisfying. Nevertheless, the series of historical reviews beginning with 9 10 has often been recognized, and, especially recently, a new start with 5 8[18]. Nyberg (p. 18) reports that the Ḥamāsa, a typical Arabic anthology, is arranged according to certain themes; within the thematic groupings, the associative principle holds. Hosea's book evidently falls into the same pattern. In length, the book, or its larger part, corresponds roughly to the standard Sanscrit śataka, which is composed theoretically, though not literally, of one hundred short poetic units with the size of Hosea's small paragraph, supposedly created by a single author[19].

The question can be raised whether the cycles within chs. 4—11 ever formed independent elements of tradition. It is hard to see why groups of oracles centered around a single topic should have been

---

[14] Already J. Eichhorn (Einleitung in das Alte Testament, III 1803³, 225) regarded chs. 1—3 4—11 and 12—14 as three parts of Hosea. H. Birkeland, emphasizing the placement of hope passages, found in addition a break after Hos 6 3 (Zum hebräischen Traditionswesen, 1939, 60).

[15] Hos 12 4-7. 10f. 13f. 13 4f. 14.

[16] E. g., S. Michelet, Norsk Teologi til Reformationsjubilæet 1917, 11.

[17] G. Ewald, Die Propheten des Alten Bundes, I 1867², 187ff. Similarly, but always disagreeing in dividing points, Keil (1866); W. Nowack, Der Prophet Hosea, 1880 (but appropriately rejected in 1922, 10); H. Frey, Das Buch des Werbens Gottes, 1961.

[18] Good's major groupings are: 4 1-3 4 4—5 7 5 8—8 14 9 1—10 15 11 1—14 1 14 2-9, based on a somewhat different theory of catchwords.

[19] S. N. Dasgupta, ed., A History of Sanscrit Literature, I 1947, 157. 399.

constructed to be transmitted without reference to other such groupings; though cycles determined by content may have been memorized
independently, it must have been clear that they were each a part of
a larger whole. Furthermore, cycle III is quite short and has a rather
weak beginning. It has some connection with the end of cycle II
(8 1ff.) and possibly with cycle IV, especially if the latter should once
have opened with a form of what is now 11 1-7, with its reference to
early Israelite history.

It is likely that chs. 4—11 and 12—14 form two collections which
do not presuppose each other. Each ends on a relatively hopeful note,
making a satisfactory conclusion possible. Furthermore, they both
begin with an oracle which contains a *rib*, a judicial process[20]. This
fact could be a coincidence; but ch. 2 opens in the same way, and the
rib theme introduces a number of collections outside of Hosea.

Thus Mi 1 2 heads the first chapters of that book and indeed the book as a
whole, while Mi 6 2 introduces the complex of Mi 6—7. Is 1 forms the opening of that
book or specifically of a smaller complex within it; Jer 25 31 is part of the introduction (or perhaps end) of the collection of oracles against foreign nations, while
Jer 2 9 probably lay early in the scroll containing Jeremiah's poetry and in any case
comes soon after the account of Jeremiah's call. In prophetic literature, only Is 3 13
and Mal 3 5 have an explicit *rib* in some other position.

The two parts of Hos 4—14 can easily have played somewhat
different roles in tradition. Since the material of chs. 12—14 parodies
cultic pronouncements, it could be used for ironic attack upon cult
assertions, while chs. 4—11 have a more general application. The two
parts, however, had a common history, as indicated by the fact that
in both of them all references to Judah (except possibly one) are
negative[21]. Those circles in the southern kingdom which preserved the
tradition — perhaps northerners who had fled south — sought to
apply its critical thrust to the southern kingdom as well.

In a decidedly contrasting manner, the tradition of Hos 1—3 is
friendly to Judah[22]. That tradition must have passed through patrioti-
cally minded circles in the south; among these it probably received its
final form relatively late, perhaps not before the Babylonian exile.

Hos 1—3 consists of three complexes, each of which has a complicated, evidently largely oral, history. Ch. 1, as will be argued below,
combines two narrative strands, one of which includes at least two
different interpretations of the name Jezreel. Two Judaistic additions

---

[20] C. Schedl, Geschichte des Alten Testaments, IV 1962, 184.
[21] Hos 4 15 5 5. 10. 12-14 6 4. 11 8 14 10 11 12 3. The obscure reference in 12 1 can be
read positively; if so, the addition of 12 1f. (and the joining of chs. 4—11 with
chs. 12—14) must have taken place after other Judean references had entered.
[22] Hos 1 7 2 2 3 5.

— 1 7 and 2 1-3 (in 2 2 "children of Judah" precedes "children of Israel," indicating a southern origin) — complete the section. A second complex begins in 2 4 with an extended passage in which Israel, or its land, is spoken of symbolically as a woman in the style of a legal process (*rîb*) against an adulterous wife (2 4-7. 10-12). Within this, two verses (v. 8f.) have been inserted which pick up earlier terms, but whose own terms are not repeated. The judicial passage is continued, either originally or secondarily, by a realistic threat against Israel (v. 13-15). Thereupon follows an announcement of discipline and renewal (v. 16-25), which can hardly represent an organic continuation of the de-claration of legal process but fits in generally with its theme. This promise has been greatly developed in the tradition, so that its original lines are difficult to determine; a number of deliberate verbal connec-tions with earlier parts of the book are apparent in the material. Ch. 3 represents an afterthought relating to one strand within ch. 1; it has itself been expanded. The three parts comprising chs. 1—3 evidently developed both independently and as a united whole, at differing stages.

Hos 1—3 was naturally placed to precede chs. 4ff., since the latter opens with the cycle centered on whoredom[23]. So far it has been taken for granted that a single author stands behind most of the tra-ditions of the book; should this be a false assumption[24], one must then speak of a tradition originating within related circles in the Northern Kingdom and continuing in varying ways in Judah.

While Hos 1—3 was sharply transformed in a long process of largely oral tradition, the remaining chapters appear to have been reduced to writing fairly early, even if primarily as a guide to memory. Only thus can one explain the survival of internal jaggedness within the individual sections and the relative lack of secondary growth. The presence of catchword connections does not necessarily antedate a written state, for such devices were used widely in the ordering of written collections at a time when these arrangements were still supportive in relation to a simultaneous oral transmission[25].

Writing could be employed in the ancient world for several standard purposes. It is thus used for letters, ownership designations, memorial inscriptions, business documents, spells, and laws, all of which are attested in the Old Testament[26]. It may

---

[23] The fact that "sons of Israel" in 4 1 and "beasts of the field and birds of the air" in 4 3 repeat expressions in preceding chapters may be taken as coincidental.

[24] As thought by H. Graetz, Die Geschichte der Juden, II, 1 1875, 93. 214. 440; Y. Kaufmann, The Religion of Israel, 1960, 369—371.

[25] So, for the Talmud, B. Gerhardsson, Memory and Manuscript, 1961, 149.

[26] Ownership (in a sense) is designated in Num 17 17f.

be noted that written spells appear typically in the negative form of curses[27]. In prophecy, the operation of written curses is emphasized repeatedly; indeed, the use of writing is mentioned primarily for words of woe, partly to give them added threatening power and partly to seal them for a later occasion since they are not accepted by the hearers[28]. There was probably a tendency to put negative pronouncements into written form, more readily than encouraging statements. Such a tendency helps to explain the survival of doom prophecies from pre-exilic times and specifically the relatively firm written tradition of Hosea's negative sayings, as in chs. 4—14.

The presence of very small sense-units within the larger oracles is puzzling. H. W. Wolff has suggested that in most cases each ("kerygmatic") unit of tradition contains several small utterances ("rhetorical units") spoken at one time or at a series of related occasions, largely in back-and-forth discussion with the prophet's audience. This interpretation rests in part on the assumption that an individual utterance must be reasonably homogeneous in form, for instance in the manner in which Israel is addressed. Violent changes of grammatical forms, however, are characteristic of prophetic style, as attested in non-Israelite prophecies as well[29], and have a content-determined rationale, as will be seen. While it has often been thought that ecstacy must produce short oracles, Lindblom's thesis that ecstatic experiences produce disconnected images and forms is more appropriate in many instances[30]. Gunkel noted that prophetic words are either short or fall into smaller utterances in which the prophet turns hither and yon[31], in other words, that no lengthy coherent exposition takes place.

In Hosea's words, it is only the larger groups (called "oracles"), which have sufficient complexity to contain the interplay of accusation, threat, lament, and irony, and the combination of different address styles, which comprise the essential structure of his prophecy. While it is possible that the originally spoken or written units were much simpler fragments (though that is doubtful), the present struc-

---

[27] Num 5 23 Zech 5 3 Dtn 29 19f. II Chr 34 24. The curses of Dtn 27 16-26 were quite likely inscribed (cf. v. 4). Written protective spells do occur sometimes elsewhere, in the Near East especially in later times (see J. Hempel, Apoxysmata, 1961, 49f.); but in the survey of A. Bertholet, Die Macht der Schrift in Glauben und Aberglauben, 1949, they constitute a very small minority, since protective formulas are generally turned negatively against evil forces.

[28] Is 8 16 30 8 65 6 Jer 25 13 36 (and 45?); 51 60-63 Ez 2 9f. Zech 5 3 are negative in character. Is 8 1 and Hab 2 2 are unclear in their major thrust; Jer 30 2 is positive. On tablets in the ancient world, J. Scharbert, Biblica 39 (1958), 3; for their use in Greece, F. Heiler, Prayer, 1932, 81. The largely positive spells of Egyptian mortuary texts are given in the form of a direction for oral recitation.

[29] E. g., J. Geffcken, Komposition und Entstehungszeit der Oracula Sibyllina, 1902, 6.
[30] E. g., Prophecy in Ancient Israel, 1962, 124.
[31] Die Propheten, 116—118.

3*

ture represents the form in which the words were made available to the public.

Most of the oracles reveal a remarkable internal unity despite their jagged style. In the translation (Chapter II), each oracle has been provided with a carefully worded heading designed to formulate its central point. Internal word repetitions help to develop most of them. The imagery of several oracles will be treated in greater detail at appropriate points below[32]. In connection with the data that can best be gathered directly from the translation, a few explanatory words are in order.

In some cases, there are signs of an internal development within units of tradition. Thus 4 1-9 was expanded by v. 10; 5 1f. was probably joined somewhat secondarily with v. 3-7; 8 1-4, perhaps with v. 5-7; while 10 9-15 and perhaps 5 11—7 7 contain three subdivisions. The parts are tied together by verbal connections that have a certain ring of artificiality; such transitions can in part be instances of poetic freedom to follow up a previous word. The combinations must have been made before the entire collection was formed, for otherwise one element of each oracle would have no verbal connections with what precedes or follows. Hos 11 1-7 may not originally have been followed by v. 8f., but this hopeful conclusion provided the place of the oracle in the collection[33]. In each case (except in 11 1-9), at least one of the parts fails to exhibit the proper form for the beginning or ending of an independent oracle, as analyzed earlier; in other words, the combinations were created — in some cases perhaps already at the original stage of production — to form genuine wholes out of somewhat divergent materials or thoughts. Several oracles (such as 9 10-17 12 3-15) appear to be in disorder regarding their internal sequence.

Hos 8 1-7 and 10 1-8 refer both to royalty and to the cult, especially to the "calf." Several explanations for such a mixture are possible: (1) the units are complex wholes with no particular specialization; (2) Hosea had some reason to connect royalty with the calf-image[34]; (3) the "king" is an ironic references to the image itself. It is hard to decide between these alternatives, but the third possibility fits best in 10 1-8.

Special difficulties reside in an analysis of the section 5 8—7 7. In the text as transmitted, its first part contains references to Judah;

---

[32] See the index as a guide to discussions.

[33] M. Buss, Diss., 1958, treated 11 1-7 and 8f. as separate oracles (thus Wolff's comment, 249); Hos 11 1-7 may conceivably have once followed 9 1-9, with its theme of a return to Egypt.

[34] So, A. Cacquot, RHPR 41 (1961), 144, specifically seeing a reference to Jeroboam I. Cf. Ward 148—151.

these have been accepted as original by many commentators, as by Wellhausen and A. Alt[35]. Several considerations, however, speak against that view. Israel is known to have trespassed the border of the south, since 5 8 expects a return blow by Judah within its own boundary. That Judah then invaded Israelite territory is not attested; if such an invasion did occur (presumably after the call of 5 8), that could not easily have been singled out as a special evil, since the Northern Kingdom itself had just committed a major transgression of this kind. Hos 5 8-10 is best taken as a single saying, with the point that Israel's action as a boundary thief will be punished. In Hos 5 11ff., a reference to Judah is absent not only from v. 11 but also from the crucial sentence of v. 13aβ, in which it is said that Israel seeks help for its malady from Assyria; to retain the name Judah elsewhere in this section, one has to insert it here by textual emendation[36]. It is simpler to assume that in Hos 5 8—6 4 the word Judah was substituted for Israel in several instances, as happened 10 11 12 3. Judah is absent also from the rest of the section, which is centered as a whole around the theme that healing is made impossible by deep social sins. No major break in continuity occurs until after 7 7, for 6 7 provides a poor beginning and the material of 6 7—7 7 is based on a single catalog of evil.

II. POETRY

If the question whether the book of Hosea contains poetry or not is to be answered in terms of feeling[37], the answer must be in the affirmative. It is clear that the emotional tenor is high. Related to emotion is involvement, as distinguished from dispassionate discursive observation; it is a high degree of involvement which elicits a strong emotion. There can be no doubt that Hosea exhibits a participation in the life of the community as it faces disaster, specifically by the threat of God. Especially pronounced is his identification with the divine viewpoint, with God's violent opposition to Israel; but he also poignantly expresses lament for the people.

If there is anything that detracts from his poetry, it is the fact that his emotion is not sufficiently restrained but too often empties itself out uncontrolledly. The finest poetry probably is created when dammed-up feeling is allowed to discharge itself somewhat gradually

---

[35] Kleine Schriften, II 1953, 163—187.

[36] That creates even more tedious repetition than Alt noted. Mowinckel seeks to ease the parallels by a use in part of Joseph or Jacob; but the passage does not read badly with Israel as the name, since Ephraim is twice mentioned alone (v. 11. 13).

[37] Cf. I. A. Richards, Principles of Literary Criticism, 1945, 273; Susanne Langer, Feeling and Form, 1953, 27; W. Kayser, Das sprachliche Kunstwerk, 1948, 274.

in sublime expression, as is possible under conditions of extreme concentration. But "surplus creative energy"[38] is not held in reserve by Hosea, so that his ecstatic form is of a relatively undisciplined variety[39].

There was a close connection between prophecy and poetry in the ancient Near East and elsewhere, so that the employment of lyrical forms by a prophet was by no means external. The poet was widely believed to speak on the basis of inspiration[40], while prophecy could be brought about by music, as attested in Israel itself[41]. Even the supernatural power attributed to the prophetic word may be compared to the magical implications of a carefully formulated poetic construction. In short, though prophet and poet are not automatically identical, they do share an attitude of receptivity, emotionality, and an emphasis on the word itself as a powerful and effective phenomenon. Like other forms of receptivity, they exhibit not inactivity but an unusually creative outburst[42].

The fact that Hosea is full of standardized phrases and forms, as will be seen later, by no means conflicts with his sense of inspiration. There is no reason why intensity of feeling should be able to find expression only in individualistic, novel formulations; if there is a heavy loss of consciousness, deliberate variations are even pushed into the background.

Among the devices and objective marks of poetry, the most important is repetition. Repetition serves the concentration of thought and the heightening of feeling[43].

Examples of repetition can be found in Hosea, for instance in the form of assonance, including alliteration. The boundary line between deliberate assonance and an accidental constellation of sounds is fluid. The more notable instances of sound repetitions in Hosea, with the exception of those to be mentioned separately below, are as follows: צָרַר רוּחַ 4 19; many words beginning with א 5 14f.; the conjunction of

---

[38] A. Culler, Creative Religious Literature, 1930, 2.

[39] D. H. Lawrence, with similarly great sexual feeling, is also said to have failed to develop disciplined art (R. P. Blackmur, Language as Gesture, 1952, 288. 300).

[40] A. Guillaume, Prophecy and Divination Among the Hebrews and Other Semites, 1938, 243—259. 309—314; J. Pedersen in: T. H. Robinson-Festschrift, 1950, 127—142; J. Hempel, Apoxysmata, 287—307; Plato, Phaedrus, 245, and Ion; I. Seierstad, ZAW 52 (1934), 39f.; A. Heschel, Die Prophetie, 1936, 42—50, and, further, The Prophets, 1962, 367. 377f.

[41] I Sam 10 5 II Kings 3 15.

[42] So, rightly, H. Steiner, Die Christliche Welt 51 (1937), 798 (with a fine collection of examples, 757—762).

[43] A. Merzbach, Über die sprachliche Wiederholung im Biblisch-Hebräischen, 1928, probably correctly connects repetition with semiconscious, affective structures. Similarly, J. Muilenburg op. cit. 102, and earlier J. Herder, The Spirit of Hebrew Poetry, I 1833, 41.

עָנָה ... הַפּוּכָה, בָּקָר ... בָּעֵר 6 6; חֶסֶד חָפַצְתִּי, רף and יח, 6 1f.;
נִדְמֹה 10 5; (?), יָגִילוּ ... גָּלָה in 9 6; קב and מ 8 10; מְעַט מִמַּשָּׂא מֶלֶךְ 7 8;
at beginning of 11 8; words with א and ק, 11 9b; רֹעֶה רוּחַ וְרֹדֵף, 12 2;
נִדְמָה מֶלֶךְ, 10 15; אַט אֵלָיו אוֹכִיל (MT) and עַל עָל, 11 4; four words with א,
יָשְׁבוּ יֵשְׁבוּ, 14 8[44]. Rather frequently, word pairs with assonance are
taken over from broader Israelitic style traditions; so עָשׁוּק רָצוּץ
(5 11)[45]; צָמָא ... צִיָּה (2 5); חַגָּה חָדְשָׁהּ (2 13); אמלל ... אָבֵל (4 3);
אֵלָה ... אַלּוֹן (4 13)[46]; שָׁרֵיהֶם סֹרְרִים (9 15)[47]. Rhyme appears rather
elaborately in the quotation laid upon Israel's lips in 2 7[48], as well as
in a proverbial jingle (8 7). Other cases of rhyme are a more or less
accidental by-product of the repetition of identical endings or suffixes,
as in 5 8f. (with ending *ā*) and rather frequently in 9 1-9 (v. 1 *an*,
3 *ayim*, 4 and 9 *am*, 6 *em*, 8 *āw*); more of these can be recognized if
Hosea's Hebrew was accented on the ultima (4 7 *am*, 7 8 *a*). Sometimes, though not strikingly often, a single root appears twice in a
single phrase[49]. The expression שׁוּב שְׁבוּת ("restoration of fortune,"
6 11) is a standard prophetic term.

Allied to assonance are the frequent plays on words evident in the
book. The names "Jacob" and "Israel" reveal a traditional relation to
the roots *'qb*, "hold a heel," and *śrh*, "struggle," in the (quoted?)
saying of Hos 12 4f[50]. "Ephraim" is joined with *p⁰rî*, "fruit" (9 16
14 9), with the verb *pr'*, "to be fruitful, flourish" (13 15, an abnormal
form of *prh* to accentuate the association), with the noun *pæræ'*, "wild
ass" (8 9), and (consciously?) with *rp'*, "to heal" (5 13 11 3). Folk

---

[44] S. Kaatz, Wortspiel, Assonanz und Notarikon bei Hosea, Jeschurun 11 (1924),
424—437, suggests further cases of assonance among which the following are prob-
ably the best: חֲרַשְׁתֶּם רֶשַׁע, סַר סָבְאָם 4 18; הָאֱוִיל הַלָּךְ, שֹׁכֵן שֹׁמְרוֹן 5 11; 10 5; חֲרַשְׁתֶּם רֶשַׁע,
10 13; כְּשֹׁד שַׁלְמָן, תֶּאְשַׁם שֹׁמְרוֹן 10 14; 14 1. Harper (clxxii) points to sounds in
5 1b. 2, and to the association of שָׁב with יֵשְׁבוּ in 9 3. Wolff sees assonances in
8 3b (5), 8 7 (יְזְרָעוּ ... יִקְצֹרוּ) and 12 9 (אוֹן and עָוֹן after מִצָּא). Additional examples by I. Casanowicz, JBL 12 (1893), 105—167; H. Lubsczyk op cit.. 41 and
Rudolph 21f. are less than convincing.

[45] Cf. Dtn 28 33, as pointed out by P. Saydon (Biblica 36 [1955], 294).

[46] For parallels to the last four examples, see I. Gábor, Der hebräische Urrhythmus,
1929, 5. 6. 8. (He also adds the pair, אַף ... עֶבְרָה, 13 11). Earlier, J. Ley, De
alliteratione, 1859, 5—7.

[47] Cf. Is 1 23 and Jer 6 28 ?

[48] Probably read פִּשְׁתִּי; but that form spoils a small rhyme in 2 11. In 2 11a, for that
matter, a certain rhyme-cadence appears in the words בְּעִתּוֹ ... בְּמוֹעֲדוֹ.

[49] Hos 2 8 4 18 9 11 10 4. 15. דָמִים appears twice 4 2; רָעָה, doubled in 10 15. H. Recken-
dorf, Über Paranomasie in den semitischen Sprachen, 1909, finds "syntactic connections between two or more root-related words" to be relatively common in
Hebrew (vii).

[50] Similarly already in the J passages Gen 25 26 32 29; no accusation is involved in
these older traditions.

etymology had already explained Ephraim in the light of the root *prh*, "to be fruitful"[51]. The place-names of Gilead and Gilgal together receive an ironical allusion from the word *găllîm*, "stone heaps," which builds on associations already known[52]. An allusion to Beersheba is probably implied or included in Hos 4 15, in a manner similar to that of Amos 5 5 and 8 14. The name of Hosea's son "Jezreel" receives varied explanations and allusions (not all of them genuine)[53]. Though Hosea is not highly original in the creation of literary symbols, he is effective in their variation.

Terms are sometimes repeated in adjacent phrases — in an ironical tone (10 1), with the implication that the punishment meets the crime[54], or for comparison[55], but also simply for the sake of crescendo[56]. Such reiteration can involve anything from the negative particle[57] to the full phrase "and he does not know it" (7 9). Stylistic and associational word-repetitions have already been discussed in a preceding section.

The most important form of repetition is rhythmical parallelism, which in Hebrew ideally means the restatement of a thought in similar terms. Often, however, the second member ("stich"[58] or "colon") of a couplet (or "period") runs parallel to the first neither positively nor negatively in content but continues the flow of meaning. The phenomenon of such "structural parallelism"[59] reflects a basic "law of duality[60]," of which ideational parallelism is merely one form. The application of duality can be expanded by doubling the basic couplet so that a four-cola unit is created. Such a quatrain employs, in effect, a combination of internal and external parallelism, i. e., within and between periods[61].

---

[51] Gen 41 52. The appearance of the word *parā*, "calf," in 4 16 is not specifically related to Ephraim. Gen 49 22, in the Joseph blessing, probably involves a play with *prh* (MT), *parā*, or *pæræ'* (E. Speiser, Genesis, 1964, 368).

[52] Hos 12 12. Gilead is associated with the word *găl* in Gen 31 46-52 (JE); Gilgal probably derives its name from the presence of a circle of stones (Josh 4 20) and is further interpreted in the light of the verb *gll*, "roll" (Josh 5 9).

[53] Hos 1 4f. (including assonance with "Israel") 2 2. 25.

[54] Hos 4 6 11 5 (using two somewhat different meanings of שוב, according to a stylistic pattern noted by C. C. Torrey, The Second Isaiah, 1928, 199—202).

[55] Hos 4 5f. (?) 10 14 12 13f. 13 6.

[56] Hos 2 18. 21f. 23f. 3 1 4 4. 5 6 4 7 8 (Ephraim) 8 11 9 5. 7 11 8.

[57] Hos 3 4 4 1 11 9.

[58] With G. B. Gray, The Forms of Hebrew Poetry, 1915, instead of "hemistich."

[59] G. Young, Ugaritic Prosody, JNES 9 (1950), 133.

[60] S. Mowinckel in: Pedersen-Festschrift, 1953, 250.

[61] According to the terminology of T. H. Robinson, The Poetry of the Old Testament, 1947, 28f.

The prominence of the four-part stanza in Hosea has been noted by Marti, Duhm, and others[62]. Pfannmüller and Mowinckel translated Hosea in such a way as to reflect regular four-line strophes, although with considerable emendation either through omission[63] or restoration[64]. Other translators have noted this organization in individual verses, sometimes independently from previous studies[65]. Many, however, have completely ignored such a structure, probably largely since no rigid scheme can be carried through the text as it stands or when following natural sense-divisions. Probably the best approach is one that allows for free variation around the general pattern of duality or repetition.

A major variation of the four-cola strophe can be seen in the three-member unit, which may often be regarded as an entity of which only one half is further subdivided into two parts. Two short cola are hardly strong enough to stand by themselves, but three or four yield together a satisfying whole. Thus most of Hosea's groupings consist of two periods, one of which contains two cola, while the length of the other is variable. (As printed in Chapter II, each long or short period begins at the left-hand margin.)

The principle of duality works in such a way that, in Hosea at least, there are no tricola in which three full-sized members are equally parallel to each other to form a sense unit. In independent formations of tristiches, two of the members can be grouped together, with the third balancing the others[66]. Altogether about fifty stanzaic tricola can be found in Hosea. Almost thirty of these stand either next to each other or adjacent to another weak stanza (see below), as it were for mutual support. Most of the rest appear at the beginning or end of major (or sometimes minor) poetic divisions[67].

---

[62] F. E. Peiser, Hosea, 1914; P. Ruben, AJSL 51 (1934/35), 30—45; 52 (1935/36), 34—42 (with a discussion of Hos 7 1-7). See also the translations by Procksch and especially Bruno.

[63] So, G. Pfannmüller, Die Propheten, 1913.

[64] So, Mowinckel (1944). His view is that lacunae developed through deterioration of papyri (ZAW 45 [1927], 42). Mowinckel arranges almost all prophetic poetry, especially before the Exile, in four-cola groups. He has championed this form in a number of studies, from Norsk TT 28 (1927), 1—31, to VT 5 (1955), 26.

[65] K. Elliger, ZAW 69 (1957), 151—160; Wolff 139. 195f. 252. 290. The writer noted the form while searching for the smallest possible units.

[66] The same observation also holds true for most of the tricola identified by S. Mowinckel, Real and Apparent Tricola in Hebrew Psalm Poetry, 1957, despite his analysis, even in the cases he specifically quotes.

[67] Hos 1 9 2 12f. 16 4 4. 9. 14 5 7. 11 7 16 9 7 10 8. 13 11 9 12 3. 15 13 1 14 1. Exceptions are 7 1. 10 (genuine?) 8 5 (?) 9 13 (quatrain?) 11 3 (after a long stanza) 12 7 (a quotation) 13 6. The edge position was noted by Wolff 39. 174, and, for other

Sometimes, three cola are balanced by a single line or by a weakly divided period to form a strophe. In two such cases, the three parallel cola are very short and are intimately parallel to each other (8 6 10 4). The rest exhibit standard degrees of parallelism within the three-cola group (2 7b. 10 ?. 15 5 1. 2. 15 7 14 10 5).

Stanzas with five or six cola often include quotations, from proverbial material (4 11f. 8 7 9 15 13 12f.), from sacred traditions (10 12 12 13f. 13 4f. 14), or from the words of those addressed (2 14 12 8f. 13 2. 10). Sometimes a fifth colon appears when one of the four basic elements is long enough to contain two phrases (2 21f. 3 1 9 1 12 12 and perhaps 4 2 11 4). Thus Hosea was free to expand the rhythmic structure[68], occasionally even to three periods in a group.

In a number of cases, two stanzas can be combined to form a double strophe, which might be resolved into a long one with five or six cola and a short one with two or three (4 13b. 14 5 12f. 9 5f. 10 7f. 11 ? 13 7-9). Furthermore, about fifteen quatrains[69] form only a loose sense unity whose component periods are not specifically related to each other, though rhythmically they belong together and their content forms a reasonable whole.

There are in evidence, however, about seventy rather closely knit quatrains, including twenty whose reconstruction is not quite certain. It is not necessary to assume that the author was conscious either of the quatrain as such or of its deviations. The rhythm, including its syncopations, was part of his poetic inheritance, in which the pattern of duality, with many possibilities of development, prevailed. Unconsciously, Hosea followed the advice of a later classical writer that the best rhetorical style uses a mixture of formed groups with looser collections of members[70].

Credit should go to Robert Lowth for already recognizing the basic pattern herewith presented. In his study on Isaiah, he notes a stanza form containing four lines, or two distiches. In addition, he recognizes triplets, usually with two synonymous members, and stanzas of five lines, with an extra colon at the middle or at the end[71]. Similarly, C. C. Torrey accepted the quatrain as a common but not ex-

---

parts of the Old Testament, by B. M. Waggoner, Studies in Hebrew Poetry, Diss. Duke, 1952.

[68] The remaining examples are explainable as follows: quotations or allusions may be present in 6 5f. 11 1f. 13 15; secondary material is probably in 2 5. 10. 15 9 4 and perhaps in 2 4 14 4. In addition, two cola each in 7 13 and 10 1 contain two short phrases.

[69] Hos 4 5. 7f. 6 7f. 7 3f. 7. 15f. 8 2-4. 10-12 9 2f. 9 10 2. 6-8. 15 13 15 (end)-14 1.

[70] Demetrius, On Style, § 15. Most of the structures not listed as exceptions form good quatrains, representing close to half of the text of Hosea.

[71] Isaiah, 1779[2], xv—xvii; 1793[3], 16—18; 1834[10], xii—xiv; with variations in detail. Lectures on the Sacred Poetry of the Hebrews, end of ch. XXVIII, for Is 14 4-27.

clusive form, to which triads, in themselves relatively weak and unbalanced, add variety[72].

The double-period group indeed can be widely found in Old Testament poetry[73] and is prominent in a large part of Akkadian and Egyptian literature[74] and elsewhere[75]. In Near Eastern traditions, strophes thus built up do not always represent rigid sense units, and variations appear frequently. Sanscrit poetry, however, developed a rigorous form of this basic pattern, namely in strongly isolated stanzas divided into two parts, each of which is composed of one or (usually) two short *padas*.

A continuation of the old form is preserved in the Masoretic versification, which breaks each verse into two parts, one or both of which are usually again subdivided. In fact, in many cases the delineation of units as conceived here coincides with Masoretic verse divisions.

Members of periods in Hosea's poetry stand regularly in *ideational parallelism*, with varying degrees of preciseness in correspondence. Complete parallelism, in which each element of one member can be matched with an element in the other member[76], occurs almost forty times. Incomplete, even if close, synonymous parallelism (with an unmatched element) occurs somewhat more than eighty times; about ten of these instances, however, are unbalanced only by a "therefore" or some other word not easily repeated. In content, parallelism can be stated either positively or negatively; but the only instances of the negative form are to be found in 2 18 9 4 ("their food will be for themselves; it will not come into the house of Yahweh") 12 1 (?) and in the wisdom addition 14 10.

In a good number of cases, however, the second colon does not simply restate the essential point of the first, but forms what may be called *directional parallelism*, in which one member builds on the other. The major types belonging to such a construction are as follows: forms expressing causality or ground, regularly introduced by כִּי, "for" or "since" (2 6 4 6 9 17 14 1. 2); sequential relations, such as the following: "They came to Baal-Peor and dedicated themselves to Shame" (9 10);

---

[72] Op. cit. 178.

[73] See the analysis and history of discussion by C. Kraft, The Strophic Structure of Hebrew Poetry, 1938. In addition, J. W. Rothstein, Grundzüge des hebräischen Rhythmus, 1909, 64ff., and Hebräische Poesie, 1914; J. Begrich, TR NF 4 (1932), 89; and many individual studies, including H. Gunkel, Die Psalmen, 1926.

[74] E. g., W. F. Albright, JPOS 2 (1922), 70; Falkenstein—Soden, 40f. 240—247. 270—273. 381f. 388; S. Mowinckel, The Psalms in Israel's Worship, II 1962, 191; S. Herrmann, Die prophetischen Heilserwartungen im Alten Testament, 1965, 26, etc.

[75] Cf. C. Budd, Chinese Poems, 1912, 22 (though this discussion is one-sided). In Syriac, Arabic, primitive, and modern poetry, the same group is a popular, though by no means an exclusive, form. For Bedouin poetry, J. Smart, JSS 11 (1966), 202 to 216; 12 (1967), 245—267.

[76] Gray op. cit. 59.

contrast, for instance in comparing Yahweh's action to Israel's response (7 13b. 15 8 12 11 2); reciprocity, with analogous mutual relations (1 9b 2 4. 25); circumstantial relations, such as, "If it should make some, strangers will swallow it" (8 7); consequence or response (4 17 10 2a. 12a. 13a); an object of thought or speech (7 2 13 10 14 3).

Without close ideational synonymy or directional organization there exists what may be called *loose parallelism*, wherein two related concepts are juxtaposed (so, 4 7 6 3a 7 2b 8 5 9 15b 10 3b 12 5 14 8. 9). This pattern, together with "directional parallelism," is often classed as "synthetic;" but this use of the term is different from that of R. Lowth, who included incomplete synonymous parallelism but expected a correspondence in construction in the two parts of the synthetic form[77].

In addition, many periods are divided into parts, one of which cannot grammatically stand by itself. Several typical constructions emerge. One part can be introduced by לְ ("to"), designating an aim when related to a verb, or a reference point when attached to a noun; כְּ ("as"), making a comparison of some sort; בְּ ("in," "when"); מִן ("from"); or עַל ("because of," "on"). Temporal designations using the word "day" (5 9 7 5 9 9 10 9. 14), direct objects (1 4. 6 2 10), and subordinate characterizations (2 14 10 11 14 8) also appear. Sometimes no clear internal division is at all apparent, except for a rhythmic caesura in a long clause (8 4b 10 15b 13 15 [end]). On the whole, such constructions may be considered a little-developed form of directional parallelism.

When a period contains only such intraclausal parallelism as was discussed in the last paragraph, it may be considered to be weakly divided. A tristich or the conjunction of two weakly divided periods may be considered to form a weak stanza. Such stanzas as a rule stand at the beginning or end of a passage (4 1 and see above for triplets) or in pairs with two weakly formed quatrains (5 9f. 7 8f.) or two triplets (6 1f. 7 5f. 8 8f. 13 9 16f.) or one of each kind (4 16-18a 6 9f. 9 10 10 11 12 10f.). Rows of three triplets occur three times (2 8f. 11 5-7 14 5-7).

Synonymy between periods is looser than between cola on the average; no very neat patterns are discernible. Relations between stanzas are even more tenuous, if present at all. Parallelism occurs also within cola, though not frequently (4 13 7 15).

To compare Hosea's poetry to that of other prophets would require a more thoroughgoing analysis than can here be attempted. The ratio of complete to incomplete parallelism appears to approximate that found in Lamentations by G. B. Gray and in Amos by

---

[77] In line with the Greek "parallelism of form" discussed by E. Norden, Die Antike Kunstprosa, 1958, 816. See Lowth, Isaiah, 1779[2], xxi; 1834[10], xvii.

L. Newman, while the phenomena of intraclausal relations bear similarity to those discussed by W. Popper in a study of Is 1—35[78]. Like parallelism, meter or rhythm is a form of repetition. K. Budde has pointed out that ancient poetry is characterized by the breaking of speech into small units[79]. The regularity of the recurrence of a break and, in some poetic traditions, of the recurrence of still smaller units called "feet" constitutes a repetitive feature. The concept of a foot, however, is probably not appropriate to Hebrew literature, unless one identifies it with a unit composed of a strong word or of a phrase including such a word. A single colon can contain from two to four, or exceptionally one or five, such units, without following a discernible rule[80]. Each unit naturally contains one relatively heavy accent; in this sense and in this sense only it is possible to speak of an accentual rhythm[81].

A strict emphasis on accents is misleading for several reasons. To begin with, regularity of distances between accents (however one locates these) is no greater in poetry than in prose[82], though meter should be a distinguishing feature of the former if it is at all relevant. Secondly, the number of accentual emphases in a single stich is highly irregular, at least in Hosea; it is thus hard to see what is gained by counting accents. Thirdly, it is still unclear which syllables bore a major stress in ancient Hebrew[83] or more specifically in Hebrew poetic language; the present Masoretic accentuation, if pronounced with appreciable emphasis, is anything but euphonic. Fourthly, accent is not as phonemically important an element in Hebrew as one

---

[78] Gray op. cit. 94; L. Newman and Wm. Popper, Studies in Biblical Parallelism, 1918—1923 (University of California Publications, Semitic Philology, I), 137—155. 440—455.

[79] K. Budde, Geschichte der althebräischen Literatur, 1906, 26. Earlier, I. Nordheimer, A Critical Grammar of the Hebrew Language, II 1841, 321.

[80] One unit only: 7 8 8 6aα 9 8 — all of them uncertain in structure. Five units: 2 11 (if *laken* is counted); 12 14 (prose ?).

[81] For older Jewish theories of word or thought units, see J. Saalschütz, Von der Form der hebräischen Poesie, 1825, 105—113; E. König, Einleitung in das Alte Testament, 1893, 545. Similarly, Gray, E. Isaacs (AJSL 35 [1918/19], 41), A. Bruno (since 1930), T. H. Robinson, S. Segert in part (Acta Orientalia 21 [1953], 481—542), H. Kosmala (VT 14 [1964], 425).

[82] That E. Sievers found meter in Genesis and Samuel illustrates the weakness of his theory, which has also been criticized by colleagues in literature as ignoring the semantic component in rhythm.

[83] A different accent is attested by Samaritan pronunciation, often in Babylonian punctuation, and perhaps by some ancient transcriptions and Qumran material, etc. Cf. R. Meyer, TL 77 (1950), 722—726; P. Kahle, The Cairo Geniza, 1959, 163f. 186f. 318—332; G. Bergsträsser, Hebräische Grammatik, I, §§ 21, 30; Kahle in H. Bauer and P. Leander, Historische Grammatik, § 9c; C. Sarauw, Über Akzent und Silbenbildung in den älteren semitischen Sprachen, 1939, 9. 25. 37.

might expect for its employment in a metrical system[84]; for instance, pausal and contextual forms of a given word can carry the accent on different syllables without a change in meaning. It is indeed likely that Hebrew was pronounced without considerable stress on any syllable but (at a later time?) with a light touch on the end of the word, as in French[85]. It is possible, however, that at least in poetry a stronger, recessive accent (as in pausal forms) was employed; this would probably yield a more pleasing rhythm than does the Masoretic accentuation[86].

In other words, the accentual system developed by H. Ewald, E. Meier, J. Ley, and E. Sievers on the basis of patterns in Germanic poetry[87] is no more adequate to represent Hebrew poetry than were syllabic analyses suggested by the Greco-Latin systems, which influenced subsequent Syriac and Arabic versifications. The nature of ancient Near Eastern rhythm (including that of Ugaritic) is still very obscure, although it is known that Indo-Iranian literature employed syllabic meters or morae. Early poetry, however, like much of modern production, usually does not employ numerically ordered rhythms. In the book of Hosea, no regular numerical pattern appears, whether based on accent, syllables, or morae[88].

Probably more significant than the accent as such for Hebrew poetry is what Slavic Formalists have designated the "interverbal pause," the division between words[89]. These divisions would naturally group the material into units of words or phrases. The question that can be asked is how pronounced these pauses are. Though it is true that one would not ordinarily take a breath between words in the middle of a colon, it is also clear that poetic material must be read more deliberately than prose and that individual words stand out in almost staccato fashion, while prose sentences read as a flowing whole.

Now it is a characteristic of poetic discourse that words, as words, are more important than they are in ordinary speech, that attention is

---

[84] E. g., R. Wellek and A. Warren, The Theory of Literature, 1956 (Harvest Book), 161.

[85] Ultima accent was explained by F. Praetorius, Über den rückweichenden Accent, 1897, 66f., as arising from lack of accentual emphasis in context. On light accentuation in modern Hebrew: A. Idelsohn, MGWJ 57 (1913), 541. Fluctuations in heaviness of stress are postulated by A. Murtonen, Materials for a Non-Masoretic Hebrew Grammar, III: A Grammar of the Samaritan Dialect of Hebrew, I 1964, 324 (arguing also for a penultimate stress, 49).

[86] Similarly, Saalschütz op. cit. 206. Cf. C. Burney, The Book of Judges, 1930[2], 159.

[87] See W. Cobb, A Criticism of Systems of Hebrew Metre, 1905, 65. 73. 89. 169; E. König, Die Poesie des alten Testaments, 1907, 11.

[88] The best measure of morae may be provided by the counting of "letters," i. e., consonants and long vowels (cf. S. Byington, JBL 66 [1947], 63—77), with the pronunciation hypothesized for classical Hebrew by Bergsträsser and Kahle. Such a counting reveals a close balance in selected verses but evidently no rigid schema; fifteen letters seem standard or average.

[89] See V. Erlich, Russian Formalism, 1955, 22. 119. 186. The employment of this concept here, however, is somewhat modified.

drawn not merely to the content but to the presentation itself. (Formal-ists have appropriately spoken of the role of the self-valuable word in poetry[90].) Accordingly, in poetic speech, words are not passed over lightly, but they are each savored and, as it were, inspected for their own value. One aspect of such a word-consciousness is exhibited in violations of normal word order within a sentence. In Israelite poetry such violations are not strictly speaking a form of "license;" for, on the one hand, Hebrew lacks rigorous rules that could be broken and, on the other, Hebrew poetry rarely employs such devices as rhyme which might require a transposition for external reasons (as in Hos 8 7). The transpositions are, rather, effective means of high-lighting the ex-pression itself; they are a part of that "organized violence"[91] which constitutes poetry.

In chs. 4—14 of Hosea, about half of all the sentences with enough words to make a transposition possible deviate from standard or ordinary word order[92]. The individual deviations are not necessarily inappropriate in a prose context, for nonstandard forms may be used especially for the sake of emphasis. The presence, however, of a sig-nificantly large percentage of such forms lends a peculiar aura to the style, while individually the deviations, with their special character, keep up a hammering rhythm which hinders a fluid reading.

Hos 1—3 exhibit a somewhat different style. Ch. 1 is almost entirely standard in word order, reflecting prose manner. Ch. 3 follows the same pattern, except for the emphatic temporal phrase "many days" (v. 3. 4). In ch. 2 only one-fourth of the sentences deviate from the norm, a pattern relatively low for poetic style; there is no signi-ficant difference between verses accepted as genuine in the present study and those not so accepted. The complex of Hos 1—3 probably passed through a lengthy phase of oral tradition, in which the material of ch. 2 was welded together into a relatively smooth unit. In any case — however the fact is to be explained — Hos 2 exhibits a more

---

[90] Ibid. 157.

[91] Ibid. 189 (from R. Jakobson). Irregularities help to create "frustrated anticipation" (Jakobson); ibid. 184.

[92] Standard word order for verbal sentences: verb—subject—any other material. For nominal sentences: subject first. The following words are ignored: (1) particles such as כֵּן, עַל־כֵּן, לָכֵן, גַּם, פֶּן, אַךְ, הֵנֵּה, negatives, interrogatives; (2) certain temporal adverbs, especially עַתָּה and אָז (Brockelmann op. cit. § 121k). The combination of לְ or בְּ with a suffix can regularly follow the verb immediately (Nyberg, ZDMG 92 [1938], 327f.). According to P. Joüon, Grammaire de l'Hébreu biblique, 1947, § 155k, verbal sentences without conjunction (including וְ) have as normal prose order: subject—object; if so, this rule is more often violated than not in Hosea, with the result that statistics of deviation to be presented below are not affected materially.

coherent style than do chs. 4—14, as has already been observed by other investigators[93]; one of them (Y. Kaufmann) has concluded partly on that account that Hos 1—3 stems from another author.

The percentage of word order deviations in chs. 4—14 easily matches and perhaps surpasses that of typical poetic style; yet it does not equal the extreme violation of normal order to be observed in proverbial literature. In the latter, nonstandard order is the rule rather than the exception, perhaps because of the compactness of the sayings. A more precise analysis must await the development of a thoroughgoing analysis of the relation of style to word order, which has not so far been attempted, though a look at randomly chosen material seems to indicate its possible usefulness[94].

It is conceivable that word transpositions — together with the operation of other factors — create a minor break within a colon, perhaps at the point at which the abnormal order becomes especially apparent. Such an intracolon break seems particularly characteristic of proverbial literature. Caesuras are marked in at least one late Mesopotamian text[95], so that it is tempting to look for internal breaks elsewhere. Yet most of Old Testament poetry such as that of Hosea reads evenly through a stich without any special grouping of units within it. Masoretic accentuation, indeed, did not develop its very detailed marking of subdivisions below the middle of the verse until post-Talmudic times and then most likely under the influence of outside systems[96]. The law of duality probably did not originally apply to a level below that of the colon, which in most Hebrew poetry is too short for a pronounced break, for convenient intonational phrases are generally at least the equivalent of two feet in length[97]. As

---

[93] C. Toy, JBL 32 (1913), 75; Kaufmann op. cit. 369 (above, p. 34).

[94] C. Albrecht, ZAW 7 (1887), 218—224; 8 (1888), 249—263, discusses the word order of nominal sentences in prose and prophetic books; Psalms, Job, Lamentations, Proverbs and Song of Solomon are excluded. Though not all data are complete, one might judge that, within the books discussed, deviations from the main rule amount to 25 per cent; an imperfect check indicates that, within these data, prose passages exhibit about 20 per cent and poetic sections about 30 per cent deviation — not a very large difference. Nominal sentence style of Hos 4—14 is close to 40 per cent nonstandard. The order of verbal sentences — which also are the more frequent type — is probably much more significant, but no large-scale data are available for it. In Hos 4—14, declarative verbal sentences are 55 per cent nonstandard; imperatives and questions are naturally more regular.

[95] B. Meissner, Die babylonisch-assyrische Literatur, 1927, 25.

[96] A. Idelsohn, Jewish Music, 1929, 67f.; further, E. Werner, IDB, III 297.

[97] G. Hölscher does not find caesuras in the seven-syllable meter common in Syriac (Syrische Verskunst, 1932, 202), although they appear in meters with eight or more syllables; Hosea's cola typically include only six or seven syllables (ignoring half-

a matter of fact, an excessive operation of duality is wearying, so that one can welcome a different pattern within the colon.

Beside word order, other syntactical peculiarities can be pointed out which set off poetic speech from prose, if not inherently then at least by the frequency with which they are used[98]. To examine these would require a full-scale treatment which cannot be attempted here. It is, however, clear that poetry moves in an expressive world of its own; few of the phrases to be found in Hosea could easily be mistaken for prose even if presented individually without parallelism, though this fact is due largely to lexical properties, i. e.. to the choice of words and symbols.

On the borderline between poetry and prose lie the words of Yahweh appearing within the narratives of chs. 1 and 3. Though they can be treated as poetry, their tone runs on a high even level with virtually equal emphasis on each stressed item and with little internal division. Such a monotony of intonation creates an effect of solemnity. In Hos 3, G. Fohrer has found "Kurzverse," i. e., a series of cola without parallelism[99]; the chapter does indeed contain an elevated form of speech, embodying a proclamation.

The two major forms of providing emphasis and expressing emotionality in Hebrew are repetition (with several varieties) and changes in word order. These have been discussed. In addition, a heightening of feeling can be brought about by other means, such as the use of figurative expressions[100] (including both metaphors and similes[101]), drastic concreteness[102], and questions[103] or commands[104], all of which are illustrated in Hosea. Furthermore, poetry is usually

---

vowels and final Masoretic vowels not supported by the consonantal text), making a consistent fourfold accentuation (as seen by some) and especially the presence of an ordered caesura unlikely. On intonational phrases, see J. Mukařovský, Archives néerlandaises de phonétique expérimentale 8—9 (1933), 153—165.

[98] Two extreme cases of grammatical peculiarities (related to word order) are: דֶּרֶךְ יְרַצְּחוּ שֶׁכְמָה (6 9) and נִדְמֶה שֹׁמְרוֹן מַלְכָּהּ (10 7). A compound subject is followed by a singular verb in 9 2 10 8 (as rarely, according to Gesenius-Kautzsch, § 125 d).

[99] TR NF 20 (1952), 254f. (following E. Balla).

[100] Hos 2 5. 9. 12 4 16. 19 5 1f. 12-15 7 4-9. 11f. 8 9 9 8-10. 16 10 1. 4. 7. 11-13 11 1-4. 10f. 13 3. 7. 15 14 6-9. On their emotionality, Eichhorn op. cit. III 6, as earlier Longinus, On the Sublime, XV.

[101] Metaphors: 5 1f. 7 8 8 9 10 1. 11 11 1. Similes: 4 16 5 12. 14 7 4. 6f. 11f. 9 10 11 4. 10f. 13 3. 7f. 14 6-9 (i. e., with כְּ).

[102] E. g., 4 13 9 14 10 8 14 1.

[103] Hos 8 5 9 5 10 9 11 8 13 10 14 9. The ironical 4 16b may be a question. (H. Mitchell in: Harper-Festschrift, I 1908, 115—129, notes the omission of the interrogative particle in Hebrew irony.)

[104] Hos 1 2. 4. 6. 9 2 3f. 4 1. 10. 15. 17 5 1. 8 8 1 9 1 10 12 12 7 14 2f.

marked by peculiarities in vocabulary, which raise its level out of the ordinary — including archaisms, rare words (especially for purposes of parallelisms)[105], terms used in a figurative sense[106], and generally more elaborate phraseology[107].

In these features, however, there arises the problem of the boundary between poetic devices and prophetic tradition. Since poetry and prophecy are closely allied, an absolute division cannot be made. As will be seen below, many of the figures used by the prophet are neither chosen arbitrarily nor new to him. Little can thus be said on the basis of images used in the writing either about the personal background of the author or about his richness of imagination; for instance, not the roaring of lions in the Jordan jungle, but a standardized stylization of enemy descriptions is responsible for references to a lion. A few of the images may be original, but Hosea's main contribution is in the free use he makes of existing figures. Poetic concreteness (though often associated with vagueness in specific predictive content) and the use of questions and commands have long been recognized as features of prophetic speech[108].

The poetic organization of Hebrew prophecy has close parallels in other seer traditions. Ancient Delphic oracle style has been described as including vagueness, pictorial images (especially with animal metaphors), and sharp assonance and alliteration derived from primitive poetry, together with sarcasm, brusque address, and sharp fluctuations in grammar[109]. H. M. and N. K. Chadwick describe Polynesian political prophecy as "highly elusive, rhetorical, and exclamatory," with rapid changes in content and address form and dominated by "metaphors and veiled sayings[110]."

The absence of the phrase "thus says the Lord" in the book of Hosea may well be due to the fact that the oracles are poetic in nature. That introductory phrase occurs much more frequently in prose than in poetry. When it does appear in connection with poetical oracles (as especially in the books of Amos and Jeremiah) it stands outside the metrical structure[111] and may not even be original[112]. The formula evidently belongs to the manner of the letter or oral message, ordinarily given in prose.

---

[105] E. g., תִּירוֹשׁ (often); הַקְשִׁיבוּ and הַאֲזִינוּ (5 1).

[106] E. g., כָּשַׁל (4 5 5 5 14 2. 10).

[107] E. g., יִשְׂאוּ נַפְשָׁם (4 8).

[108] E. g., Gunkel in: H. Schmidt, Die großen Propheten, 1915, lviif.; ZAW 42 (1924), 183—189; Rinaldi 85—89.

[109] H. Parke and D. Wormell, The Delphic Oracle, II 1956, xxiii—xxv.

[110] The Growth of Literature, III 1940, 340f. (comparing also the Abyssinian Galla).

[111] Balla op. cit. 8.

[112] Cf. Jer 26 18 with Mi 3 12.

III. NARRATIVE

Beside poetry, the book of Hosea contains narrative material. Within prophetic stories, a distinction has been made between "biographical" and "autobiographical" narrative[113]. These two types differ overtly in their use of the third or first person, respectively, when referring to the prophet — provided that the grammatical form is employed in an ordinary manner. The essential difference between the two types, however, is provided by their situation and function. That is, a story can have its *Sitz im Leben* either in the circle of prophetic disciples or in the life of the prophet himself.

If a story has a place in the life of the prophet, it is part of that prophet's literature or word. Prophetic first-person narration covers a rather large field. One type of such narrative is that of the report of a vision, which usually includes an audition. Another, a very common, type is the report of a simple audition, especially with a command to bring a certain message. Still another is the account of a symbolic act, which usually includes the report of an audition and may in some cases describe a merely visionary experience. Unfortunately, prophetic autobiographical narrative has not yet been studied systematically with a survey of its entire field rather than of single aspects.

These autobiographies focus on the prophetic message or, in part, on the divine origin of that message. Unlike Nehemiah's memoirs, they do not glorify an activity but stand in the service of the divine word. Glorification of a prophet (or of the god whom he serves) belongs to the function of third-person accounts, the prophetic "legends".

For an analysis of the stories in Hosea[114], it is wise to begin with ch. 3, since the situation here is relatively clear. This chapter is a prophetic "sermon", namely one leading to a message of hope after considerable discipline. What matters fundamentally is not the situation of the prophet, but rather the relation of Yahweh to Israel.

As a narrative of the prophet's life, ch. 3 leaves much to be desired. Some important elements of story-telling are lacking, especially all descriptions of time and place[115]. These elements are generally absent from prophetic narrative sermons, whether they report visions, symbolic acts, or simple conversations between Yahweh and the

---

[113] So, especially, T. H. Robinson (ZAW 42 [1924], 209—221, and elsewhere).

[114] For surveys of opinions, see Harper 208—210; H. H. Rowley, Men of God, 1963, 66—97; G. Fohrer, Die symbolischen Handlungen der Propheten, 1953.

[115] E. Robertson considers three elements to be "necessary" for a story: "something must be done, by someone, and in some place" — so that there is activity with a "setting" (The Old Testament Problem, 1950, 210).

prophet, while they are usually present in prophetic "legends[116]." The absence of setting is, of course, only apparent, since the real setting of the sermon stories is in Israel's life with God.

Ch. 3 begins with the words, "And the Lord said to me," a phrase which often occurs in first-person narratives to introduce a word of Yahweh to the prophet. There is no reason to believe that such words were literally private; in most cases they are obviously told by Yahweh with the intent that others hear of this conversation. This seems to be the purpose in Hos 3.

God's words in Hos 3 1 begin with a command. Such an opening is very common in prophetic oracles, even in such as do not present a narrative sermon. From Mari prophecy to Jeremiah and still later, a saying often begins with the report of a command by God to the prophet before the message itself is given[117]; that this report was presented in public speech seems to be clearly implied in several places in which a prophetic word is quoted[118]. Commands are particularly important in symbolic narratives, just as questions are prominent in visions.

Next, in Hos 3, the interpretation of the action commanded is given in the form of a comparison of the deed with Yahweh's relationships to Israel. Thereupon follows a report of the prophet's action, couched in mysterious terms which supply a high degree of concreteness characteristic also of other reports of symbolic actions. The action includes a word to the woman bought by the prophet, which apparently points to an enforced seclusion for the time being. The ending of the chapter is related to the future situation of the people.

The chapter plainly contains allegorical motifs, which are generally strong in sermonic narratives, especially in visions and symbolic reports[119]. The connection of such stories with dreams, which also bear symbolic character, has been noted repeatedly[120]. In how far the symbolic acts which are reported autobiographically were carried out

---

[116] The presence of time references in biographies of Jeremiah — contrasting with their absence in first-person narratives — has been noted by H. Schmidt op. cit. 277.

[117] So, already, J. Hänel, Das Erkennen Gottes bei den Schriftpropheten, 1923, 187, For Jeremiah, H. Wildberger, Jahwewort und prophetische Rede, 1942, 49ff. See Lindblom, Die literarische Gattung der prophetischen Literatur, 1924, 25, for medieval parallels; and W. von Soden, Die Welt des Orients 1 (1950), 397—403, for Mari.

[118] Jer 45 4 Ez 24 21. Cf. Is 21 6.

[119] Gunkel in: Kultur der Gegenwart, I: VII 1906, 84; Gressmann, Die älteste Geschichtsschreibung, 1910, 324.

[120] M. Sister, MGWJ 78 (1934), 422—425; E. Ehrlich, der Traum im Alten Testament, 1953, 123.

literally can hardly be determined on a stylistic basis, just as it is
difficult to decide on that basis whether genuine visions lie behind
visionary accounts. Actually, to the prophet's mind, there may not
have been a sharp distinction between ecstatic experience and what
the modern mind considers reality. Moreover, first-person form is
often used in Near Eastern fictional narratives[121]. In the last analysis,
it does not matter greatly whether the actions were executed literally
or not. Human life operates essentially on the level of symbolic structures. Its physical, "literal," aspects are, in themselves, incidental and,
if seen in isolation, subhuman. Thus, leaving the question open, one
can say, with R. G. Moulton, that there is here, whether "in reality or
in a parable," an "emblem prophecy[122]."

Yet, a few critical observations may be made, which at least raise
doubts about a literal interpretation. The fact that the author reports
his own symbolic action speaks against its actuality rather than for
it. For self-reported actions commonly exhibit a tendency toward
nonhistoricity, as in the following cases.

Altogether unhistorical are the events of Jer 25 15-29 (action with a cup of
wrath); Ez 2 8—3 3 (the eating of a scroll); Zech 11 4-17 (a shepherd allegory). Elements of significant foresight are involved in Is 8 1-4 (the birth of a male child);
Jer 32 6-15 (the coming of an uncle); ch. 35 (the action of the Rechabites); Ez 24 15-24
(the wife's death); though none of these events are very unusual and some are easily
anticipated, the prophet stresses in his presentation miraculous or unobservable
aspects[123]. The actuality of the rest of the self-reported events is debated, but one
may make the following tentative judgments. Jer 13 1-11 (a waist-cloth in the
Euphrates), if genuine, is a visionary experience; Jer 18 1-12 (a potter's vessel) is an
interpreted event, analogous to the class involving foresight; the muteness of Ez 3 26f.
and 33 21f. was either voluntary (thus not literal) or else interpreted in hindsight;
a possible original form of the very difficult Ez 12 1-16 (an exile's flight) remains as
a potentially straightforward symbolic action, but its problem cannot here be discussed. In summary, it is clear that several of the self-reports are completely unhistorical, while others involve tendentious elements[124].

For a truly concrete and public action, no account of one's deed
is necessary, at least in its original situation; only the report of a
divine command, which is a non-public event, needs to accompany the
action in order to legitimize and interpret it.

---

[121] G. Misch, A History of Autobiography in Antiquity, I 1951, 46ff.

[122] The Literary Study of the Bible, 1899, 375. 503.

[123] A. van den Born, Profetie Metterdaad, 1947, classes these and some others as
natural events symbolically explained.

[124] Similarly A. Groenman, Het Karakter van de symbolische Handelingen der oud-
testamentische Profeten, 1942. Even verbal expressions — not only marvelous
acts — can be "signs" in Israel (see C. Keller, Das Wort OTH, 1946, 36).

Reports of the execution of the action are thus appropriately absent from the following prophetic words: Jer 16 1-9 (denial of family life, mourning, and festivities); 19 1-2a. 10-11 (breaking of a flask), which is probably a first-person sermon later incorporated into a third-person legend highlighting the prophet's subsequent suffering; Jer 27 2ff. (carrying a yoke) and 28 11 (Hananiah's action), two first-person words incorporated into a legend which celebrates Jeremiah's encounter with Hananiah; Jer 43 8-13 (stones in Tahpenhes), surviving as a third-person report; Ez 4 1-17 (the symbolization of a siege); 5 (actions with hair); 12 17-20 (trembling); 21 11-12 (sighing); 13-22 (a sword); 23-28 (marking of crossroads); 24 1-14 (a pot with meat); 37 15-28 (two sticks); Zech 6 9-15 (a crowning ceremony). In all of these cases, the prophetic word accompanies an at least potentially observable action which is not itself narrated[125]. Is 20 3-6 (naked walking) forms a special case in that it alludes to a (literal?) three-year action already accomplished. Strictly third-person accounts do include reports about the symbolic action — as in I Kings 19 19-21 22 11 and II Kings 13 14-19 — but not within the words quoted from the prophet himself.

Though the situation is far from perfectly clear, one may conclude that the presence of an autobiographical report of the action engenders suspicion rather than confidence. In the case of Hos 3, one can argue that the marital relationship is sufficiently non-public, so that it needs to be narrated. But that consideration shows only that an actual execution is a possibility, not that it is necessary or even likely on the basis of the self-report.

The presence of concrete details, especially in v. 2, is no argument for actuality, for that phenomenon can be evaluated with at least equal justice as a deliberate stylistic device[126] or as making a significant point. In the context of the narrative, the purchase price underscores a permanent relationship — even if as with a "kept" woman — since the price is too high for a temporary liaison[127]; its point appears to be the incisiveness of the divine activity. The woman here is not a harlot, but evidently one sold because of unfaithfulness to her husband.

---

[125] It is far from certain, however, that Ezekiel's symbolic actions were actually carried out. The non-symbolic events of Ez 8—11, including Pelatiah's death in 11 13, most likely constitute a visionary experience. According to W. Irwin (The Problem of Ezekiel, 1943) and H. Guthrie, Jr., Ezekiel 21, ZAW 74 (1962), 280, Ezekiel's descriptions of symbolic action were originally in brief poetic form; did they accompany some gestures? Fohrer (Ezechiel, 1955, 30) thinks that Ezekiel at least "started" to perform the actions of ch. 4, while Irwin speaks of "pantomimes" — somewhat incorrectly, since that word indicates silent action. In either case, their literal character is impaired. Zech 6 is also problematical, despite the mention of witnesses.

[126] So, e. g., Marti 36; A. Regnier, RB 32 (1923), 391f.

[127] Prostitutes could be either bought or rented in the ancient world (H. Herter, Jahrbuch für Antike und Christentum 3 [1960], 78. 81). Marriage, ownership, and temporary hire (of a woman) are distinguished also in Islam. (N. Coulson, A History of Islamic Law, 1964, 110).

The purchase form is not a regular marriage contract but is that of an acquisition of a concubine or slave woman, which yielded the man greater power[128].

Ch. 1 of Hosea is more complicated in structure. Certain features of a legend or report are present; but others are absent, and contrary indications can be seen.

"Biographical" character appears most obviously in the use of the third person for Hosea[129]. There is no evidence, however, of the usual interest of a legend in the person of a hero, who in prophetic stories ordinarily appears as an able prognosticator or determiner of the future[130], as a miracle worker[131], or as a sufferer[132], with an ultimate emphasis on divine action through or in him.

On the other hand, "autobiographical," or sermonic, features are present. To begin with, the structure of Hos 1 is very similar to that of the autobiographical Is 8 1-4, which may be called a naming-sermon. They share the following items: God gives a command, a woman "conceives and bears" a child, and God "says: Call its name ..., for ...;" an effort is made in both to provide for realism. Even assuming that the chapter is a report by someone other than the prophet, it is likely that Hosea presented one or more naming-sermons, either in an oral or a written form, which then became the basis of the report as it has survived. In other words, some first-person message form undoubtedly lies behind the present text.

A sermonic feature of Hos 1 appears in the fact that the story contains both accusation (v. 2) and threat, which are to some extent pointed toward each other. The three threatening names with their

---

[128] M. Schorr, Urkunden des altbabylonischen Zivil- und Prozeßrechts, 1913, 4, points out the purchase form, which lacks a provision for a divorce, in the acquisition of a concubine in Babylonia; for purchase of a slave woman in Ugarit, cf. A. Rainey, Orientalia 34 (1965), 19. Hos 3 2 thus does not support a view of Hebrew marriage as a purchase (rejected also by M. Burrows, The Basis of Israelite Marriage, 1938, 138). Similarly, Kraeling.

[129] That Hosea himself used the third person, as has been supposed by Gressmann, Guthe, A. Allwohn (Die Ehe des Propheten Hosea, 1926, 14f.), and Fohrer (Studien zur alttestamentlichen Prophetie, 1967, 104) is theoretically possible, but not likely, as the discussion will show.

[130] Cf. J. Meinhold, Die Jesajaerzählungen, Jesaja 36—39, 1898; O. Plöger, Die Prophetengeschichten der Samuel- und Königsbücher, 1937, 53.

[131] J. Hempel, Worte der Propheten, 1949, 65—68. 81. Miracles are a legitimating sign of charismatic leaders in Shamanism, Islam and "messianic" groups, as well as in older times. On Yahweh as ultimate author, G. Quell in: Rudolf-Festschrift, 1961, 256.

[132] See Am 7 Hos 9 8 Mi 3 7; O. Steck, Israel und das gewaltsame Geschick der Propheten, 1967, 243—250; etc.

explanations can be understood, if necessary, by themselves without standing in the narrative context; even the accusation can be conceived of as standing alone. Yet in the present context the accusation of harlotry provides the background for the threats, especially for those given in the names "Not-pitied" and "Not-my-people[133]." It is indeed likely that the chapter contains an extended message in which marriage and children are combined, and not simply four separate announcements[134].

The most independent element in the story is the name Jezreel. It has no direct relationship to the reproach of v. 2, but rather carries an accusation in itself. It is much more enigmatic than the other two names and is surrounded by a circle of different explanations.

It is likely that the chapter combines two traditions. One concerns the naming of a son Jezreel. This name is ambiguous; like the names of Isaiah's two sons, it can be interpreted either positively or negatively as hope or judgment for the people. Though awkward, it can be used, perhaps only on occasion, as the actual call-name of a boy, partly because of its potentially positive meaning. When questioned about the name, the prophet can tell a naming-sermon which would bring his interpretation. The other tradition revolves around the second and third children, together with a reference to their harlotrous mother. In this part of the story, the names are unambiguously negative and hardly the actual call-names of two children. The supposition that the last two names formed originally a unit independent of the first name is strengthened by the stylistic anomaly that the process of weaning is mentioned only between these two children. The two traditions differ in point. "Jezreel" is directed toward the life of politics; the mother and the other two children indict religious harlotry[135].

The name Diblaim may belong to the second story, indicating harlotry in some form[136]. The name "Gomer" (better, "Gamar") can belong to either one; it is probably a simple personal name[137]. The second story does not state that the children were Hosea's. It is likely, though not certain, that it intends to say that the woman remained a

---

[133] "Not-my-people" can include an accusation; its force here, however, seems to be declarative and thus threatening.

[134] Against Wolff 9.

[135] H. G. May (JBL 55 [1936], 289) points out that the name Jezreel ("God sows" or "may God sow") is appropriate for a prostitute child. Yet to designate such as a child of *God* would spoil the point of the message, unless Hosea once held a view from which he later recoiled.

[136] "Two-fig-cakes" may be a prostitute name (W. Baumgartner, ZAW 33 [1913], 78); but see Rudolph.

[137] As on Samaritan ostraca. Cf. Jacob; Gordon, Ugaritic Textbook, 1965, 380; S. and S. Rin, BZ NF 11 (1967), 176.

prostitute[138]. Certainly this is the literal meaning, since harlotry rather than adultery is described. But reconstruction is made difficult by the fact that Hos 1, as it now stands, is a secondary structure. If the story is not literally true, the somewhat curious mixture of prostitution and adultery in the accusations of chs. 1—3 forms an inessential problem.

If one seeks a biographical reconstruction, one may accept Jezreel as a real son of Hosea, born of Gomer or perhaps of a woman whose name is not preserved; his name received more than one interpretation. The rest is most easily, though not with certainty, seen as an ecstatic naming-sermon (or sermons), in the same style as an ordinary, historical one[139]. No one would have been misled about the character of Jezreel's mother; for Israelites were polygamous. Asiatic shamans, indeed, commonly spoke about a celestial or underworld marriage paralleling their earthly one[140].

The two naming-sermons of ch. 1 were combined at some time by a hand other than that of the prophet, who himself would have smoothed out the narrative more coherently. It is probably at this point that a change from the first person to the third person took place. Such a change of persons is comparable to a similar process in some other cases in which a prophetic word has become incorporated into an expanded account by a prophetic disciple.

A final observation can be made. Hos 3 1 begins with the words, "And the Lord said to me again[141]," thus implying a previous narrative. The phenomenon of a second command with a second act occurs also in other symbolic stories. In each case, the second scene constitutes a contrast to the earlier one, specifically the reversal of a preceding

---

[138] It is not clear whether Babylonian marriages with hierodules were consummated or how often their offspring was destroyed; cf. C. H. § 144 (partly against G. Driver and J. Miles, Babylonian Laws, I 1952, 366f. 370f.). Reversing the theory of Tushingham (JNES 12 [1953], 157), the story may intend that the children were Hosea's legally, though not actually. Thus Hos 1 2 can stand as it is (against Rudolph 47). The father's naming would execute an adoption (Driver and Miles op. cit. 333; H. Hoffner, JNES 27 [1968], 201); but cf. below, pp. 88, 111.

[139] An alternative explanation might involve relationships with three women; perhaps these were not all to be consummated, so that Hosea's sexuality may have rested in vicarious phantasy more than in execution, even then. Also a proleptic interpretation of 1 2 is possible, on the basis of prophetic style alone.

[140] M. Eliade, Shamanism, 1964, 75—81. 421 (with literature). On spiritual journeys (unreal events) of seers in Asia (including Mesopotamia ?), Europe, and Africa, see N. K. Chadwick, Poetry and Prophecy, 1942, 90—100.

[141] When the term עוֹד carries the meaning of "again," it follows the verb to which it belongs (as in 1 6); so, rightly, R. Gordis, HUCA 25 (1954), 29. Preceding the verb it means "still," "besides," etc.

outlook[142]. The first person pronoun in 3 1ff. shows that the original
author of this section still had available to him the first-person form
of the story concerning the marriage with a harlot. That probably indicates a relatively early date, though this fact does not prove a common authorship with the first; a disciple may be responsible for it.
Later modifications of the story are likely. Its basic pattern, however,
fits closely the inner structure of the relatively hopefully oriented
portions of Hosea, especially in ch. 2.

While historical details may be uncertain, the symbolic structure
of the narratives, with the interest to which they are oriented, is
relatively clear. They express the same content as the poetic oracles,
but in a different mode. In their dramatic nature, the stories involve
the person of the prophet, even if only in imagination, so that it is
possible to speak with Abraham Heschel of a "sympathy" of the
prophet with God[143], though this is hardly their major point.

---

[142] Is 8 5 Jer 13 3 (the contrast is explained in v. 10f.) Zech 11 15 (where a contrast
to an earlier good-shepherd figure [v. 4-8] is intended).

[143] The Prophets 55. 307—323.

Chapter IV: The Word as Communication

I. INTRODUCTION

Prophetic word, unlike possibly some other literature, functions as a word from one person to another[1]. It is not merely a means to give expression to joy or sorrow on a certain occasion but seeks to establish a bridge between the originator and the recipient, that is, to communicate.

Accordingly, prophetic utterances, including Hosea's, can begin with such calls as "Hear the word of Yahweh" or "Hear this" (Hos 4 1 5 1), just as a royal messenger begins his speech with "Hear the words of the Great King"[2]. H. W. Wolff has argued that doubled or tripled formulations of this phrase moved from early songs and wisdom to law instruction and from there to prophecy[3]; such a reconstruction appears to be too artificial and certainly more than can be proved. The usages listed, however, do represent several notable specializations of the opening-formula. The phrase appears in Hos 4 1 and 5 1, introducing a legal procedure. As a mantic formula, a two-fold call occurs already in Num 23 18; in prophecy the call appears as a rule in non-divine speech.

Now it is true that in the book of Hosea the use of the second person is very limited, so that it has been repeatedly supposed that many of the oracles were not spoken in public[4]. Such a supposition may

---

[1] For analyses of presentational types, see N. Frye, Anatomy of Criticism, 1957, 246—250; W. Kayser op. cit. 335—348 (aboze, p. 37).

[2] Is 36 13. J. Lindblom points out that "Hear this" is a typical opening for public speeches (Hosea 69, with reference to an earlier study of his in the Buhl-Festschrift, 1925).

[3] Pp. 82. 122f., with useful listings of occurrences. Its role in wisdom had been noticed by Gunkel (Gunkel—Begrich 390).

[4] Lindblom (143) will accept only 9 1-9 as spoken in public. Sellin recognizes 2 4ff. 4 1-19 5 1-7 9 1-6 — and perhaps also 5 8—6 6 14 2-9 — as public oral words, otherwise assuming an immediate writing or perhaps a speaking in a small group (1929, 7. 19f., after recognizing even fewer words as oral in the first edition). Others with similar views include B. Duhm (Israels Propheten, 1922², 100), Marti (5), K. Beyer (Spruch und Predigt bei den vorexilischen Propheten, 1933, 101, regarding Hos 9 10—14 1 as monologues of reflection, together with 4 11-19 2 16-25 8 4-14), Lippl (9, for Hosea from 9 10 on), and Weiser (3). Wolff thinks of private instruction in the circle of disciples as the place of most utterances after 9 10.

indeed be correct; nevertheless, it is clear that the words were put into a form in which they were designed to become known, for the book of Hosea is hardly a diary which happened to be discovered contrary to the intention of the prophet. To some students, Hosea's messages have appeared stylistically as "monologues[5]." Yet the third-person style should not keep one from recognizing the true intent of the words. Style is a precarious basis on which to rest reconstructions of the precise physical circumstances of an individual saying, since it indicates only the functional place of the word. The use of the second person does not prove an actual face-to-face encounter, nor does the use of the third person deny it. The style of Hosea's words reflects a situation deeper than the physical setting, namely a confrontation of Israel by God, i. e., by the ultimate reality on which its life depends. Thus the message transcends a mere communication between prophet and audience.

II. THE SPEAKER

First, attention may be paid to the speaker, the source of the word. Like most prophets, Hosea uses the divine "I", presenting God as speaking in the first person. On occasion, however, God is mentioned in the third person; in these passages presumably the prophet is the speaker. Many statements, or even groups of such, do not refer to God at all, so that it is hard to tell whether God or the prophet is thought to be the source. In these, the determination of the speaker can perhaps — but not with certainty — be made through an attempt to feel oneself into the words and to judge whether they emanate from Yahweh or from a human being. An element of empathy has played a role in the development of the analysis that is to follow, but the discussion of the problem will naturally emphasize more observable data upon which a clear decision must necessarily be based.

The most important question confronting the student is whether there is a difference in content between divine words and prophetic words, that is to say, whether the change in style is significant in meaning or not. Accordingly, a useful procedure is to mark the sayings for grammatical style, for subject matter, and for feeling — in line with Gunkel's emphasis on form, content, and mood — and to note

---

[5] So, already, C. Cornill, The Prophets of Israel, 1895, 51; similarly Wellhausen, Israelitische und jüdische Geschichte, 1897[3], 115. E. Balla, Die Botschaft der Propheten, 1958, 98, considers Hosea's words as "divine monologues." N. Bratsiotis, ZAW 73 (1961), 35f., again finds many monologues in Hosea, presumably as a stylistic concept.

any correlations that might appear. The results may be treated
separately for each type of subject matter; for content is often the
best organizer of forms. In connection with such data, the life-situation
of the forms will be discussed.

A. Threats

In threatening statements it is striking that words in which the
divine "I" is prominent are far less specific than other words in the
description of the evil that is to come. Divine words are full of figurative speech and generalized terms, many of which will appear below
(in Chapter V) as technical expressions. Divine words also tend to be
highly threatening in emotion.

Figurative speech is central in Hos 2; Yahweh addresses Israel
personified as a woman, threatening to strip her naked or to bar her
ways (2 5. 8. 12). Later on, Yahweh declares himself to be a lion,
leopard, or she-bear coming to rend and devour Israel (5 14 13 7f.).
Or he can speak of himself as a "moth" and as "rottenness" (5 12). He
threatens to throw a net (7 12) and to be himself a "fetter" (5 2).

A *threatening emotion* is expressed by the words for wrath, which
in Hosea invariably appear on Yahweh's lips. "My wrath" is poured
out (5 10 13 11), God says; "my anger is hot against them" (8 5[6]).
To put it another way, God "hates" Israel, and "will not love them
again" (9 15). Indeed, he will not forgive or have mercy (1 6 2 6). No
compassion exists for his enemies (13 14[7]). He throws a "woe to them"
in Israel's face (7 13 9 12) — "no one can rescue" from his ferocious
attack (2 12 5 14).

Yahweh's threat is delivered, then, in highly *personal* terms. One
form of divine judgment, indeed, consists simply in saying that Israel's
evil is being recognized. Israel's sin is "revealed" and has come before
God's eyes (7 1f.). God "knows" Ephraim; it is "not hid" from him
(5 3). He "remembers" their evil (7 2). The expression "not-my-people"
is already a threat (1 9). The response of Yahweh to Israel's sin is to
"cast them out of my house" (9 15), to reject them as they have
rejected him (4 6).

Announcements of punishment are held in a *general tone;* even the
occasional concrete descriptions are relatively stylized. Yahweh will
"visit" or "return" Israel's sin (1 4 2 15 4 9) and "chastise" (or "bind")
them (7 12 10 10). Yahweh threatens shame (4 7), bereavement (9 12. 16),

---

[6] Cf. 11 9 14 5 (negated in promises) and 13 11.
[7] חֶם is best translated as "compassion," since the repentance involved is said to
be "hid" from God's eyes, an expression rather inappropriate for "wrath."

the gathering of peoples against Israel or its own being "gathered"
(8 10 10 10). Devastation of the land and an end to festivals are announced, however, in fairly concrete terms in ch. 2 (v. 5. 11-15).

Threats are somewhat less frequent outside of divine speech.
When they do occur in the *prophet's own words*[8], they are often quite
specific about what will happen. Thus, the altars will be broken down[9],
the calf of Samaria will be carried away or become splinters[10], sacrifices will cease[11], and the holy places will lie deserted[12]. The king of
Israel will disappear, and princes will fall[13]. Exile and a return to
Egypt is announced[14].

Prophetic threats feature *descriptions or visualizations* of future
events. "They will be ashamed of their altars[15]." They will not find
God, and all their riches will "not be found[16]." Israel itself will disappear[17]. Terrifying descriptions of the horrors of war and vivid
pictures of the devastation of the land to be expected are given in
crass detail[18]. Hunger will rule[19]. How strongly the prophet lives in
the future in his mind's eye is reflected in his repeated use of the
"prophetic perfect," wherein the perfect — and perhaps the imperfect
consecutive — instead of indicating the past is used for future events[20].
In many cases, indeed, it is difficult to determine whether the present
or the future is meant, especially since the Hebrew imperfect is
ambiguous[21]. The prophet is fond of the adverb "now," though it
also appears on the lips of Yahweh[22].

The prophet's descriptions of Israel's predicament today and
catastrophe tomorrow often carry a tone of *lament*. In picture after

---

[8] For reasons that will become clear, all sentences in which Yahweh does not appear
in the first person will be regarded as the prophet's own.

[9] Hos 10 2. 8. So also 12 12 ?

[10] Hos 10 5f. 8 6.

[11] Hos 3 4 9 4.

[12] Hos 9 6 10 8.

[13] Hos 3 4 7 16 8 10 10 3. 7 (?). 15 (MT). On Yahweh's lips: 1 4b. 5 (secondary?). (The
Yahweh-words 7 7 and 13 10 refer to the past.)

[14] To Egypt: Hos 8 13 9 3. 6 11 5. Exile in general: 9 17. To Assyria: 9 3 (not genuine?).

[15] Hos 4 19.

[16] Hos 5 6 12 9.

[17] Hos 13 3.

[18] Hos 10 14f. 11 6 13 15 14 1.

[19] Hos 4 10 8 7.

[20] Hos 4 19 (twice, if one repoints) 7 7 (?) 8 8 (twice?). 10 (?) 9 7. 16 (?) 10 5. 6 (?). 7. 13
(twice?). 14 (twice?). 15 (twice?) 12 12 (twice?) 13 9. 15 (?). Other possibilities of
occurrences exist — but no certain ones in divine speech (10 10 13 7. 11).

[21] E. g., 9 11.

[22] Hos 4 16 5 3. 7 8 8. 13 10 3 13 2. By Yahweh: 2 12 (with]) 8 10, as in Ps 12 6 Is 33 10.

picture he draws the lines of Israel's futility[23]. As already noted, individual units often begin on a lamenting tone. On one occasion, the prophet, true to his role of intercessor, breaks through with his emotion to ask God to prevent the birth of children so that they may not be killed (9 14). Often it is hard to tell whether the lament is real or only the prophet's style for presenting a threat. For instance, in the exclamation just quoted Hosea may merely intend to say that childlessness will appear merciful in comparison with what else will happen; in that case, the plea is an ironical intercession. Yet the prophet's fellow-suffering is everywhere evident.

The element of *warning* is strong in prophetic speech, usually intertwined with visualization. "The days of visitation have come" (9 7). The exclamation "Blow the trumpet in Gibeah!" is stylistically typical of prophecy, reflecting war calls[24]. After all, the prophet is the "watchman" of Israel[25], a role not unrelated to the tradition of Holy War. Allied to warning are the repeated announcements of judicial prosecution[26]. The prophet is probably speaking in the declaration, "among the tribes of Israel I announce the truth" (5 9), which is comparable to the watchman's conclusion in Is 21 10, "what I have heard from the Lord of hosts ... I announce [with the same grammatical form of a different verb] to you."[27]

It is characteristic of the prophet's own words that the future of Israel grows out of the present almost automatically. Hosea, in other words, points out the *direction* of Israel's life. This is even expressed as though it were a conscious and deliberate choice[28]. Prophetic words are, in general, considerably more rational in character than are Yahweh's own declarations, in which his personal opposition and destruction are emphasized.

---

[23] Particular attention may be drawn to 4 14b 5 11 7 8f. 11. 16 8 8 9 11. 13. 16 11 7. See below, p. 123, for the "futility curse."

[24] Hos 5 8. Hos 8 1 also belongs in this context, if it does not represent an address of Yahweh to the prophet.

[25] Hos 8 1 (?) 9 8.

[26] Hos 4 1 12 3. So, probably, also 5 1.

[27] This form is related to, but different from, the "Bekräftigungsformel" (von Rabenau, WZ Univ. Halle, G.-s. 5 [1955/56], 678) "I, Yahweh, have spoken" (or its third-person form, cf. Lindblom, Hosea, 78); for a divine declaration need not stress that it speaks the truth. It is close to the "Legitimierungsformel" of seer words (D. Vetter, Untersuchungen zum Seherspruch im Alten Testament, Diss. Heidelberg, 1963, 226f.), which is continued in prophetic books (including reports of inner struggle, as in Jer 6 11). Also elsewhere oracles end in a protestation of truth (D. Jennes, The Life of the Copper Eskimos, 1922, 211).

[28] Hos 5 11 8 4 12 2 (discussed below, p. 121); cf. 5 4.

The distinction between divine and prophetic speech is strong enough so that there is very little overlapping in significant terminology. In Yahweh's threats, there occur words signifying emotion: עֶבְרָה (5 10), אַף (8 5), אהב (for Yahweh's: 9 15), רחם (1 6), שׂנה (9 15), probably עַמִּי (1 9 4 6. 8. 12 6 11), אוֹי (7 13 9 12); some general or figurative verbs of negative action: אסר־יסר (7 12 10 10), נצל (2 11f. 5 14), גרש (9 15), שׂכח (4 6), hiph. of שׂבת (1 4 2 13), פשׂט (2 5), שׂוֹך (2 8), גדר (2 8), a good number of figurative nouns and associated figurative verbs: מוֹסֵר (5 2), רֶשֶׁת (7 12), שַׁחַל (5 14 13 7), כְּפִיר (5 14), נָמֵר (13 7), דב (13 8), רָקָב and עָשׁ (5 12), שׁוּר (13 7), פגשׁ (13 8), טרף (5 14), קרע (13 8, but literally in the prophet's word 14 1), and, finally, the personal word פָּנַי (5 15 7 2).

To be found exclusively in prophetic speech are some descriptions of disaster: לַעַג (7 16), שָׁאוֹן (10 14), חֶרֶב (7 16 11 6 14 1), כלה (11 6), יָבֵשׂ (9 16 13 15); ססה (13 15), שְׁבָבִים (8 6), שׂמד (10 8), לבט (4 14 ?), בושׂ (4 19 10 6), שָׁמָּה (5 9), ערף (10 2), נפל (7 7 ?. 16 14 1), כשׁל (4 5 5 5 14 2. 10 — not all genuine), שׂדד (10 2, cf. שׂד below), שׂוּב (to Egypt: 8 13 9 3 11 5), שׂחת (13 9), and the following terms describing Yahweh's action: יום (5 9 9 5. 7)[29], ריב (4 1 12 3), יכח (4 4 5 9), שְׁלָם (9 7).

Some notable words appearing in both types of contexts are: פקד, "visit" (Yahweh: 1 4 2 15 4 9. 14; Prophet: 8 13 9 9 12 3), אשׂם, "suffer in guilt" (Yahweh: 5 15; Prophet: 4 15 10 2 13 1 14 1), שׂד, "destruction" (Yahweh: 7 13, in a curse; Prophet: 9 6 10 14 12 2), גלה, "uncover" (Yahweh: 2 12 7 1) or "depart" (Prophet: 10 5), זכר, "remember" (Yahweh: 7 2; Prophet: 8 13 9 9), מאס, "reject" (Yahweh: 4 6; Prophet: 9 17), דמה, "undo" (Yahweh: 4 5f.; Prophet: 10 7. 15), הֵשִׁיב (Yahweh: 4 9; Prophet: 12 3. 15), also the very common לקח.

Admittedly, the substantive distinction between the two types can be upheld only if one credits to divine speech no more than those sayings in which the divine "I" explicitly occurs. But two arguments point in favor of assigning doubtful cases to prophetic speech. First, the prophet is the actual speaker; "divine speech" is merely a term for those words in which an "I" other than the prophet's becomes stylistically prominent. The burden of proof lies on the side of an assignment to Yahweh. Secondly, and more important, in content and evidently in feeling, grammatically neutral statements are closer, as the above analysis has shown, to clearly non-divine statements than to clearly divine ones. Thus they should be grouped with the former.

---

[29] The phrase "the time comes" appears in Ezekiel similarly within the third-person style of *Durchführung*, as described by K. von Rabenau, in: von Rad-Festschrift, 1961, 70f.

The opinion has been advanced by some that Hosea contains almost entirely divine speech[30]. Behind such a view there usually lies the assumption that within a given unit only Yahweh or the prophet can be speaking; thus a single instance of divine "I" in a passage leads to an assignment of the whole to God[31]. One of the results of this assumption was the breaking up of prophetic writings into small units[32]. Yet in Hosea one cannot lead a single style consistently through every unit, however one may divide the book. Lindblom rightly recognized and championed the changeableness of grammatical style within prophetic speech, though he appears to have assumed that the alternation of speaker was arbitrary. Rather than being predominantly composed of divine speech, the book of Hosea reveals itself as prophetic word with divine style appearing occasionally, in a manner somewhat reminiscent of the "quotations" of divine speech noted by H. Wildberger within Jeremiah's own words[33]. Such an analysis of Hosea with succinct divine speech has been anticipated by Paul Riessler, who did not, however, pay attention to the significance of content in association with the form[34].

As a result of the conclusions reached here, it is no longer necessary to exclude the book of Hosea from the generalization that there is a distinction between divine and human word in prophecy[35]. Their close relationship within a single order, however, indicates that prophetic speech and divine word are not separable genres existing independently but that they are factors of style, perhaps even not necessarily rigid ones.

The nature of the variations in Hosea agree closely with those noted in other contexts. E. Balla lists as characteristics of the "oracle of disaster" the following: (1) the prophet himself speaks; (2) the prophet speaks of the future as though it has

---

[30] So, Sellin 17 (with considerable emending of the text); H. Hertzberg, Prophet und Gott, 1923, 107; Lindblom 138f. More extensive prophetic speech has been accepted by F. Giesebrecht, Die Berufsbegabung der alttestamentlichen Propheten, 1897, 42f., with better recognition of the changeableness of speaker. Fairly frequent divine speech is assumed by Deissler (63. 77. 80f. 95).

[31] So also Wolff passim. His designation of Yahweh-sayings is very similar to that of Giesebrecht, but he sees them as separable rhetorical entities.

[32] So, for instance, L. Köhler, Amos, 1917, who assigns each small piece to either the prophet or God.

[33] Op. cit. (e. g., 81).

[34] P. Riessler at one time regarded individual sentences of divine speech as the "Grundstock" of Hosea (Die kleinen Propheten, 1911); later, his translation (Die Heilige Schrift des alten und neuen Bundes, 1956[8]) marks numerous very short quotations of divine speech, though a little more generously than the present study does.

[35] Wolff excludes Hosea and Habakkuk (ZAW 52 [1934], 6; Das Zitat im Prophetenspruch, 1937, 107).

already happened, using the perfect; (3) a "demonic-enigmatic tone;" and (4) an abrupt, jumpy style[36]. To generalize for prophetic literature, non-divine style is more detailed and more extended[37] than the divine. It is more visionary[38] and employs more frequently the "prophetic perfect" (though the latter phenomenon is admittedly somewhat uncertain)[39]. Its feeling is more on the side of the people, as reflected in the laments and dirges widely used in prophecy. As in the work of ancient seers, it is inclined to be rational and to analyze the inherent drift of events[40].

The two styles of divine and human speech reflect two different structures which may have been originally separate. They probably belong to the God-possessed *nabî'* ("prophet"), on the one hand, and to the objective "seer" who serves human need, on the other[41]. Another possibility is that the role of the priest or cult prophet lies behind one style, while the independent prophet (not necessarily a reform prophet) stands in the background of the other[42]. The two possibilities are probably closely allied, since the *nabî'* was evidently closely related to the regular cult, while the seer could operate privately[43]. If a distinction is made, it can be noted that a pronounced "ecstatic" style — abrupt, poetic, and visionary[44] — belongs not to the *nabî'*-words but to the structure of the human seer-words. That means then that a formal identification with Yahweh and an experi-

---

[36] Droh- und Scheltworte 48f. (He does not find this in Amos.)

[37] Cf. K. Elliger, Das Buch der zwölf kleinen Propheten, II 1950, 12 (in a comment on the book of Nahum).

[38] So, also, Wildberger op. cit. 121, for Jeremiah.

[39] Already K. Keil (Manual of Historico-Critical Introduction, I 1869, 275) stated that "the prophets in the Spirit behold the future as if it were present." Similarly, G. Hylmö, Studier över stilen i de gammaltestamentliga profetböckerna, 1929, 44. A. Jepsen, Nabi, 1934, 129, speaks of the "perfect of simultaneity," with which may be compared the perfect of execution (Gesenius—Kautzsch § 106m); in accordance with this usage (cf. Westermann, EvTh 24 [1964], 363), the perfect is also occasionally found in divine speech at the beginning of the "oracle of answer," namely at Is 41 10. 14 43 1 49 8. That the prophetic perfect is found above all in non-divine, and especially in visionary, speech can be gathered from an examination of listings by S. Driver, A Treatise on the Use of Tenses in Hebrew, 1881, 22—24, and also A. Lamorte, Le problème du temps dans le prophétisme biblique, 1960 (in the data of the latter, especially Jer 4 7. 29 6 22. 24 Neh 2 2. 3. 11 3 18; many other examples given are waw-perfects). It is a feature of the seer-word, which is never divine in form (D. Vetter op. cit. 216).

[40] See below, p. 123—125.

[41] Cf. M. Jastrow, JBL 28 (1909), 56; Hertzberg op. cit.

[42] Mowinckel, Psalmenstudien III, 1923, 93—96. The opposite viewpoint is, wrongly, implied by G. Driver, Problems of the Hebrew Verbal System, 1936, 133—135.

[43] So, H. Junker, Prophet und Seher in Israel, 1927. As in Greece; see A. Heschel, The Prophets, 455.

[44] As described by H. Gunkel (so already in: Kultur der Gegenwart, I: VII, 85).

ence of visions belong to different aspects of prophecy and are not to be grouped together as a single form of ecstacy in any specialized sense.

The duality of the two structures appears to be world-wide and not merely the result of an accidental combination within Palestine. Mesopotamian religion knew both the possessed *maḫḫu* and the seer *baru*, the latter employing omens and relating himself to Shamash, the god of justice. The oracle of Delphi combined Dionysiac intoxication with that Apollonic rationality which included a moral emphasis and the observation of signs[45]. It has been suggested that the ecstacy of both the *maḫḫu* and the Delphic Pythia, as well as of Canaanite prophecy, derive specifically from a Dionysiac religion centered in Asia Minor[46]; though such a development may perhaps have occurred as a factor in Near Eastern history, similar forms of possession have been observed in Arabia[47] and in wide-spread shamanistic traditions[48]. An important root of the form of divine speech lies in the operation of the regular cult, especially in the word of a priest or priestess as represented by the oracles of Ishtar of Arbela.

Whatever the precise historical or genetic considerations may be, a functional complementarity exists between the two forms, even if not developed in an identical manner in different cultures. They both appear in Hosea, as also in other Israelite prophets, so that this prophet combines within himself "Dionysiac" abandon and "Apollonian" rationality[49]. These two aspects are probably not to be understood in narrowly psychological terms[50], but represent two symbolic structures embodying dual dimensions of human life. Divine speech gives adequate expression to the element of receptivity toward the Other, and human speech to that of man's activity and comprehension.

---

[45] The combination of ecstacy and rational observation of the future was noted by Plato, Phaedrus, 244 (somewhat differently in Timaeus, 72, with the rational prophet interpreting the other, in line with the role of the Greek "exegete," for which see A. Bouché-Leclerq, Histoire de la divination, II 1879, 215).

[46] G. Hölscher, Die Propheten, 1914; W. Albright, From the Stone Age to Christianity, 1940, 233; G. Pfannmüller, Tod, Jenseits und Unsterblichkeit, 1953, 24 (on Delphi); A. Neher, L'essence du prophétisme, 1955, 29—32.

[47] E. g., A. Haldar, Associations of Cult Prophets Among the Semites, 1945, 180f.

[48] R. de Nebesky-Wojkowitz, Oracles and Demons of Tibet, 1956, 548: the spirit speaks through an unconscious shaman, with words that need to be interpreted. A. Jensen, Myth and Cult, 1963, 223: deities address the assemblage through the Venezuelan shaman.

[49] Similarly F. Böhl, Het Profetisme, Nieuwe Theologische Studiën 16 (1933), 138f., with Nietzsche's distinction in mind.

[50] Noteworthy, though not fully adequate, is T. Andrae's distinction between auditive-exalted and visionary-hypnotic inspiration (Mohammed, 1935, 48f.).

B. Accusations

It is more difficult to make a distinction between human and divine word in accusation than in threat. The terminology used by the two styles overlaps, no matter what principle one uses in separating the two. Continuity of mood, indeed, often speaks against too rigid a boundary around divine word; in many cases, one may want to be more liberal in assigning accusations to Yahweh than has been done in the course of the translation above.

Nevertheless, a certain tendency appears. On those occasions in which the divine "I" is prominent, accusation often has a highly *personal* tone. The people, or the priests, are accused of having sinned against Yahweh (4 7), and of having broken his covenant (8 1). They are said to have rebelled against him (7 13f.) and against his "knowledge" and law (4 6 8 1), to have acted treacherously (6 7), or to have departed from him (11 2. 7). They have made kings "without me" (8 4); they have forgotten God (2 15 13 6) or his law (4 6 8 12), failing to call to him (7 7. 14). They do not discern his leading (11 3). Indeed, God complains that "they speak lies against me," "devise evil against me," and "surround me" like enemies (7 13. 15 12 1). It is natural, of course, that accusations involving the divine "I" are highly personal; yet it is significant both that similar statements appear less often with Yahweh in the third person[51] and that the personal references appear as frequently as they do.

A further tendency can be seen in that prophetic accusation is on the average more *concrete* than is divine reproach, especially if Yahweh's words are taken with a narrow construction, though it is possible that this difference should not be stressed. Divine first-person accusations, when not personal, tend to be general. They speak of Israel's "evil" or of their "deeds" or "ways[52]." In one instance, Yahweh uses the symbols "snare", "net," and "pit," without specifying the transgression[53]. The most specific divine accusations are that the priests "eat the sin of my people," if this refers to the exploitation of sinofferings (4 8), and that "my people" inquire of wood and staff (4 12) — assuming that "my people" is said by Yahweh. Specific transgressions, like murder (including "blood")[54], cursing or perjury[55],

---

[51] Hos 4 10 5 7 7 10 9 17 14 1.
[52] "Evil:" 7 1f. 9 15 (non-divine: 7 3 10 15). "Deeds:" 4 9 7 2 9 15 (non-divine: 5 4 12 3). "Ways:" 4 9 (non-divine: 12 3).
[53] Hos 5 1f. (non-divine: 9 8).
[54] Hos 4 2 6 8f. 12 15.
[55] Hos 4 2 10 4.

various kinds of falsehood[56], oppression and robbery[57], adultery and drink[58], sacrifice and idolatry[59], political and social strife[60], international activity[61], as well as opposition to the prophet himself[62], are not, as a rule, mentioned directly by Yahweh in a first-person statement. Though some of these specific evils are described in close connection with a divine threat, they rarely outside of chs. 1—3 form an integral part of its phrasing, though they do sometimes form an integral part of the prophet's own word[63]. In addition to these and some generally worded accusations, the prophet presents the term זנה, "whoring" (outside of chs. 1—3)[64], and proverbial expressions[65].

Since the evidences of evil are open for all to see, no special revelation is required. In a similarly human manner, in Egypt, the "Eloquent Peasant" and Ipu-Wer denounced the evil they saw in the land[66]. Nevertheless, in Hosea divine words have a part in the pointing out of evil. It is doubtful that either the human or the supernatural element can be assigned temporal priority in Hosea's consciousness. The elements undoubtedly form a structured whole.

C. Positive Motifs. Relations to the Cult

"Exhortations," or appeals, in prophecy can either come from the prophet himself or be cast as divine speech. So also in Hosea. The *protective calls* of 4 15 and 14 2 are non-divine. In two general demands (10 12 12 7), a curious stylistic phenomenon occurs. Judging from the introduction of the preceding verse, a divine word might be indicated; but the exhortation mentions Yahweh in the third person. These two belong to *parenesis*, or cultic wisdom, for which the word שמר (as in 12 7) and promises of blessing are typical[67]. An authoritative *instruction* is given as a divine word in Hos 6 6. Parenesis and instruction reflect levitical and priestly *torā*.

---

[56] Hos 7 1 10 2. 4 12 8. (But see also 12 1.)

[57] Hos 6 9 7 1 12 8.

[58] Hos 4 2. 11f. 14. 18 7 4f.

[59] Hos 4 13f. 17 8 4. 11 9 10 10 1. 8 12 12 13 2f.

[60] Hos 5 10 7 3. 5. 7 9 9 10 9.

[61] Hos 5 13 7 8. 11 8 9 10 13 (in a sense) 12 2. Yahweh, however, threatens to end Israel's going elsewhere, if the beginnings of 7 12 8 10 are his word.

[62] Hos 9 8.

[63] Hos 8 5 10 2. 6. 8 12 15. But see note 61.

[64] Hos 4 11f. 18 5 3f. 6 10 9 1. Note also the mixture of style in 1 2 3 1.

[65] Hos 8 7 9 15 (?) 10 13.

[66] ANET 407—410. 441—444.

[67] N. Lohfink, Das Hauptgebot, 1963, 90—97; J. Malfroy, VT 15 (1965), 53.

References to history are typically phrased in the form of divine speech, especially when God's goodness is recited[68]. After all, according to a widespread outlook, not only the future, but also the past, can be the subject of divine revelation[69]. More specifically, these pronouncements reflect sacred traditions of a priestly type, as will be developed more fully below (Chapter VI).

Hope passages in Hosea evidence both divine and prophetic speech. Most of the words with non-divine style are secondary (2 1-3 3 4f. 11 10f., conceivably 14 8, but probably not 14 6f., which might however also be considered a part of divine speech). From the point of view of content, the latter, especially the secondary ones, are fairly concrete in their announcements. The basic hope sayings tend to rest in a personal promise of God to Israel, just as the cultic "oracle of answer" typically comes from Yahweh. The non-divine style reflects the tradition of the seer or singer. In addition, it represents a somewhat artificial situation, in which a revered prophet of the past (Hosea) is believed to speak to the later situation.

The presence of these positive sayings raises once more the question of a cultic situation. In Hosea, as in other prophets, there is clearly a combination of two approaches, the confrontation with God— in his anger, claim, and love — and the elucidation of the position and direction of Israel through human thinking surrendered to, and inspired by, God. It appears that the second approach should not simply be called one of "dispute[70]," as though the prophet were by nature an enemy of the people; the prophet, often, is "pastor" to his people[71], or intercessor for them before God, acting as a homo religiosus[72]. The confrontation with God fulfills a very important function in Israel, as for any group of men. Every society has its religion by which is relates itself to the source of its existence and to the authority over its life — in other words, to that which defines its life and determines its prospect. The exercise of this relationship is called "cult," whatever its form may be. In Israel, this cult centers around divine speech, to which human word can be related as acknowledgement, request, elucidation, or own insight. The elements of divine speech noted in Hosea — as within instruction, references to history, and declarations of promise — stand fairly close to the official tradition of

---

[68] Hos 10 11 11 1. 3f. 12 10 13 4f. Other historical references occur in 10 9 11 2 12 4f. 13f.

[69] E. g., H. M. and N. K. Chadwick, The Growth of Literature, I, 452. 634.

[70] So, for Hosea, Wolff, e. g., 105. "Word of dispute," however, has become for him a technical term for non-divine speech, somewhat different from Gunkel's use of it for altercations (Die Kultur der Gegenwart, I:VII, 87).

[71] "Seelsorger." (So, already, W. Erbt, Jeremia, 1902, 284, presumably following Gunkel.)

[72] Cf. E. Hoebel, Man in the Primitive World, 1949, 414.

Israel in style and often in content. The symbolic structure of divine threats probably points toward a ritual background of these also, but they have been given a new and unexpected turn in their radical direction against Israel.

III. THE ADDRESSEE

It is the people of Israel who are confronted by the prophetic word of Hosea, whatever may have been the exact nature of his actual audience. Two main styles, however, are used to designate these recipients, namely direct address in the second person and indirect address or reference in the third. The issue to be discussed, then, is not the identity of the addressee but the manner in which he is designated or in which he appears.

The use of the third person for Israel is by far the most common form in Hosea. The second person is used especially for promise and exhortation, while indirect address is the almost exclusive form of threats and reproaches (with exceptions confined to certain relatively well-defined special cases to be discussed). In addition, there are quotations of words in which Israelites speak in the first person.

Direct address in *exhortation* and *instruction* (4 15 6 6 10 12 12 7 14 2f.) is not surprising. Indirect speech for such a purpose is rather awkward and is represented in the book of Hosea only by the wisdom-style conclusion (14 10).

Both direct and indirect address appear in the *promises* of the book of Hosea, but the indirect style tends to be associated with sayings that are not genuine. All of the non-divine hope sayings, most of which are secondary, have the form of indirect reference. But also those third-person promises that are laid on the lips of Yahweh are frequently suspect.

The indirectly phrased 2 20. 23-25 are prose — even if rhythmical — and therefore hardly genuine. Indeed, v. 20 breaks the flow of the passage; in content it is reminiscent of later descriptions of paradise. Thus the phrase "to dwell securely" is almost a cliché in certain post-exilic promises, although, it is true, it already appears earlier[73]. The theme of fertility in v. 23f. has a good parallel in later descriptions, though, of course, ideal conditions of nature are an old theme[74]. V. 25 (like v. 1-3) is based on a combination of the two elements making up the tradition of symbolic action in Hosea and thus is presumably secondary. In the long oral history of the whole complex of Hos 1—3,

---

[73] See Dtn 33 12. 28; and below, Chapter V.
[74] A. De Guglielmo, CBQ 19 (1957), 307.

assimilations to later expressions of hope took place; the phrase "in that day," at least in 2 20 and 23, probably belongs to such a development.

Two or three further third-person words reflect growth in the tradition. Hos 2 17a is at least out of place and is an awkward sentence. Probably, either v. 18 or v. 19 is secondary; most likely the latter, since it is extremely similar in wording to the probably late Ex 23 13b and to Zech 13 2.

A characteristic of the indirect sayings is a desire to picture concretely a situation of welfare, going beyond the merely metaphorical. Thus the formal observation can be made that all of those verses concretely describing the future rather than promising it in a personal fashion are cast in the form of indirect address; such an observation can be harmonized even with a developmental analysis, since later traditionists undoubtedly had a weaker personal but stronger applied interest than the original proclamation did. If it is true that all or most indirect promises in Hosea are secondary, one can compare with this circumstance the fact that in Jeremiah many indirect promises are similarly not genuine[75].

Most likely genuine is the progression 2 16. 17b. 18 (?). 21f.[76]. The first verses in this sequence continue the indirect form of the preceding threat describing a chastising and cleansing action of Yahweh. At the point of his solemn declaration of betrothal in v. 21f. (or already beginning in v. 18?), Yahweh shifts into direct address. The exclamation of Yahweh in Hos 11 8f. uses for the most part direct speech; Israel, however, is mentioned in v. 9 to underline Yahweh's unwillingness to annihilate the nation he has created[77]. Hos 14 5-9 presents a conditional promise as an incentive to turn in the form of indirect address, except for the final expression, "From me your fruit is found."

A final decision on the historical issues concerning the genuineness of material must await the execution of a complete survey of Old Testament hope statements. For the present discussion it is sufficient to point out that promises in the book of Hosea have their center in direct speech, the form employed in the assurances by priest or singer in sacred rites. Both the cultic "oracle of answer," as reconstructed by Begrich[78], and the majority of the unconditional promises given in

---

[75] So, according to the analysis of Wildberger (op. cit. 54—75), whose summary, however, fails to note that it is particularly the indirect *promises* which are secondary, while indirect threats are usually genuine.

[76] Similarly, N. Micklem, Prophecy and Eschatology, 1926, 139; S. Herrmann op. cit. 111.

[77] This is the meaning of "again." (With 2 11 and already Marti.)

[78] ZAW 52 (1934), 81—92.

psalms[79], as well as most oracles of promise recorded in the area of the Fertile Crescent[80], employ second-person speech. The use of the third person has its place primarily in descriptive "portrayals of salvation" which C. Westermann has attributed to the form of the seer[81], occasionally in what Westermann calls "announcements of salvation[82]," as well as partially in the description of "external consequences of divine action" noted by K. von Rabenau in Ezekiel[83]. In addition, the third person is characteristic of conditional promises in the psalms[84]. It is not necessary to suppose that the same usage will hold true for all Old Testament promises, but these data are enough to present analogies to the tradition of Hosea.

Two short passages of a special character, 12 10f. and 13 4-5a, address Israel similarly in the second person. These statements are characterized by a tone and cadence which seem to place them within the *cultic tradition* of the actualization of a sacred past. The first is most naturally read as a call to the assembled populace at the feast of Tabernacles, an invitation — and promise — to experience the days of meeting between Yahweh and the people. It is not necessary that the Israelites dwelt in literal tents on such an occasion in order to have them regard their dwellings (such as huts) ceremonially as extensions of the earlier situation[85]. The placement of עֹד in the prepositive position indicates continuity and extension rather than repetition, appropriate for a sense of unity with the primordial past. Prophetic revelation is promised for the occasion. The second passage (13 4-5a) is clearly part of, or related to, a traditional recital. As soon as an accusation follows upon this, the style of address changes to an indirect form.

---

[79] So: Ps 2 8f. 68 23f. (no pronoun in v. 23) 110 1. 4 132 11f. But the third person occurs in the generalized triumph word of 60 8-10 (= 108 8-10), in the word to Nathan (?) about David quoted by Ps 89 20-38. (Ps 85 10-14 and 126 5f. are not divine words, against the comparison by Wolff 302.)

[80] So, by Baal-Shamaim, Ishtar, Enlil, Atum-Re (AOT 444; M. Jastrow, Die Religion Babyloniens und Assyriens, II 1912, 152—172; ANET 449—451; Falkenstein—Soden, 292—294; Haldar op. cit. 66; etc.).

[81] In B. Anderson (ed.), The Old Testament and Christian Faith, 1963, 209.

[82] So, Is 41 17-20 49 9-12 (EvTh 24 [1964], 365 f.); these are conditioned by need (cf. in Anderson op. cit. 207).

[83] Von Rad-Festschrift 74. Ez 34 28 36 38 37 25.

[84] Ps 12 6 (for the poor) 50 23 81 15-17 (emended at end) 91 14-16. (But the conditional divine promise of Is 58 13f. employs the second person.) Also, in effect, Ps 132 12. On Hos 14 5-9, see also below, p. 128.

[85] See H. Kraus, Worship in Israel, 1965, 61. 132, for theories. J. Pedersen thought of the passover season (ZAW 52 [1934], 175). If the fall festival is intended, the present passage in Hosea attests its historicization as already accomplished.

To a certain extent, these cultic statements may be actual quotations on which the prophet desires to comment. Quoted or artificially created *statements on the lips of Israel* can also be found, in which the addressee is thus represented as speaking in the first person. These include a statement of opposition to the prophet (9 7) and an expression of over-confidence (12 9). A pilgrim song[86] (6 1-3) and a prayer of penitence (14 2-4) are suggested by Hosea to the people for their words in turning to Yahweh. Yahweh's address to Israel, "Where is now your king, to save you, and all your princes, to judge (defend) you, of which you have said, 'Give me a king and princes'" (13 10), takes up the request, "give us a king that he may judge us," transmitted in I Sam 8 6, as well as the theme of I Sam 10 27 11 13 that Saul had brought "salvation," even through his enemies had doubted that he could.

The difficult Jacob-passages in ch. 12 give the impression of being actual quotations, perhaps slightly modified. V. 4f. sound like a proud, almost bragging, saying[87]. V. 6 is clearly liturgical, probably designed to connect Yahweh-Sebaoth with the town or god Bethel[88]. It is best to recognize in v. 6f. the reflection of a ritual form, according to which the deity speaks to Jacob (and thus to his descendents), in a piece of cultic wisdom which may antedate Israelite religion. The juxtaposition in v. 13 of Jacob, who herds for a wife, with Moses, who shepherds Israel out of Egypt, sounds like a popular religious jingle. Hosea does not reject the sacred tradition as such, but the context makes it clear that he cannot share his countrymen's exuberant enthusiasm.

Parody — both satirical and innocent — was to become one of the major forms of humor of later Judaism[89]. The instances just discussed show that already in Old Testament times Israelites could use sacred narratives in a light-hearted way and that Hosea found it appropriate to use both popular and solemn presentations as a background for his severe message. Old Testament prophets regularly used actual quotations or ironical creations of sayings by the people, just as words by enemies are quoted in the Psalms. Somewhat analogously, the Delphic oracle regularly commented on, or criticized, queries it received[90].

In *accusations and threats*, Israel is usually spoken of in the third person. In fact, the emphatic pronoun "they" is used derisively and

---

[86] Rightly, Gunkel-Begrich 430. It is not a song of penitence, as frequently held with the erroneous view that 6 4-6 is an answer to it. Cf. Is 2 3.

[87] That Jacob is victor is likely in view of a verbal similarity with Gen 32 29. See also J. Scharbert, Solidarität in Segen und Fluch, I 1958, 209, with literature. The "speaking" of v. 5 parallels Gen 35 15 (P ?), probably with an indirect relationship.

[88] The employment of the name Sebaoth at Elephantine points to an association with Bethel (A. Vincent, La religion des Judéo-Araméens d'Éléphantine, 1937, 90).

[89] I. Davidson, Parody in Jewish Literature, 1907.

[90] Parke and Wormell op. cit. II xxix.

ominously[91]. Direct address, however, occurs under certain definable conditions. First, it is used for rhetorical commands. "Hear the word of Yahweh" (4 1), "Hear this ..." (5 1), "Do not rejoice, Israel ..." (9 1), "Plead with your mother!" (2 4); calls of alarm (5 8 8 1) are a special form of command. Secondly, the second person is used in ironical or perturbed questions: "What will you do in the day of the feast?" (9 5), "Where is your king ... ?" (13 10), and, "What shall I do with you?" (6 4)[92]. Thirdly, a statement of reasoning appears in such a form: "He is not able to heal you" (5 13).

Further, in three passages direct address occurs with sayings of a peculiar structure, which begin with a subordinate clause introduced by a causal *kî* ("because" or "since"). In these three, the threat given is expressed in terms which imply an appropriate consequence or reversal of the situation described by the accusation: "since you have rejected ..., I will reject ..." and "since you have forgotten ..., I will forget ..." (4 6); "since you have trusted in your (military) might ..., war tumult will arise ..." (10 13b-14); "since you have become a snare ..., I will become a fetter (?) to you" (5 1). (The same construction probably appears in the proverb of 8 7a, in the third person: "since they sow the wind, they will reap the whirlwind," and perhaps in 4 16.) A prepositive causal *kî* is extremely unusual[93], occurring elsewhere, as far as can be determined, only in the following cases: Gen 3 14. 17, curses on Adam and the serpent; Judg 11 13, a quasi-legal form; Is 28 15, against brazen words (and perhaps Is 17 10[94]); Hab 2 8, emphasizing appropriate reversal; and, probably, Num 15 31 in cultic law. Second-person address is employed in all of these cases, except in the last-listed, which has a general application.

The only other cases of direct address, besides words immediately preceding or following the structure just mentioned (4 5 10 15), are represented by 1 9, probably influenced by a legal formula of disavowal; 9 7, a direct answer to a statement by the people; and 13 9, evidently reflecting Dtn 32 38, since the pattern of Dtn 32 10-18. 37-39 dominates Hos 13 1-11.

---

[91] Hos 3 1 6 7 7 4 8 4. 9. 13 9 10 13 2, also 4 14. Similarly, Is 1 2 63 10 Jer 5 5 Ps 106 43. So probably then Ps 62 10 63 10 94 11 120 7 (against J. Patton, Canaanite Parallels in the Book of Psalms, 1944, 37).

[92] For prophetic questions and imperatives, Hylmö op. cit. 47—53 (above, p. 66).

[93] On the otherwise wide usage of *kî*: J. Muilenburg, HUCA 32 (1961), 135—160. Wolff relies on the theory of a "deictic" *kî* to explain the usage in Hos 8 7 10 13b, as in other cases (90. 102. 114. 173. 236 etc.), probably too imprecisely at least for 10 13. The meaning of "as" appears in Hos 8 10f. Possibly related but ambiguous are instances listed by R. Frankena, Vriezen-Festschrift, 1966, 95, 98.

[94] So, R. B. Y. Scott op. cit. 180, who also lists Is 30 9. 15 (see above, p. 29, n. 5).

The question must now be asked, why the third person is used as often as it is in threat and accusation. Several reasons suggest themselves. The most obvious interpretation, a physical one, is that the people are literally absent, the words being either written with hardly anyone present or else being orally addressed to a small group of disciples[95]. In the delivery of extremely harsh threats and reproaches such a situation would not be surprising, for the audience would dwindle or become hostile. Another explanation, a semipsychological one, can be based on the theory that the prophet reports what Yahweh has said to him about the nation[96], perhaps as a speech within the divine council[97]. A third type of interpretation is that the form has a stylistic rationale in a dependence on legal processes or on the style of oracles against foreign nations. The two possibilities within the third type are not mutually exclusive, for the conceptual systems of legal procedure and of concern with enemy nations interpenetrated each other; for instance, Israelites commonly thought of enemies as opponents in a law suit, and vice versa[98].

Though these hypotheses are not always mutually exclusive, they must be examined in turn. The physical and psychological explanations suggested suffer from the fact that the indirect style is not uniform but is broken by instances of direct speech, which would then have to be explained, perhaps stylistically. To theorize that the change in persons is due to the prophet's turning from one audience to another does not fit well with the observation made that stylistic variations fall into describable patterns. These patterns of variations indeed run through the entire book, or at least through chs. 4—14, so that it is not appropriate to suppose a situation for the final chapters different from that of the earlier ones.

The possibility of legal style, championed by Wolff, requires careful analysis, especially since it is difficult to evaluate. For legal processes could employ both direct and indirect speech, each as a rule having its own sphere of operation. One must distinguish three phases: (1) controversy in direct confrontation with an opponent, (2) arguments and testimony before an assembled court, (3) the judgment or sentence, including formulas accompanying execution. The process outside of a court is a *rîb*, usually executed in the second person, with accusing questions introduced by "why"

---

[95] Deissler (90) explains the frequent changes in form as alternations between addressing the actual hearers and a speaking of Israel in general.

[96] So, Beyer op. cit. 67, for shorter oracles (see above, n. 4).

[97] Cf. F. Cross, JNES 12 (1953), 274—277.

[98] The designations are used parallelly in Ex 23 4f. Explicitly in regard to oracles against foreign nations: Jer 25 31, referring to chs. 46—51; similarly, Is 34 8 Jer 51 36. For Egyptian, cf. J. Zandee, Death as an Enemy, 1960, 217. A. Dupont-Sommer, Les inscriptions Araméennes de Sfiré, 1958, 131f., translates *rîb* as "entre en conflict" in the treaty passage III, 17, 26. See below, p. 83. 95. 115.

or "what[99]." If the *ríb*, unsettled, is brought before a court, the opponent is typically accused in the third person, though the defense leads once more to altercating forms of direct speech[100]. The judgment issued by the proper authority is cast, when possible, in direct address; but it employs the third-person form when circumstances make that the logical style, for instance when the defendent is absent[101].

Of formulas accompanying execution, three are recorded in the Old Testament, all expressed in the second person; their central point is that the execution is the appropriate consequence of the guilty person's actions. Thus Joshua says to Achan at the stoning: "Why did you bring trouble on us? The Lord brings trouble on you today" (Josh 7 25). Samuel declares to Agag as he is about to lay a sword to him: "As (כַּאֲשֶׁר) your sword has made women childless, so shall your mother be childless among women" (I Sam 15 33). David addresses the killer of Saul, as he is being hewn down, giving the confessed deed as reason (II Sam 1 16). In addition, in connection with commands of execution, David "seeks" Ish-baal's blood from his murderers (II Sam 4 11) and Solomon declares that Yahweh will bring back Joab's blood on his head (in the third person, since Joab is absent) and tells Shimei, "You know . . . all the evil you did . . .; so the Lord will bring back your evil upon your own head" (I Kings 2 32f. 44). The death of Haman is ordered by the phrase, "Hang him on that" (Esth 7 10), i. e., on the gallows he had prepared for Mordecai, underlining the appropriateness of the sentence[102].

It is now possible to test the style of the prophet's sayings against these legal forms. The accusing question introduced by "why" or "what" is absent from Hosea, though it occurs within the controversy forms of other prophets, including those of pre-Israelite Mari[103]. Third-person accusations in Hosea hardly reflect legal style, since there is no forum to which they are referred, for even a human king dispenses with the court situation for his own cases[104]. The style of the declaration of judgment is too variable to provide a firm analogy; if a legal

---

[99] Partly with H. Boecker, Redeformen des Rechtslebens im Alten Testament, 1964, 26—34. 48—61. It should be noted that the term *ríb* refers especially to "prelegal" (better: "extralegal") controversies, though a *ríb* can then also be brought to a court for help.

[100] Ibid. 71—111.

[101] Ibid. 122—150 fails to distinguish between general declarations applying to anyone who commits a certain evil, which are stated in the third person, and specific judgments, which may use either the second person (I Sam 14 44 22 16 Ps 82 7) or the third, the latter when determining a punishment in absentia (Gen 38 24 Num 15 35 II Sam 12 5f. I Kings 2 24) and when otherwise convenient (I Kings 3 27).

[102] I Sam 22 16-18 and I Kings 2 23-25 bring a reason in a different way. Num 15 35f. (the only remaining account of an execution?) is closely associated with the *kî* form of 15 31. See also p. 123 and K. Koch, VT 12 (1962), 396—416.

[103] Is 3 15 Mi 6 3 Jer 2 5; less precisely in Is 1 5. 11 5 4. See C. Westermann, Grundformen prophetischer Rede, 1960, 102—104; A. Malamat, Congress Volume 1965 (SVT, XVI), 215; that this is part of (Sumerian) controversy style, can be seen from E. Testa, Bibbia e Oriente 8 (1966), 161.

[104] As pointed out by H. Boecker, EvTh 20 (1960), 408.

framework is assumed, a sentencing in absentia can provide the background of indirect speech. Probably the closest point of contact appears in the execution formula, which reveals significant similarities, in address form and intent, with the appropriate-consequence form in Hosea, though not so close as to produce an identity.

The legal execution formulas do not open with *kî* or with some other word for "because," as does Hosea's appropriate-consequence form. In this respect, the latter is closer to that prophetic form which opens with *yă'ăn*, "because," and continues with *laken*, "therefore," a form which may have grown out of the one employed by Hosea[105]. The peculiar use of *kî*, however, may have been conditioned by its employment for "if" in juridical and priestly laws. As in the legal forms, the main sentence following the *kî* clause is not introduced by *laken* but simply by ן (literally, "and") or not by any introductory particle at all[106]. Whether the fact that Akkadian *šumma* is used both for the legal "if" and for the mantic "if" in prognostication can illustrate a possible intermingling between law and prophecy is hard to say; Mesopotamian prognostication, however, was a powerful force toward the development of a theory of moral retribution, including an emphasis on reversals for pride[107].

More directly relevant is the fact already noted (p. 75) that the appropriate-consequence form with causal *kî* occurs in God's curses on Adam and the serpent and probably in the general judgment of Num 15 31 for a person who deliberately opposes Yahweh, "Because he has despised the word of Yahweh ..., that person shall be utterly cut off; his iniquity (shall be) upon him." A similar structure with "because" appears also in a Mesopotamian incantation[108]. One can conclude that the form belongs to sacral law, with its curses. Num

---

[105] *yă'ăn* has a secular nonprophetic use probably only in I Sam 30 22 (a legal situation?). *laken* outside of threats or promises tends to represent a response to another person's word (so, Gen 30 15 Judg 8 7 11 8 I Sam 28 2 Job 20 2 34 25 42 3, similarly often within divine speech); on this, further, S. Blank, HUCA 21 (194 8), 334. The *yă'ăn-laken* style is standard in the deuteronomic work of history (E. Schütz, Formgeschichte des vorklassischen Prophetenspruchs, Diss. Bonn, 1958, 146), Ezekiel, and P (Num 20 12). Isaiah uses *yă'ăn kî* together (Is 3 16 7 5 8 6 29 1 3, sometimes with *laken*) or one of these alone (*yă'ăn*: 30 12; *kî*: 28 15, followed by *laken*). Am 5 11 has *yă'ăn* but with prefixed *laken*, a still informal structure?

[106] ן in the Hosea passages, in Judg 11 13, and in the law Ex 21 19 (after אם). No introduction in Gen 3 14. 17 Num 15 31 Hab 2 8 and in most laws. *laken* does appear in Is 28 16.

[107] F. Kraus, ZA 43 (1936), 77—113; F. Böhl, Der babylonische Fürstenspiegel, 1937.

[108] "Because thou hast said this, O worm [desiring to cause a toothache instead of accepting a gift from Ea], may Ea smite thee with his mighty hand!" (C. Gadd in S. Hooke [ed.], Myth and Ritual, 1933, 66.)

15 31, just quoted, spoke of a person's "despising" (בזה) the word of Yahweh. Some word for "despising" (usually the more common מאס) occurs at least sixteen times in the Old Testament as ground for judgment in quite similar formulations, including the one in Hos 4 6 with *kî*[109]. It is clear that the declaration of sentence follows a very definitely formed tradition in sacral pronouncements. Prophetic circles were undoubtedly the primary guardians of such announcements of judgment.

Wolff has linked exhortations with proposals for bringing a controversy to conclusion[110]. Wolff himself, however, has listed in addition three other possible roots for the exhortation[111]. In Hosea, there is not sufficient reason to specify a legal background for them, except perhaps for the indirect form in Hos 2 4. The major exhortations are probably either quotations attributed to an older situation (10 12 [with Sellin] 12 7) or constitute a standard prophetic call to turn (14 2f.).

To sum up, Hosea hardly had a direct relation to secular judicial forms, as has repeatedly been supposed for him or for other prophets. Rather, the prophetic tradition in which he lived already had some contact with legal structures, more or less cultic in nature, for instance in the form of curses or condemnation proceedings.

Closer still is the relation of Hosea's style to the form of oracles against foreign nations, especially to those that appear in the book of Jeremiah. Jer 46—51 is largely cast in third-person form; exceptions to this rule fall into the following classes: imperatives[112], questions[113], a duel-formula[114], exclamations sounding like warnings[115], and a series of threats announcing the downfall of the proud or selfconfident[116]. The similarity between these instances of direct addresses with those in Hosea is very strong. The last-named class may be compared with the reversal structure described. In fact, one example in that group reads thus: "Since you have trusted in your works ..., you also will be taken" (Jer 48 7), closely resembling Hos 10 13f., although employing *yă'ăn* instead of *kî* for its introducing particle.

---

109 Elsewhere: Lev 26 15. 43 Num 11 20 (Moses to Israel) I Sam 15 23. 26 (Samuel to Saul) II Sam 12 10. 14 (Nathan to David) Am 2 4 Is 5 24 8 6 30 12 Ez 5 6 20 16. 24.

110 So, for Hos 2 4 4 15 8 5 (emended).

111 ZAW 76 (1964), 56, adding priestly *torā*, wisdom, and a call for lament.

112 Jer 46 11. 14 b. 19 48 6. 18f. 28 49 3. 8. 11. 30 — as addresses to the endangered nation. (These and others are discussed, not entirely convincingly, by R. Bach, Die Aufforderungen zur Flucht und zum Kampf, 1962.)

113 Jer 47 5 48 14. 27 49 4. 12.

114 Jer 50 31 51 25. See P. Humbert, ZAW 51 (1933), 101—108.

115 Jer 48 43 50 42.

116 Jer 48 2. 7 49 4 (with question). 15f. 50 24 (?) 51 13f.

Rather similar phenomena can be observed in other foreign oracles, though stylistic traditions can vary. Some reveal a tendency to express reproaches, including the accusation of pride, in the second person; this tendency, when not determined by the form of an accusing question (as in Nah 1 9), is allied to the declaration of an appropriate consequence. Thus the long second-person stretch of accusation in Ob 10-16 ends on the note, "as you have done, it shall be done to you" (v. 15, and similarly v. 16). The use of direct speech in reproach may well be connected with the use of the second person in statements of reasoning, which are allied to accusation in function. Sometimes, however, not only threats but also accusations employ the third person (e. g., Is 16 6). In neighboring countries, divine threats against enemies were ordinarily expressed in indirect speech, sometimes as part of an oracle of promise directed to a certain king[117].

Hosea's words are earlier than Israelite foreign oracles considered. Yet it is not likely that the latter are based on Hosea in form and content. Rather, one must assume that their style traditions reaches far back, representing one of the forms of hope prophecy. In oracles against foreign nations, the use of the third person is quite natural, since those cursed are far away. More generally, in cultic action the faithful community is presumed present, so that exhortation, direction, and promise are addressed to it by the priest or cult prophet. The enemy is absent; even the internal enemy, the "wicked," is supposedly outside, excluded from the covenant community[118].

The tradition of cursing enemies and evil powers, whether human or demonic, is old. The shattering fact in Hosea is that the object of such a curse is the whole nation of Israel, treated as an enemy of Yahweh.

---

[117] S. Strong, The Babylonian and Oriental Record 6 (1892/93), 1—9; Jastrow, Die Religion, II 155. 167. 171; S. Langdon, Tammuz and Ishtar, 1914, 147 (etc.); F. Böhl, Opera Minora, 1953, 70; ANET 328 (execration texts). The second person, however, is used (in connection with an accusing question) in a Mari word (Malamat op. cit. 215).

[118] Cf. G. von Rad in: Bertholet-Festschrift, 1950, 418—437, and further M. Buss, JBR 32 (1964), 321.

Chapter V: The Word as Message: Terms

I. INTRODUCTION

Communication is meaningless apart from its content. Content itself can be viewed under two aspects — the individual motifs as building blocks and the structured whole. The individual elements may be called "terms"; they are separable entities, but fulfill a function within the larger whole.

A proper recognition of terms involves simultaneous attention to language, mood, and life-situation. The following exposition is an attempt to scratch the surface of the problem of symbolic analysis. It will deal especially with words which occur more than once in the book of Hosea and will compare them with similar occurrences elsewhere. An exploratory form of organization will be used in order to be able to group similar materials together.

Since comparisons with material outside Hosea will be made, one issue needs to be raised, at least in the form of a problem. To what extent are later writings directly or indirectly dependent on Hosea? It seems to be possible, on the basis of vocabulary and thought, to show that there is a stream of tradition which includes Hosea, Deuteronomy, the Asaph psalms, the Deuteronomistic historians, Jeremiah, and Ezekiel. After the Exile, the influence of this school is very broad, fused with other currents. Within this tradition there can easily have existed direct knowledge, on the part of any one representative, of earlier writings. Yet similarities that exist between two members can also be due to the tradition rather than to literary dependence of one on the other.

Between Jeremiah and Hosea, for instance, K. Gross has found numerous connections[1]. These, however, reside often in such subtle similarities of style that his conclusion that Jeremiah studied Hosea to acquire them is anything but convincing. It is more reasonable to regard Jeremiah as part of the same tradition to which Hosea belonged, though an occasional direct allusion is possible. Again, the inter-relationship between Hosea and Deuteronomy is complicated. The opinion has been gaining ground — though admittedly not without contrary views — that Deuteronomic antecedents in the Northern Kingdom lie behind Hosea, presumably largely in an unwritten form.

---

[1] Die literarische Verwandtschaft Jeremias mit Hosea, 1930.

If one asks in what kinds of circles the tradition was current, the possibility suggests itself that groups are involved which include both priestly and prophetic elements. Jeremiah is known definitely to have been of priestly descent. That Hosea belonged to a priestly family has long been suggested, though that is hardly more than a speculation. Hosea speaks of enmity existing against him "in the house of his God" (9 8), probably revealing a personal connection with the sanctuary, even though its precise nature is not clear. The Asaph psalms reflect the work of cultic singers. For Deuteronomy and Ezekiel a combination of priestly and prophetic motifs is well known. In addition to prophetic and priestly elements, however, many of these works — excluding perhaps Jeremiah and especially Ezekiel — reveal a wisdom background. One may hypothesize that the distinction between priest, prophet, and wise man was less sharp in the Northern Kingdom than it was in Judah where a definite functional division is attested (Jer 18 18)[2], but one may also have to distinguish between priestly and royal types of wisdom. In any case, Hosea presupposes a complex torā tradition, related to Shechem, which probably involves the still somewhat vaguely known levitical stream leading to the book of Deuteronomy; this movement seems to have included a pervasive element of moral wisdom, developed within the orbit of Yahweh religion. It was centered in the figure of Moses and in part expressed itself in covenant terms[3]. The whole movement, up to Ezekiel, shall be called here the "levitic-deuteronomic tradition."

A central document reflecting the northern tradition is Dtn 32, to which repeated reference will be made[4]. Though its date continues to be a heavily debated issue, a considerable amount of its material can be reconstructed as belonging to the Northern Kingdom on the basis of what is presupposed by Hosea. Its pattern continued to play a major role in Samaritan religion until modern times[5]. Its influence on Judean writings can be seen in Is 1, though not yet in any other (earlier) genuine words of that prophet[6], and perhaps in Mi 1 2.

Canaanite religious forms undoubtedly created tensions in the Northern Kingdom, especially during the Omri dynasty. It is not

---

[2] Differently, Wolff 95 f.

[3] See M. Buss, JBL 82 (1963), 382—392; VT 16 (1966), 503. Related to it are the "covenant lawsuit" and probably also Prov 1, which shares much of its phraseology with Hosea.

[4] The major similarities with Hosea lie in v. 5f. 10. 15-18. 20f. 35. 37-39, and in the use of negatives (see index).

[5] See especially the Zain hymn for the day of atonement (A. Merx, Der Messias oder Ta'eb der Samaritaner, 1909, 10—13).

[6] See A. Dillmann, Die Bücher Numeri, Deuteronomium und Josua, 1886[2], 394; M. Gaster, The Samaritan Eschatology, 1932, 79.

likely, however, that the official cult consciously deviated from exclusive Yahweh worship during the time of Hosea, though ostraca show that many names given in the eighth century were compounded with Baal (probably as an epithet for Yahweh)[7]. It is thus perhaps somewhat too one-sided to see Hosea as a member of an opposition group which had to nurture Yahwistic faith outside of the official cult; but divisions and hostilities undoubtedly existed[8].

II. NEGATIVE TERMS

A. General Negative Terms

Several groups of negative motifs transcend a distinction between accusation and threat and may be treated first. The most prominent of these groups involves the theme of enmity.

1. Enmity

Hosea once exclaims, "Israel has rejected the good — the enemy will pursue him" (8 3). The enemy! One can hear a cry of anguish from the lips of Israel. Enemies are a prominent feature in psalms of lament. There they appear to be a stylization for all the evils that threaten man, often identified with (invisible) accusers[9]. That the enemy "pursues" (רדף) is standard terminology[10].

In the socio-political realm, from a certain ideological perspective, "stranger" and "enemy" are virtually synonymous terms. Hosea accordingly speaks of the "strangers" that devour Israel's strength (7 9 8 7), in words related to a similar usage elsewhere[11].

---

[7] W. F. Albright, Archaeology and the Religion of Israel, 1942, 160f.; Y. Kaufmann op. cit. 138.

[8] Wolff designated Hosea's circle as a "prophetic-Levitic community of opposition" (TL 81 [1956], 85—94).

[9] G. Widengren similarly regards enemies as mythical representations covering different types of evil (Radin-Festschrift, 1960, 480f.). For mythical accusers in Egypt and later Judaism, see G. Roeder, Urkunden zur Religion des alten Ägypten, 1923, 46 ff.; C. Schedl, Biblica 43 (1962), 170.

[10] Dtn 30 7 II Sam 24 13 Am 1 11, often in laments. Enemies are sometimes simply called "pursuers" (Gunkel-Begrich 196; ANET 384). Pestilence, fever, and drought (Dtn 28 22), curses (Dtn 28 45), "blood" (Ez 35 6), and "evil," i. e., misfortune (Prov 13 21), can "pursue."

[11] Especially close are Prov 5 10 Is 1 7. See, further, P. Humbert, Opuscules d'un hébraïsant, 1958, 112—115; L. Snijders, OS 10 (1954), 1—154.

Psalms of lament often describe enemies as laying traps; also in other contexts evil is symbolized by this figure of speech[12]. In 5 1f., Yahweh accuses the Israelites of having become a "snare[13]," a "net[14]," and a "pit[15]." Hosea describes the Israelites as seeking to snare him, the prophet (9 8). Yahweh threatens to be a trapping iron himself (as in Is 8 14), or to throw his net over Israel[16]. It is indeed common, not only in the Old Testament but also elsewhere, to picture deity as coming with a net[17]; it occurs in a threat against a foreign city by a Mari prophet[18].

Another symbolic presentation of enmity speaks of wild animals, especially the lion, for which Hebrew has several different words. In two passages, Hosea has Yahweh announce himself as destructive animals: once as a moth and a lion (5 12-15) and then as a lion, leopard, and bear (13 7f.). The leopard or the bear are often mentioned together with the lion in Old Testament literature, for the sake of parallelism[19]. In typical language, a lion "rends" (טרף) and a bear "encounters" (פגשׁ) its object in a hostile fashion[20].

"Lion" is a favorite expression for the enemy in psalm language and prophecy[21]. Just as a Mesopotamian or Egyptian king or deity can

---

[12] I. Scheftelowitz, Das Schlingen- und Netzmotiv im Glauben und Brauch der Völker, 1912; M. Eliade, Images et symboles, 1952, ch. III; H. Kees, Ägypten, 1933, 26; J. Zandee op. cit. 226—234; W. Wuellner, The Meaning of "Fishers of Men", 1967 75—131.

[13] פַּח can mean anything threatening: Job 18 9 22 10 Ps 69 23 Is 24 17f. Jer 48 43f. The verb פחח is used similarly in Is 42 22, as well as the family נקשׁ/יקשׁ (Hos 9 8).

[14] רֶשֶׁת. Cf., in addition to psalms, Ez 19 8 Job 18 8 Prov 29 5. Outside Hosea, חֵרֶם, Mi 7 2 Hab 1 15-17 Ez 32 3.

[15] שַׁחַת. Cf. psalms and Ez 19 4. 8 Prov 26 27. Further synonyms (מְצוּדָה, שִׁיחָה, מְשַׁחִית) occur outside of Hosea.

[16] Hos 5 2 7 12. The word מוֹסֵר, 5 2, seems to be connected with the root יסר־אסר, "to bind," which may appear in 7 12 10 10. It is just possible that the motif of "binding" reflects the ritual "fettering" of demonic enemies by a Mesopotamian sorcerer, as also in the Christian text discussed in S. Euringer, "Das Netz Salomos," ZS 6 (1928), 76—100. 178—199. 300—314.

[17] Ez 12 13 17 20 32 3 Lam 1 13; M. Farbridge, Studies in Biblical and Semitic Symbolism, 1923, 184; E. Van Buren, Symbols of the Gods in Mesopotamian Art, 1945, 11f.; F. Horst, Die zwölf kleinen Propheten, 1954, 177; ANET 115, etc.; Falkenstein-Soden 107. 132. 230. 353; A. Falkenstein, Sumerische Götterlieder, I 1959, 20; II 1960, 14. 76. Against his own people: B. Meissner op. cit. 36 (above, p. 48).

[18] Malamat op. cit. 215. 217.

[19] Is 11 6 Jer 5 6 I Sam 17 34. 36f. Am 5 19 Lam 3 10 Prov 28 15.

[20] טרף is hence often used in a figurative sense.

[21] So, אַרְיֵה, כְּפִיר, and לָבִיא (the latter typically as a parallel word). For שַׁחַל, cf. Job 10 16 (Yahweh) and usage in wisdom for danger or evil.

be described as a roaring lion going out for battle[22], so also an Israelite king[23] and, especially, Yahweh himself[24]. The lion, in fact, has long been employed in the Near East (as in many other areas) as a pervasive symbol for destructive and hostile forces[25]. The stylization of the enemy as a lion is so strong that Yahweh can even accuse Israel of being "a lion" toward him (Jer 12 8).

The lion image has a certain, though subtle, connection with sexuality, expressing — generally negatively — the strongly emotional struggle between life and death[26]. In such a way, it relates closely to Hosea's message. But it is clear that Hosea did not create the lion symbol; representations of lions, indeed, were prominent in the Samaria of his day[27].

A characteristic expression connected with the picture of a lion is the phrase "there is none to deliver." Indeed, the entire phrase "I will rend, and there is none to deliver" of Hos 5 14 also appears in the Asaphite Ps 50 22. It occurs elsewhere in slightly varying forms[28]. In Dtn 32 39, the phrase occurs again in a context which also has other similarities with Hos 5 13—6 2[29], evidently reflecting a liturgical form on which Hosea depends. In Near Eastern religion generally, divine power is viewed as irresistible in its wrath[30].

---

[22] Falkenstein-Soden 107. 126. 131; ANET 381. 384; H. Grapow, Die bildlichen Ausdrücke des Ägyptischen, 1924, 70—72; U. Schweitzer, Löwe und Sphinx im alten Ägypten, 1948, 18—21. 51; A. Falkenstein op. cit. I 110. 120. 123f.; II 76.

[23] Prov 19 12 20 2 28 15. For officials: Ez 22 25 Zeph 3 3. For a nation or tribe: Dtn 33 20 Mi 5 7 Ez 19 1-9.

[24] Is 31 4 38 13 Jer 25 38 49 19 Lam 3 10 Job 10 16. He is often described as "roaring" (Hos 11 10 Am 1 2 Job 37 4, etc.).

[25] So in texts, carvings, etc. See M. Witzel, Der Drachenkämpfer Ninib, 1920, 147. 176. 191f. 212; E. Van Buren, The Fauna of Ancient Mesopotamia as Represented in Art, 1939, 3—7; H. Bonnet, Reallexikon der ägyptischen Religionsgeschichte, 1952, 428f.; E. Goodenough, Jewish Symbols in the Greco-Roman Period, VII 1958, 37—86; B. Goff, Symbols of Prehistoric Mesopotamia, 1963, 63f.; etc.

[26] One of its major connections (though not to be exaggerated) is with Ishtar; cf. Hempel, Apoxysmata, 18f. Some overt association with fertility appears in Egypt; cf. Goodenough op. cit. VII 49f. 77f. See further the data and theory of A. Moortgat, Tammuz, 1949; also, H. J. Kantor, JNES 21 (1962), 93—117, with an image of naked women on lion heads.

[27] J. and G. Crowfoot, Early Ivories from Samaria, 1938, 22—25; A. Parrot, Samaria, 1958, 67. 77f.

[28] Ps 7 3 Mi 5 7 Is 5 29. Without the verb "to rend," but in connection with a wild animal: Dan 8 4. 7. Further, of Yahweh: Dtn 32 39 Is 43 13 Job 10 7.

[29] Including the double "I" as in Hos 5 14. (See also Hos 13 4.)

[30] A. Haldar, Studies in the Book of Nahum, 1947, 104f.; W. Lambert, Babylonian Wisdom Literature, 1960, 201 (cf. 188), in connection with a lion figure.

The word "moth" appears in the Old Testament only as a technical expression for destructive enmity[31]. According to Ps 39 12, for instance, God consumes "like a moth," as in Hos 5 12.

Israel's evil is enmity, so much so that Yahweh can accuse the people in these words, "They devise evil against me" (7 15); this follows a phraseology typically employed to described enemies[32] and closely parallels a prophecy accusing Nineveh of plotting against Yahweh (Nah 1 11). Like enemies in the psalms, Israel "speaks lies against me" (7 13; cf. Ps 5 7 58 4) and "has surrounded me," using "falsehood" as its weaponry (12 1)[33]. Yahweh, for his part, also acts as an enemy, as is explicitly stated elsewhere[34]. In Hosea's symbolism it is quite clear that God and the people are enemies.

2. *Separation and Negation*

Hos 4 6 has Yahweh say to the priest, "Since you have rejected the 'knowledge,' I will reject you from being priest to me." Numerous parallels speak of a rejection of God and his word by man or of a rejection of man by God[35].

Psalms of lament complain that Yahweh forgets, forsakes, drives out, and casts off the one who is praying[36]. Each of these words occurs in Hosea for either man's or God's action, or for both (4 6. 10 8 3. 5. 14 9 15 13 4-6). The statement that Israel lifted up its heart when it was satisfied and thus forgot God its Savior (13 4-6) is closely paralleled by Dtn 8 11-16 and other passages[37]. The similar word of Hos 8 14 (genuine?),

---

[31] A moth is also mentioned in the Aramaic curse reported by J. Fitzmyer, JAOS 81 (1961), 185. The translation "pus" does not have adequate support in Arabic, besides ignoring the symbolism.

[32] Ps 35 4 41 8 140 3 Gen 50 20 Jer 48 2 Zech 7 10 8 17 Neh 6 2. For Yahweh: Jer 26 3 36 3. Similar phrases are found in Ps 21 12 35 20 36 5 52 3.

[33] For the correct usage of סבב, e. g., Ps 22 13 109 3. In Hos 7 2 the evil deeds similarly "surround" Israel. See also p. 102.

[34] Jer 30 14 (with a context strongly reminiscent of Hos 5 13) Lev 26 40f. Lam 2 4 Is 63 10, indirectly elsewhere (e. g., Is 8 14 Job 13 24). Cf. S. Mowinckel, Psalmenstudien II, 1922, 339. 250—252; P. Volz, Das Dämonische in Jahwe, 1924, 17; A. Weiser, Die Prophetie des Amos, 1929, 45; H. Fredriksson, Jahwe als Krieger, 1945.

[35] Hebrew: מאס. Man rejects God (Num 11 20 [JE] I Sam 8 7 10 19). Man rejects God's *torā* (Is 5 24 Jer 6 19 Am 2 4), word (I Sam 15 23, etc.), judgments (Lev 26 43, etc.), and statutes (II Kings 17 15, etc.). God rejects man (Am 5 21 I Sam 15 23 16 7 Jer 2 37 7 29 14 19 31 37 33 24. 26 Ps 53 6 78 59. 67 89 39).

[36] Gunkel-Begrich 192.

[37] Dtn 6 12 32 15-18. Without the motif of fullness: Ps 106 21 Is 17 10. The emphasis is often on "your" or "their" God who is forgotten (Hos 13 4 Dtn 8 19 Judg 3 7 I Sam 12 9 Jer 3 21, etc.).

that Israel has forgotten its maker, resembles Dtn 32 18 and Is 51 13. The forgetting of God by man is a theme characteristic particularly of the levitic-deuteronomic tradition and of psalms allied to it[38].

Separation in a family situation may express itself in divorce. It has been suggested that a divorce formula lies behind the phrase, "She is not my wife and I am not her husband" (Hos 2 4)[39]. The matter, however, is more complicated. If Yahweh were divorcing Israel in an ordinary fashion, he would be required to bestow on her a proper financial settlement and explicitly renounce all future claim on her. As a matter of fact, Hos 2 4ff. is designed to elaborate the opposite of this situation. It justifies and announces Yahweh's withdrawal of support, to which a marriage contract ordinarily obligates a husband unless the woman commits adultery, with the specific aim of motivating Israel's return. Rather than instituting divorce, Yahweh is making public the fact that no proper marriage exists and engages in a judicial procedure designed to win her through discipline.

The formula quoted has no precise parallel in Israelite, Jewish, or Near Eastern divorce terminology, but is rather a negated marriage formula, intended here primarily as an accusation. Near Eastern divorce documents use the positively worded formula, "I divorce (repudiate, hate, etc.) you (or, her)," together with an appropriate renunciation and settlement[40]. The typical marriage formula states that "You are (or, she is) my wife," occasionally with the addition, "I am her husband," or similarly[41]. A negated form of the marriage formula occurs in an Old Sumerian law and in Old Babylonian marriage contracts[42], which provide generally as follows. If a man says to his wife, "you are not my wife," he must forfeit a sum; and if a wife says to her husband, "you are not my husband," she is to be thrown into a river, cast from a tower, or stripped naked. It is clear especially in the

---

[38] Ps 44 21 50 22 78 7. 11 103 2 106 13. 21 and often in Ps 119. (These are clergy psalms or late.)

[39] So, in an unhappy phraseology, C. Kuhl, ZAW 52 (1934), 102—109, while his analysis is not actually incorrect. Hos 2 9 may imply a divorce, but is not an original part of the chapter.

[40] So in Sumerian, Akkadian, Nuzi, Aramaic, Egyptian, and Jewish forms: L. Blau, Die jüdische Ehescheidung, II 1912, 14—40; C. Gordon, ZA 43 (1936), 162; E. Neufeld, Ancient Hebrew Marriage Laws, 1944, 180f.; A. Falkenstein, Neusumerische Gerichtsurkunden, I 1956, 107f.; P. Pestman, Marriage and Matrimonial Property in Ancient Egypt, 1961, 58—72. The only exception is a medieval Karaite text (based on Hos 2 4?), whose form is expressly rejected as illegal by the Talmud (Kidd. 5b).

[41] A. Van Selms, Die Formule "Yy is my . . .; ek is jou . . .", Hervormde Teologiese Studies 14 (1959), 130—140; W. Edgerton, Notes on Egyptian Marriage, 1931, 1.

[42] Especially, M. Schorr op. cit.

latter case that the negative expression is not itself a legal divorce form but a prelegal or extralegal expression of repudiation, indicating a desire for separation or a refusal to comply with the relationship, an expression which can lead to judicial action. In Hammurabi's code (§§ 142f.) a repudiation by the wife in the form, "you may not have me," leads to a legal process ending either in a divorce, if the husband has unjustly disparaged her, or in a punishment for the woman.

Marriage contracts in the Near East (especially in Egypt) specified that the husband furnish his wife with certain, sometimes carefully stipulated, amounts of food, clothing and personal supplies[43]. Yahweh announces that he will withdraw these marital provisions, especially since the land has improperly credited her lovers with having given them to her as hire; he will apply the sanction of nakedness, appropriate for unfaithful wives[44]. (But the promise of 2 16-22 holds out gifts after "speaking kindly" to the woman, in order to avoid divorce[45].) The children become involved in the proceeding since their status and welfare are threatened; Yahweh takes them to be illegitimate offspring (2 6), so that any eviction and non-support that is meted out to her applies to them, too. It is thus in their interest to settle the matter.

Somewhat sharper divorce terminology is used elsewhere. Among the Hebrew words for divorce is גרשׁ, "to drive out;" a common term for the sexual or personal revulsion leading to a separation is שׂנא, "to hate[46]." These two words occur together in Hos 9 15. The passage Hos 9 10-17 is indeed generally pervaded with sexual terminology, including references to birth and conception; the verb מאס in its final announcement (v. 17) can denote the rejection of a wife, as in Is 54 6.

Allied to divorce is disinheritance or the reversal of an adoption. Old Sumerian and Babylonian legal texts present formulas for repudiation, "you are not my son" or "you are not my father," which are punishable, except for serious cause after an elaborate legal process[47]. The "not" of these formulas has probably influenced or colored the fateful names "Not-my-people" and "Not-Pitied," and the declaration, "you are not my people and (thus?) I will not be for you" (1 9).

These usages of the word "not," however, belong, to a special tradition of negative expression. Dtn 32, to which Hosea is related, speaks of Israel as "not his children" (v. 5), "not wise" (v. 6, similarly

---

[43] L. Epstein, The Jewish Marriage Contract, 1927, 53f.; L. Dürr, BZ 23 (1935/36), 155—157; E. Lüddeckens, Ägyptische Eheverträge, 1960.

[44] C. Gordon, ZAW 54 (1936), 277—280; R. Gordis op. cit. 20f. (above, p. 57).

[45] See Judg 19 3 and R. Patai, Family, Love and the Bible, 1960, 105.

[46] Already L. Blau op. cit. I 18—21.

[47] M. David, Die Adoption im altbabylonischen Recht, 1927; Van Selms op. cit. 131ff.; C. H. §§ 168f.

v. 28), "children which are not faithful" (v. 20), serving what is "not-God" (v. 17, 21), so that God will provoke them with a "not-people" (v. 21)[48]. In a similar style, the goddess Inanna refuses her temple and city: "My house you are not (any longer) .... My city you are not. ... I will not (again) dwell there ..."[49]. The words אַיִן ("no") and לֹא ("not") occur often in Hosea for threats and accusations and for a lamenting note that Israel is not wise (4 14 7 11 13 13) and does not know what is happening to it (2 10 7 2. 9); the laments are comparable to the wisdom aspect of Dtn 32[50].

The sharpest form of negativity lies in the fact that its sins have so firmly separated Israel from Yahweh that they will not let it truly return (5 4); a ritual search for him will come to naught, since Yahweh has "pulled off" (חלץ, 5 6). This search is related to a theme of vain love seeking in Cant 3 1f. 5 6 (cf. Hos 2 9) and perhaps to a cultic theme of a departed God[51].

B. Terms of Threat and Destruction

1. Judicial Controversy (rîb)

"Hear the word of Yahweh, children of Israel, for the Lord has a controversy with those that dwell upon the earth" (Hos 4 1). With these words Hosea opens an oracle. In Hos 12 3, again, he announces that "Yahweh has a controversy with Israel." No elaboration of the details of the controversy are given; the style appears to be a technical one known to the audience. In 4 1-3, in fact, Hosea seems to reflect the words of his contemporaries. That passage contains a number of elements not found elsewhere in Hosea's oracles — the expression "word of Yahweh," a formal catalogue of sins in v. 2, and the description of the suffering of nature in v. 3. In v. 4, Hosea appears to reject a judicial speaking by the cultic leadership on the ground that it itself is no better than the people and is indeed responsible for the conditions in the land (4 4-8). Hos 4 1-3 evidently represents a pattern of cultic word current in Hosea's time, which is also reflected in Mi 7[52].

It is one of the fundamental convictions of Near Eastern, including Israelite, religion that suffering is due to divine wrath, presumably

---

[48] The repeated use of "not" was in large part recognized by O. Eißfeldt, Das Lied Moses, 1958, 7f.

[49] Falkenstein-Soden 184f.

[50] The phrase לֹא חָכָם occurs only in Hos 13 13 and Dtn 32 6; for אֵין לֵב, cf. the somewhat softer חֲסַר לֵב, common in Proverbs, and לֶב אַיִן in Prov 17 16.

[51] H. G. May, AJSL 48 (1931/32), 77. 83; E. Jacob, RHPR 43 (1963), 255f.

[52] B. Reicke, HTR 60 (1967), 349—367, regards this chapter as basically North-Israelite. See especially v. 1-6. 9. 15 for comparison with Hos 4 1-3 9 9 12 10, etc.

for some "sin" however superficially it might be viewed. A common
pattern for fast days, then, was to express penitence through various
rites and to offer sacrifices. Sin-offerings — undoubtedly old in Syria-
Palestine[53] — had a particular connection with the priests, who derived a large part of their support from them either in the form of
money or in the form of meat from animal sin-offerings, which were
eaten by the priests rather than by the laymen[54]. The priests thus had
a vested interest in pointing out sinfulness, thereby encouraging sacrifices. Hosea accuses them of "lifting their appetite" toward Israel's
guilt, i. e., of deriving satisfaction from Israel's sin (4 8). They have
interest, Hosea says, not in preventing evil but in profiting from it.
They have rejected the *torā* of instruction (4 6) in favor of an apparatus
of expiation.

The priest did not necessarily engage in denunciatory speech himself; a cult prophet — or any accusing prophet, who would thus earn,
at least provisionally, the approval of the priest — can properly be the
one to speak those words. The Hittite king Mursilis prays in a confession during a plague that the gods would reveal the offending sin
through prophet, priest, or vision[55]. Already in primitive society, an
ecstatic prophet could have a part in a regular ritual in order to lay
bare evils from which the hearers would then purge themselves[56]. In
Hos 4 1-3, the phrase "word of God" may hint at prophetic speech.
The (cult-)prophet is indeed mentioned together with the priest in the
threat that follows (4 5).

The description of natural disaster in Hos 4 3 has numerous parallels. "Mourning" and "withering" are two terms which often appear
together, both in laments and in announcements[57]. The words indicate
clearly a condition of drought, as it is sometimes expressly stated[58];
each of them is etymologically connected with a stem that means both
"to dry up" and "to mourn," a duality finding ritual expression in the
Tammuz cult[59]. The disaster strikes "all that dwell upon the earth (or,

---

[53] ANET 502f.; R. Dussaud, Les origines cananéennes du sacrifice israélite, 1921;
Ugaritic texts 2. 5. 9.

[54] Money: II Kings 12 17 Lev 5 15f. 24f. Num 5 7f. Meat: Lev 6 19. 22 7 6f.; priests
thereby "bear" Israel's guilt (Lev 10 17).

[55] ANET 396.

[56] See M. Buss, JBR 32 (1964), 324.

[57] Laments: Jer 14 2 Joel 1 10. 12 Lam 2 8 Is 33 9. Future: Is 19 8 24 4. 7. אבל elsewhere: Jer 12 4. 11 23 10 (laments), Is 3 26 Jer 4 28 Am 8 8 9 5 (threats), Am 1 2
(general). אמלל elsewhere: Jer 15 9 (lament), Nah 1 4 (general).

[58] That sin causes drought continues as an important theme in later Judaism (R. Patai,
HUCA 14 [1939], 264—269).

[59] So, Haldar, Studies in the Book of Nahum, 23, and A. Kapelrud, Joel Studies,
1948, 37.

in the land)," including the beasts, the birds, and the fishes, according to a description typical of similar contexts[60]. The phrase "people as priest" (4 9) seems to be part of a description of universal catastrophe[61], though now ironically used by Hosea as a threat.

The condition of chaos thus described is a result of the fearful appearance and wrath of God, as evident in many Old Testament passages[62] as well as in Tammuz liturgies[63]. Mesopotamian liturgies in calamity include powerful descriptions of the fearful "word" (cf. Hos 4 1), causing the earth to shudder and devastating field and herd[64].

A counterpart to Yahweh's controversy is a "contending" (or "arguing") by the people with Yahweh in their distress. Such complaints (and the general theme of a *rîb*) are a common phenomenon of Israelite and Mesopotamian religious literature, in both individual and communal form. Elaborating the style of individual laments, Job engages in a controversy (*rîb*) with God[65]. In Jer 2 29, God refers to Israel's contending (*rîb*), evidently in response to a collective lament. Hos 4 4 can refer to such a human contention, though the context speaks against it. According to Hos 8 2, Israel "cries"[66] to God, basing its appeal on the fact that Yahweh is its God: "My God, we, Israel, know thee!" The singular possessive pronoun in this address should not be emended, since the phrase "my God" is typical of Near Eastern laments and prayers[67], including Israelite prayers of a collectivity mediated through a leader[68]. In fact, the expression "my God" becomes a stereotyped term for Yahweh, like the better-known "(my) Lord" (אֲדֹנָי), particularly on the lips of a professional such as a prophet like Hosea[69]. The exclamation of 8 2 probably was presented by a cultic

---

[60] Hos 4 1. 3 Am 9 5 Jer 1 14 6 12 7 20 25 30 Zeph 1 2f. (with the verb אסף as in Hos 4 3) Ps 33 14 Joel 1 2. 14 Is 24 1. 5 26 21, etc.

[61] Cf. Is 24 2 Joel 1 9ff. (in late attestations).

[62] E. g., Am 1 2 8 8 9 5 Nah 1 4.

[63] Haldar, Studies in the Book of Nahum, 104.

[64] S. Langdon op. cit. 111f.; O. Grether, Name und Wort Gottes im Alten Testament, 1934, 140—143.

[65] Job 9 3 10 2 (for Yahweh) 13 6 40 2. Even the verb יכח can be used for human arguing with God (Job 13 3. 15).

[66] זעק: Hos 7 14 8 2. The word is common as a synonym for "howl" (e. g., Is 14 31) and, especially, as an expression for calling to God in trouble (e. g., Judg 10 14).

[67] For Babylonian and other traditions: W. Baudissin, Kyrios, III 1929, 561ff.; the term even becomes "erstarrt" (566). For Egyptian: H. Grapow, Wie die alten Ägypter sich anredeten, 1960², 60. Reflected in the Amarna tablets (passim), addressing Pharaoh as deity.

[68] Gunkel-Begrich 122; P. de Boer, De Voorbede in het Oude Testament, 1943, 148f. So, especially, Ps 83 14 Ezra 9 6 II Chr 6 40 Dan 9 18f.

[69] See O. Eißfeldt, ZAW 61 (1945—48), 3—16 (Kleine Schriften, III 1966, 35—47), and Hos 8 2 9 8. 17. (The LXX always translates, quite properly, simply "God.")

liturgist representing a chiding plea to God on the basis of Israel's acquaintance with him. Similarly, in their "distress" (a common time for turning to God[70]) the Israelites are expected to seek God, according to Hos 5 15, and to use words that include once more a reference to "knowing" God (6 3) as a technical term for a good relationship.

Closely related to "controversy" is the term "judgment," which appears more than once[71]. One element of judicial process is the recognition of a trespass. Yahweh declares that he "knows" Ephraim; Israel is "not hid" from him (Hos 5 3). Similar statements occur elsewhere.[72]

Thus Yahweh "will remember their guilt and visit their sins" (Hos 8 13 9 9). "Remembering" — better, "having in mind" or "taking account of" — is threatened also in Hos 7 2, being often a technical cultic or forensic term[73]. Thus Ps 74 22 cries out, "Arise, God, plead your cause, remember the reproaches of the impious against thee!" The threat of "visitation" is brought in Hos 4 9 and 12 3, connected with the announcement of a controversy, as well as in 1 4 2 15. Threats of a visiting frequently appear as part of a form with two parallel parts[74], as just cited. A "returning" of Israel's sin appears in parallelism both with visitation (4 9 12 3) and with the synonym "leaving" (12 15). The returning of deeds expresses an intimate tie between offense and punishment[75].

The term "to be guilty" or "to suffer in guilt" (אשם) belongs to cultic law[76]. Hosea employs it for the state of the offense (4 15 13 1) and especially for the resultant calamity (5 15 10 2 14 1).

Without suffix the term occurs in Hosea only in compound phrases and as a general designation of "deity" represented by an angel: 4 1 6 6 12 4.

[70] צַר; cf. Ps 18 7 107 6, etc. Similarly צָרָה.

[71] Hos 5 1. 11 6 5 10 4. Cf. Mal 3 5 and parallels with *rîb* in the Psalms and elsewhere (Gunkel, ZS 2 [1923/24], 152).

[72] Yahweh "knows:" Is 29 15 Jer 29 23 48 30 Am 5 12 Job 11 11. Sins are "not hid:" cf. Jer 16 17 Ps 69 6.

[73] Num 5 15 I Kings 17 18 Ez 21 28f. 29 16 Ps 79 8 109 14 137 7, etc. On the word, see now W. Schottroff, "Gedenken" im Alten Orient und im Alten Testament, 1964, and C. Price, Remembering and Forgetting in the Old Testament, Diss. Union, 1962 (summarized in DA 23 [1963], 2607).

[74] So, Hos 4 9 8 13 9 9 12 3 Is 13 11 26 21 Jer 5 9 9 8 14 10 (borrowed from Hosea?) Ps 89 33 Lam 4 22. (Is 26 21 and Lam 4 22 have "uncover" as parallel; the same stem appears in Hos 7 1.)

[75] E. g., in the psalms. Often this and similar terms are followed by the preposition לְ (so, Hos 12 3). "Blood" or "reproach" are connected with הֵשִׁיב in Hos 12 15 II Sam 16 8 I Kings 2 32f. Ps 79 12 Neh 3 36.

[76] So, clearly, Jer 2 3. A "curse" leads to a state of being guilty according to Prov 30 10; similarly, Is 24 6. See Wolff 112f.

2. *"The Day of Yahweh" and Terms for War and Destruction*

A large complex of motifs is represented by "the day of Yahweh," designating a terrifying appearance of Yahweh in victory over his enemies[77]. The Babylonian fire god had a similar "day," as is revealed in the prayer of a sick man:

I call to you as to Shamash the judge,
Judge my case, render my decision [cf. Ps 35 1. 23 119 154],
Overcome the sorcerer and the witch,
Devour my enemies, tear my wicked [i. e., hostile] ones,
May your fearful day overtake them[78].

It is typical of prophetic announcements that the "day" is declared to be near, to have "come[79]." Hosea accordingly announces, "The days of visitation have come, the days of 'fulfillment' have come" (9 7). "Yet a little while" (1 4) is a characteristic expression in warnings of the punishment of evil[80].

The phrase "the day of visitation" is a very common one in prophecy[81], and "the time of (judicial) 'fulfillment'" is also mentioned twice outside of Hosea[82]. The "day of reproof" announced in Hos 5 9 is similarly predicted elsewhere[83]. The semi-technical[84] term "in that day" introduces Hos 2 18 and 23 (probably not genuine). Even the phrase "many days" (3 3f.) is not chosen arbitrarily, as it appears also on the Moabite stone and in Ez 38 8 and Is 24 22, in each case as a designation for a time of disaster.

---

[77] In the Old Testament, as elsewhere in the Near East, the "day" is described as one of darkness and horror. The opposite view is based on a misunderstanding of Am 5 18-20, wherein Amos reminds the hearers of the character of the day; cf. Zeph 1 15 Joel 2 2, etc. See L. Černý, The Day of Yahweh and Some Relevant Problems, 1948, passim (especially Appendix I). A. Haldar, Studies in the Book of Nahum, 110, refers to the dark "day" of Tammuz.

[78] Maqlû I, 107—121; similarly, II, 114—121. (Mentioned by G. Hölscher, Die Ursprünge der jüdischen Eschatologie, 1925, 13, but not by M. Weiss, HUCA 37 [1966], 29—60.)

[79] קָרוֹב: Dtn 32 35 Is 13 6 Ez 30 3 Joel 1 15 2 1 4 14 Ob 15 Zeph 1 7. 14. בָּא: Is 13 9 Ez 7 2. 6f. 12 21 30. 34 39 8 Joel 2 1 Am 8 2 Mi 7 4 Lam 4 18. Cf. Am 6 3 ("you who think that the evil day is far away") Is 8 1 (Mahershalal-hashbaz). This group of expressions is basically threatening. If it served originally as a cry in battles (G. von Rad, Old Testament Theology, II 1965, 124) it must have been directed against the enemies.

[80] Is 10 25 Jer 51 33 Hag 2 6 Ps 37 10. Hopefully: Is 29 17. In Jon 3 4: "Yet forty days" (a more specific short time).

[81] יוֹם פְּקֻדָּה or similarly; see Wolff 201 and also Is 24 21.

[82] יוֹם שִׁלֻּם: Cf. Is 34 8 Dtn 32 35 (probably).

[83] יוֹם תּוֹכֵחָה: Is 37 3. Cf. Ps 149 7.

[84] See S. Mowinckel, Norsk TT 59 (1958), 52.

War is an important element in the religious tradition of Israel and one with which prophecy is closely connected[85]; for all ancient war was basically "holy" (even though kings could also employ "wisdom"). Hosea, just like Amos, expects a "day of war[86]." Yahweh, the God of "hosts," speaks (12 6). Trumpet sound is to be raised, according to an alarm typical of prophetic war songs and descriptions of enemies[87]. By the "sword," the Israelites will "fall[88];" it will "devour (them)[89]." Yahweh's threatening sword can be either his own, or one which he "sends[90];" in Hosea it is the latter. In the probably secondary 8 14, Yahweh threatens to send into the cities "devouring" fire, a standard form of divine weaponry[91].

One of the few instances in which divine speech seems to include a specific threat is the announcement that peoples will be "gathered" against Israel (Hos 10 10). Though more concrete than most other sayings on the lips of Yahweh, this word is nevertheless a highly stylized one. The gathering of peoples is a standard motif in announcements of Yahweh's victory[92]. The enemies assemble themselves in attack, only to be defeated; or else Yahweh himself gathers them, whether for the destruction of Israel[93] or for their own judgment[94]. This variable use of the image makes possible also the following declaration: "Now I will gather them [the Israelites]!" (Hos 8 10), as similarly in Ez 22 19.

The day of Yahweh is typically described in terms of devastation. Is 13 9 describes it in terms of Yahweh's wrath, "to turn the earth into desolation (לְשַׁמָּה)." Hosea cries out, "Ephraim is destined to desolation (לְשַׁמָּה) in the day of reproof" (5 9). The phrase לְשַׁמָּה is

---

[85] Max Weber, Ancient Judaism, 1952, 30—117; J. Pedersen, Israel, III—IV 1940 125—127.

[86] Hos 10 14 Am 1 14. Already W. Smith, The Prophets of Israel, 1882, 397, pointed out that in Arabic "day" frequently means "day of battle." "War" is mentioned further in Hos 10 9. 14 (negatively in 1 7 2 20).

[87] Hos 5 8 8 1; Lindblom 76; Horst op. cit. 161. 175. For the use of the trumpet in war, see H. Seidel, WZ Univ. Leipzig, G.-s. 6 (1956/57), 589—599. It is associated with the lion and trap figures in Amos 3 3-8.

[88] Hos 7 16 14 1. Cf. Num 14 3 Is 3 25 Ps 78 64, etc.

[89] Hos 11 6. Cf. Dtn 32 42 Is 1 20 Jer 46 10, etc.; J. Steinberg, Der Mensch in der Bildersprache des Alten Testaments, 1935, 15—22; J. Fitzmyer op. cit. 185 (in the Sefire treaty: "every sort of devourer").

[90] Yahweh's own: Dtn 32 41 Judg 7 20 Jer 12 12 Am 4 10 Ps 7 13, etc. He "sends" one: Am 9 4 Jer 9 15 (etc.) Ez 5 12 (etc.).

[91] F. Lang, TL 79 (1954), 56; P. Miller, CBQ 27 (1965), 256—261.

[92] Gressmann, Der Messias, 1929, 94. 99—102. 113f. etc.

[93] Jer 21 4 Zech 14 2.

[94] Zeph 3 8 (אסף as in Hos 10 10) Joel 4 2 (קבץ as in Hos 8 10).

heavily used in Jeremiah, especially in its prose sections and foreign oracles, and in other prophetic writings[95]. "Destruction" (שֹׁד) is another term used to characterize the fearful Day[96] and is employed repeatedly by Hosea[97]. So awful is the catastrophe that, as Hosea says (10 8), "they will say to the mountains, 'Cover us,' and to the hills, 'Fall over us,'" in a manner reminiscent of Is 2 10-21, with its theme of hiding at Yahweh's day against everything exalted.

A very strong word is "wiping out" (שׁחת), which frequently appears in a negative construction denoting something to be avoided[98]. The story of the total devastation of Sodom and Gomorra — or, as in Hos 11 8f., where that word is used, of Admah and Zeboiim — seems to have been a favorite of prophetic circles[99], whose professional interest is probably reflected in the account of Abraham's intercession. In Hos 11 8f., Yahweh expresses hesitancy about such a destruction, but in 13 9 no help is in sight to prevent a wiping out.

The war, destruction, and "day" themes are by no means independent of the controversy structure, as the examples cited have shown. Indeed, ancient men thought of war in terms of a controversy between the kings involved or between their deities[100]. The judicial form may have been especially appropriate for wars with unfaithful vassals[101], but it is not limited to such.

3. *Other Threatening Terms*

Hosea uses several synonyms to designate God's anger (as discussed in Chapter IV). The terms are exceedingly common in the Old Testament and the emphasis on divine wrath is widespread enough in Near Eastern literature that no proof needs to be given for Hosea's connection herein with tradition. Standardized terminology determines even details of phrasing, such as the expression "I will pour out … my wrath" (5 10) and the idiom "the heat of my wrath" (11 9). Even

---

[95] In Joel and Zephaniah also לִשְׁמָמָה.

[96] Is 13 6 Joel 1 15 (both כְּשֹׁד מִשַּׁדַּי).

[97] Hos 7 13 9 6 10 14 12 2.

[98] In pleas: titles of Ps 57 58 59 75 Is 65 8, etc. In assurances: Gen 18 28 II Kings 8 19, etc. (On the stem, M. Pope, JBL 83 [1964], 269—278.)

[99] Dtn 29 22 Am 4 11 Is 1 9 13 19 Jer 49 18 50 40 Zeph 2 9 (largely with Fohrer, Studien, 156f.).

[100] R. Press, ZAW 51 (1933), 232—234; for Hittite war, A. Goetze, Iraq 25 (1963), 126f.; J. W. Jones, The Law and Legal Theory of the Greeks, 1956, 249. See above, p. 76.

[101] See W. Moran and J. Harvey (separately), Biblica 43 (1962), 103. 180ff. 318.

Yahweh's "hating" has parallels outside Hosea[102]. "Woe to them" (7 13 9 12) reflects a standard curse form.

Among the results to be expected from divine attack is shame. A typical construction introduces with מִן ("from") the object of which a person will be ashamed. The item thus designated is usually something in which he had trusted or delighted[103], but can also simply be his "wickedness[104]." According to Hosea, Israel will be ashamed of its "altars" (4 19) and of its "counsels" (10 6). "Ignominy" (4 7. 18) is a synonym for dishonor. The motif of a substitution of "shame for glory," as expressed in 4 7, reappears in Hab 2 16. To put it in other words, there is "stumbling"[105] and "falling[106]." A rather obscure passage (11 7) seems to say, "no one raises them," with which one may compare Jer 50 32:

> The proud one will stumble and fall,
> and no one will raise him up.

Hos 13 3 employs the images of chaff (מֹץ) blown away by the wind and of vanishing smoke (עָשָׁן), both applied typically to the fate of the wicked or of Yahweh's enemies. The same verse adds the double picture of a disappearing morning cloud and of an early-vanishing dew, probably metaphors created by the prophet himself and used also in another context (6 4) to illustrate the instability of Israel's love.

Concrete threats announce hunger, infertility, and the death of children. The sentence, "they will eat but not be satisfied," as it appears in Hosea and several other places[107], is a variation of the standard positive phrase, "to eat and be satisfied[108]." Infertility and lack of progeny — as threatened for the people seemingly safely settled in Palestine (9 11. 16) — is a typical element of curses guarding treaties and inscriptions known from Mesopotamia and Asia Minor[109]. Bereavement will be caused by Yahweh himself[110], indeed so thoroughly

---

[102] Hos 9 15 Dtn 1 27 9 28 Jer 12 8 Mal 1 3 Ps 5 6 11 5 31 7 (in addition to a hating of evil deeds).

[103] Is 1 29 20 5 Jer 2 36 48 13 Mi 7 16.

[104] Jer 22 22 Ez 36 32 (?).

[105] Hos 4 5 5 5 14 2. 10 (as often elsewhere).

[106] Hos 7 7 (besides references to falling by the sword mentioned earlier).

[107] Hos 4 10 Lev 26 26 Is 9 19 Mi 6 14 Hag 1 6. Variations in vocabulary also appear.

[108] Often in Deuteronomy. Elsewhere: Ruth 2 14 Neh 9 25 Joel 2 26 II Chr 31 10 Ps 22 27 78 29.

[109] H. Bauer, AfO 8 (1932), 7 ff.; H. Hirsch, AfO 20 (1963), 73; F. Fensham, ZAW 75 (1963), 159. 169. So still in later Jordanian curses (T. Canaan, Studii Biblici Franciscani Liber Annuus 13 (1962/63), 110—135 [ZAW 76 (1964), 219]).

[110] Hos 9 12. 16. Similarly, Jer 15 7. Bereavement through some agency other than Yahweh is a judgment in Lev 26 22 I Sam 15 33 Ez 5 17 14 15.

that there will be "no man" (מֵאָדָם). The last-mentioned phrase is identical with, or very similar to, the expressions "no man" and "no inhabitant" in the book of Jeremiah[111]. The horrors of war are pictured by saying, in highly standardized phraseology, that children will be dashed in pieces and pregnant women ripped open[112].

Other specific threats include the destruction of altars, the downfall of the king, a drying of the land, and an exile. These predictions, too, contain symbolic or traditional motifs. The destruction of altars is announced also by Amos and Ezekiel. The statement, "Undone will be the king of Samaria, like a snapped twig on the water" (10 7), not only uses the widespread phrase "undone"[113] but may also allude to flooding water which figures as a means of destruction in the Old Testament as in its neighboring religions[114]. The "wilderness" (2 16) has to some extent the connotation of the netherworld[115]. The strong[116], drying "east wind" of 13 15 is a destructive image; it is called "the wind (or spirit) of Yahweh," a concept which may carry some mythological meaning[117]. The threat of exile at the hand of a conqueror is current in Near Eastern words[118].

The threat that Israel is to return to Egypt (8 13 9 3 11 5) has a symbolic meaning. Dtn 28 68 lists as a consequence of disobedience this: "The Lord will make you return to Egypt in ships, on the way which I had told you you would not see again," presupposing a promise now lost. Earlier in the book a direction had forbidden a ruler to "return the people to Egypt," since God had promised — or commanded — that Israel never go on that way again (Dtn 17 16). A command along these lines may have had its roots in a reaction against Solomon's international practice; more certainly, the directive or promise has some connection with the persistent theme of wilderness stories that the murmuring people desire to return to Egypt[119]. Some

---

[111] מֵאָדָם: Jer 50 3. מֵאֵין אָדָם: Jer 33 10. 12. מֵאֵין יוֹשֵׁב: Jer 33 10 46 19 48 9 51 29. 37.
[112] Hos 10 14 14 1. Cf. II Kings 8 12 15 16 Am 1 13 Is 13 16 Nah 3 10 Ps 137 9.
[113] Cf. Hos 10 15 (other forms of דמה: 4 5f.) Is 6 5 15 1 (Moab) Jer 47 5 (Ashkelon) Ob 5 (Edom) Zeph 1 11.
[114] Cf. Nah 1 8 (Haldar, Studies, 106); and Langdon op. cit. 15; also, O. Kaiser, Die mythische Bedeutung des Meeres, 1962².
[115] Pedersen, Israel, I—II 463; A. Haldar, The Notion of the Desert, 1950, 110f.
[116] O. Ungewitter, Die landwirtschaftlichen Bilder und Metaphern in den poetischen Büchern des Alten Testaments, 1885, 24.
[117] So, Gressmann, Der Ursprung der israelitisch-jüdischen Eschatologie, 1905, 22. Cf. Ex 14 21 ?
[118] C. H., end; Fensham op. cit. 165; D. McCarthy, Treaty and Covenant, 1963, 122. So, Hos 9 3 (probably secondary). 17.
[119] Ex 16 3 17 3 Num 11 5. 20 14 3f. 20 4 (source attributions are difficult, but probably several strata are involved.). For Dtn 1 40, see N. Lohfink, Biblica 41 (1960), 116. Another version appears in Ex 13 17 (E), and see also Ex 14 11f.

form of this tradition is most likely presupposed by Hosea, though in theory he can also have devised the symbolism of return independently. Egypt stands for the chaos out of which Israel was once saved.

Sheol appears as a negative image in Hos 13 14, which can only be read as a declaration of victory over it. The announcement, "I will redeem them from the hand of Sheol" is virtually identical with the word of confidence expressed in Ps 49 16. But this hope is rejected by Hosea (13 15).

A group of statements view disaster as the natural outcome of Israel's life. Israel is eating the "fruit of falsehood" (10 13), just as, according to Is 3 10, the righteous are to "eat the fruit of their deeds." Hosea declares Israel to be a "warped bow" (7 16, cf. Ps 78 57) or an "undesirable vessel" (8 8, cf. Jer 22 28 48 38). They are caught in "vanity[120]."

C. Terms of Accusation

1. General and Moral Evil

Descriptions of evil in Hosea are quite generalized. A number of terms simply accuse Israel of doing wrong. The broadest word is "evil[121]." The phrase "because of the evil of your evil" is partially paralleled in the book of Jeremiah by the shorter "because of their evil[122]." Typical is the expression "the evil of their deeds[123]." The very term "deeds" has ordinarily a bad connotation, as does often the word "ways[124]." "Badness" is committed and will be reaped by Israel[125]. "Wickedness" has been "plowed[126]." "Villany" is done; "evil-doers" fill a city[127]. Israel acts "corruptly[128]."

---

[120] שָׁוְא (Hos 12 12) is elsewhere parallel to tohû or to falsehood (Š. Porúbčan, Sin in the Old Testament, 1963, 48).

[121] רָעָה: Hos 7 1. 2. 3 9 15 10 15. רַע: 7 15. רֹעַ: 9 15. Forms of this stem appear, e. g., in the prophetic words of I Kings 14 9 16 7 21 20 II Kings 21 15 and in Ps 50 19.

[122] מִפְּנֵי רָעַת רָעָתְכֶם: Hos 10 15. Cf. Jer 7 12 and 44 3.

[123] רֹעַ מַעַלְלֵיהֶם: Hos 9 15. The same phrase occurs in Dtn 28 20 Is 1 16 Jer 4 4 21 12 23 2. 22 25 5 26 3 44 22 Ps 28 4.

[124] מַעֲלָל: Hos 4 9 5 4 7 2 9 15 12 3; so usually in the Old Testament. דֶּרֶךְ in a potentially bad sense: Hos 4 9 12 3; a largely though not consistently negative connotation continues to develop in Jeremiah (both prose and poetry), Ezekiel, and some other later literature.

[125] Hos 10 9 (עָוְלָה). 13 (עַוְלָה). "Sons of badness" (10 9), as in II Sam 3 34 7 10 Ps 89 23 I Chr 17 9.

[126] רֶשַׁע: Hos 10 13. Cf. Prov 4 17.

[127] זִמָּה: Hos 6 9; פֹּעֲלֵי אָוֶן: 6 8.

[128] שׁחת: Hos 9 9; as in Ex 32 7 Ps 14 1 53 2 Dtn 4 16 9 12 31 29 32 5 Is 1 4 Judg 2 19 Jer 6 28 Ez 16 47 20 44 23 11 Gen 6 11f. (P), i. e., basically levitic-deuteronomic.

All these terms, as well as some others to be discussed, are especially common in the levitic-deuteronomic tradition and occur not
infrequently in the Psalms, in Job, and in the moralistic strain of
Proverbs. Within the psalms, the watching-song Ps 5 contains an
especially large number of such expressions; but the terminology is
scattered throughout the Psalter.

Israel is accused by Hosea of "sinning"[129] or of committing
"iniquity[130]." Both of these terms, it may be noted, appear often in
requests for remission of sin[131], but are ordinarily too weak to describe
adequately the doings of enemies[132]. Specifically, a "greatness of
iniquity" is seen[133].

Another group of words denotes falsehood, for which the Hebrew
language has many synonyms. "Wrongness," "deceit," "falsehood,"
"lying" — all have about the same meaning; their different nuances
elsewhere are overshadowed by their symbolic stylization[134]. They are
used in the Psalms to describe enemies whose existence or activity is
wrong, from the point of view of the speaker. Falsehood forms not
a special type of evil among others, but rather represents the very
character of wickedness. It violates what the Egyptians called *ma'at*,
"truth, order, right[135]." The same pattern appears in Vedic and Zoro-
astrian terminology and throughout the Semitic language area[136].

The concept of falsehood leads naturally to a consideration of
specific moral evils. Hosea accuses Israel of using "deceitful balances,"
following a standard idiom[137]. This he calls "oppression," a common
concept in prohibitions[138]. The saying Hos 12 8f., in which these terms

---

[129] Root חטא: Hos 4 7f. 8 11 10 9.
[130] עָוֹן: Hos 4 8 5 5 7 1 8 13 9 7. 9 12 9 13 12 14 2f.
[131] Cf. R. Knierim, Die Hauptbegriffe für Sünde im Alten Testament, 1965.
[132] The noun "sinners," however, occurs in the wisdom-style contexts of Ps 1 25 26
51 104; some prayers ask that the "iniquity" of enemies not be forgiven (Knierim
op. cit. 223).
[133] רֹב עֲוֹנְךָ: Hos 9 7 Jer 13 22 30 14f. Ez 28 18. Similar structures can be found in
Ps 5 11 Lam 1 5.
[134] Root כחש: Hos 4 2 7 3 10 13 12 1. מִרְמָה: Hos 12 1. 8. שֶׁקֶר: Hos 7 1. כָּזָב: Hos
7 13 12 2. Also, חלק לָבָּם 10 2.
[135] E. g., ANET 378; H. Schmid, Wesen und Geschichte der Weisheit, 1966, 159.
[136] "Truth" in Vedic religion: ṛta; in Zoroastrianism: asha (opposite: drug). The Vedic
druh (druj), "lie," is applied to all evil, whether moral or demonic (J. Gonda, Die
Religionen Indiens, I 1960, 38). On the Semitic tradition, already V. Ryssel, Die
Synonyma des Wahren und des Guten in den semitischen Sprachen, 1872. Somewhat too limited in perspective is M. Klopfenstein, Die Lüge nach dem Alten
Testament, 1964, though otherwise useful for meanings.
[137] מֹאזְנֵי מִרְמָה: Hos 12 8 Am 8 5 Prov 11 1 20 23.
[138] עשק: Hos 12 8; W. Richter, Recht und Ethos, 1966, 149.

7*

occur, threatens loss of gain thus gotten, in a manner resembling the following declaration of a prayer to Shamash:

> Whoever gives money for deceit and does violence —
> what advantage has he?
> . . . .
> Whoever takes the balance
> and acts villainously,
> Whoever changes the weights of the bag —
> lowers the entire gain.
> He throws away the profit,
> and ruins his possession[139].

"Deceit" occurs elsewhere in connection with bloodshed, violence, or other sorts of trouble-making[140]. Similarly, "wrongness" (כחש) is connected with robbery and oppression[141].

An important figure for evil, both in the Old Testament and elsewhere, is that of the falsehood of a close associate[142]. In Hos 7 5-7 this takes the form of intrigue against the ruler; the persons who engage in such activity are called "deriders," or "scorners," a term typical of wisdom contexts. The destructive man "lies in wait" (Hos 7 6) on one and all, even to kill[143]. Another proverbial form of villainous evil is the moving of boundary marks, which in Hos 5 10 is applied to the relation between Judah and Israel.

The sin-catalogue of 4 2, probably a quotation by Hosea, lists cursing, lying, killing, stealing, and adultery. A similar pattern appears in Hos 6 8—7 6. Here are listed murder (6 8f., with the standardized image of a "bloody town"[144]), robbery (6 9 7 1), theft (7 1), adultery (7 4), intrigue (7 5f.). Jer 9 1-7 and Ps 50 16-21, in a related manner, list as general descriptions of wickedness: falsehood, stealing or oppression, adultery, and secret machinations against associates[145]; Job 24 13-17 mentions murderers, thieves, adulterers, and house-diggers (?) as friends of darkness. "Cursing" (אלה) is a designation for

---

[139] Following Falkenstein-Soden 244; cf. ANET 388.

[140] Zeph 1 9 Ps 5 7 35 20 38 13 55 24 Prov 12 5f., etc.

[141] Nah 3 1 Lev 5 21f. 19 11. See, further, Wolff 84.

[142] So, Ps 55 21f. Am 1 11 Mi 7 5f. Lam 1 2; ANET 115. 409. 445; Lambert op. cit. 35. 195. 232. In an African proverb: E. Loeb, Kuanyama Ambo Folklore, 1951, 334. Examples from other cultures could be given.

[143] ארב: Ps 10 9 Prov 24 15 Lam 4 19. For "blood," Prov 1 11 Mi 7 2.

[144] עִיר הַדָּמִים: Nah 3 1 Ez 22 2 24 6. 9. Cf. Is 4 4 Jer 22 3 Mi 3 10 Hab 2 12, etc.

[145] Like Hos 7 6, Jer 9 7 speaks of an "ambush." Probably the difficult קרבו of Hos 7 6 is connected with the בְּקִרְבּוֹ of Jer 9 7 and should be pointed קִרְבּוֹ. (Similarly already Schorr [see Harper], but קֶרֶב can take a singular instead of a plural suffix; cf. Gen 24 3 Ex 10 1 Is 63 11. The word לְבָּם is then probably to be omitted as a gloss or to be kept with W. Smith, The Prophets of Israel, 1902²).

the evil words of enemies in Ps 10 7 59 13 (cf. Hos 10 4). That "all are adulterers" (Hos 7 4) is hardly correct literally, but is said also in Jer 9 1 and reflects the style tradition that "all" are evil[146].

There is an obviously close connection between the sin-register just discussed and several members of the moral decalog, so that a direct dependence has been suspected. The lists cited, however, are more similar to each other than they are to the decalog and have considerable affinity to Near Eastern descriptions of evil, especially in negative confession or incantations for cleansing, as well as to those of other culture areas[147]. The function of such a list was probably that of designating the character of the "wicked," as happens explicitly in Ps 50 16. The decalog is clearly based in part upon such a tradition of negative moral description, just as apodictic law in general had roots in a wisdom background[148]; the tradition itself, however, might continue to live on its own. Whether or not the decalog was already in existence in his time, Hosea quotes more broadly from what may be called a catalog of vices[149].

In addition to these indirect connections with the decalog, the prohibitions of idolatry and of the worship of other gods (as reflected also in Ps 81) appear in Hosea. Absent is any reference to the positively worded commands to keep the Sabbath and honor the parents; perhaps indeed the oral or written antecedent of the decalog is to be seen in a double list of cultic and moral evils, each with four or five elements[150]. In a very broad sense, then, Hosea stands within what was or came to be the decalogic tradition[151].

Not specifically denounced by Hosea are a lack of concern for the poor and the weak and such evils as bribery — violations castigated sharply by Amos, Isaiah, and Micah[152]. Since these three prophets

---

[146] Gunkel-Begrich 363. Add, e. g., Jer 2 29; ANET 406. 443—445; Hos 41 Mi 7 2.

[147] "The Book of the Dead," ch. 125, especially in its first part directed to the "high-god" (C. Maystre, Les déclarations d'innocence, 1937, 139); Shurpu, II. A Greek list with stealing, adultery, and falsehood: W. Schilling, Religion und Recht, 1957, 122. A Vedic ritual tradition characterizes enemies to be conquered as thieves, robbers, waylayers, betrayers, plotters, and double-tongued (S. Rodhe, Deliver Us From Evil, 1946, 48). Ward (244) rightly compares Lev 19.

[148] According to E. Gerstenberger, Wesen und Herkunft des "apodiktischen Rechts," 1965, 49, the negative form in apodictic law represents "das Böse, Nichtige, Gemeinschaftszerstörende oder -gefährdende." Among other studies, see R. Kilian, BZ NF 7 (1963), 185—202.

[149] For such lists, see also von Rad, Gesammelte Studien, 1958, 281—296; Mowinckel 62.

[150] H. Schmidt in: Gunkel-Festschrift, I 1923, 78—119, hypothesized a list of ten negative laws; see now Richter op. cit. 89.

[151] Partially with Mowinckel, Le Décalogue, 1927, 55; The Psalms in Israel's Worship, II 1962, 71f.

[152] Am 2 6-8 5 12 8 4-6 Is 1 23 3 14 5 23 Mi 2 6-11 3 1-4. 11.

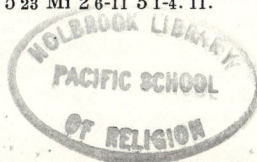

were Judeans, it is possible that different traditions of social concern obtained in the two neighboring states. On the other hand, Hosea's silence may be explained by a desire to emphasize that even the major crimes — committed by "wicked" men — were rampant in the nation, while the other prophets (less critical in a way or else more sensitive) concerned themselves with somewhat finer points which make a claim on positive goodness. In any case, the laws of the decalog form a different line from that of more positive and humanitarian prescriptions[153]; Hosea depends only on one of these, the one dealing with grosser sins.

2. Sins More Specifically Against Yahweh

Sins against Yahweh are expressed in a number of ways. To begin with, there is a group of terms meaning "revolt[154]," "rebellion" (or "stubbornness")[155], and "disobedience[156]." Egyptian execration texts and other Near Eastern writings employ a common terminology for "sin" and for enemies who "rebel[157]." Specifically, rebellion means the breaking of Yahweh's covenant, a motif important in the leviticdeuteronomic tradition[158]. God complains that his laws appear to be "strange" to Israel (8 12). Israel's action toward Yahweh is called "unfaithfulness[159]." The nation directs "reproach" (חֶרְפָּה, 12 15) against Yahweh, as do his enemies in Ps 74 22 79 12. "Turning" from Yahweh[160], Israel "turns aside" toward other gods[161]. It "goes after" these instead, in typically levitic-deuteronomic terminology[161a].

A technical term in Hosea for Israel's apostasy is "whoredom" (prostitution). Its background is puzzling. References to it outside of chs. 1—3[162] seem to presuppose an understanding of the concept independently of the story of the first three chapters. In fact, the

---

[153] G. Dilloo, Der alttestamentliche und der altorientalische Sittenkodex, Diss. Bonn, 1941.

[154] פשע: Hos 7 13 8 1 14 10. For the phrase פָּשְׁעוּ בִי (7 13), cf. Is 1 2 43 27 Jer 2 8. 29 3 13 33 8 Ez 2 3 20 38 Zeph 3 11.

[155] סרר: Hos 4 16 9 15. In 7 14 (repointed), with בְּ.

[156] מרה: Hos 14 1.

[157] ANET 329; Zandee op. cit. 290. 295f.; A. Van Selms, De Babylonische Termini voor Zonde, 1933, 109—111 (German summary).

[158] Hos 6 7 8 1 Dtn 17 2 31 16. 20 Josh 7 11. 15 23 16 Judg 2 20 II Kings 18 12 Jer 34 18 Ez 16 59 17 16. 18 44 7. Further, Is 24 5. Yahweh is implored not to break it, in the people's lament, Jer 14 21.

[159] בגד: 5 7 6 7. In each case the verb is constructed with בְּ, like פשע and סרר.

[160] שוב: Hos 11 5. 7. Cf. Num 14 43 (JE) 32 15, etc.

[161] פנה: Hos 3 1. Cf. Dtn 31 18. 20 (especially close in phraseology) Lev 19 4. 31 20 6.

[161a] Hos 1 2 2 7. 15; F. Helfmeyer, Die Nachfolge Gottes im Alten Testament, 1968.

[162] Hos 4 11f. 18 5 3f. 6 10 9 1. In essence, 8 9f.

early chapters may themselves presuppose the outlook that false worship is whoredom, seemingly taking it for granted without much explanation. No certain use of it before Hosea, however, is attested[163]. After Hosea, presumably in at least partial dependence on him, the metaphor spread very quickly. Mi 1 7 speaks of a harlot's hire in connection with idolatry, while Is 1 21 calls Jerusalem a harlot for being unfaithful to Yahweh in social matters[164]. In the Asaphite Ps 73 27 the verb means "to be false" to Yahweh. The Holiness Code designates false cultic activity, including dealings with demons and spirits, as "whoredom[165]." Harlotry thus figures partly as a cultic term; it is naturally connected with the expression "uncleanness," as it is also in Hos 5 3 and 6 10[166]. International intercourse is intended in some later prophecies, probably retaining the original symbolism if it should be older than Hosea[167]. The motif expresses an impersonal, commercial promiscuity.

The two main aspects of "whoredom" in Hosea are the international activity of Israel[168] and its false worship[169]. Hosea opposed these, as well as the establishment of the kingdom[170], as acts which did not express full allegiance to, or reliance in, Yahweh. In the realm of worship, idols come sharply under attack[171], the "calf" is derided[172], and divination is an object of head-shaking lament[173].

Though Hosea lacks oracles against foreign nations, he regards other nations as "Gentiles," whose ways should not be imitated (9 1) and with whom Israel should not be allied[174]. To appeal to other powers for a healing from Yahweh's blows is folly (5 13)! Making a covenant with other nations (12 2) or lightheartedly with anyone (10 4) reflects insincerity and instability of commitment, as does a direct breaking of a covenant with Yahweh (6 7 8 1).

Opposition to idolatry is by no means a late creation but probably goes back to the beginning of Israel. Relevant terminology was suffi-

[163] Possible, but highly doubtful, anticipations are in Ex 34 15f. Num 14 33 25 1 Dtn 31 16.
[164] Mi 1 6f. is taken as a misplaced Hoseanic saying by A. Jepsen, ZAW 56 (1938), 97—99; its interest in Samaria quite likely indicates a close relationship.
[165] Lev 17 7 20 5f.; as a general term for defilement: 19 29.
[166] Similarly Ez 23 17 Ps 106 39.
[167] Nah 3 4 (v. 5 parallels Hos 2 12!) Is 23 17. (Cf. also Ez 16 28 23 30. 43.)
[168] Especially 7 11 8 9f. 12 2 14 4.
[169] Especially 2 7. 15 3 1 4 12f. 14f. 18f. 7 14 8 11 9 1. 10 10 1. 5. 8 11 2 12 12 13 1.
[170] Hos 8 4 10 9f. (?) 13 10f., etc.
[171] Hos 2 10 (secondary) 4 17 8 4 11 2 13 2 14 9.
[172] Hos 8 5f. 10 5f. (or, here, "calves").
[173] Hos 4 12; cf. Is 2 6, as part of foreign relations.
[174] Alliances outside of covenant relations are confessed as an evil by Kaštiliaš (J. Harvey op. cit. 182; see above, p. 95).

ciently developed by Hosea's time so that he had the choice of at least
three synonyms to designate an idol[175]. Only one of these words ever
carries a relatively neutral meaning; the irony of "hewn" or "molten"
images shines through in the other two[176]. Hosea speaks repeatedly of
the "making" (עשׂה) of idols, an expression that is standard in laws
against idolatry and also in other denunciation[177].

Hosea's opposition to the kingdom has affinity with, and may
depend on, a broader tradition which cannot here be traced. The preference of loving-kindness and knowledge of God over sacrifice (Hos 6 6)
has a counterpart in the saying by Samuel to Saul which is in some
way associated with the tradition opposing royalty (I Sam 15 22f.):

> Behold, to listen is better than sacrifice;
> to hearken, than the fat of rams.
> . . . .
> Since you have rejected the word of Yahweh,
> I also will reject you from being king [cf. Hos 4 6].

A pre-Mosaic Egyptian instruction already declares, "The goodness of a just man is more acceptable to God than the sacrificial oxen
of the unjust[178]." Apollo's oracle at Delphi refused — at least in
theory — to give an answer to evil men and insisted that ritual
cleansing is not effective for a wicked person[179]. Israelite psalmists
repeatedly expressed a preference for their verbal praise over sacrifice,
a theme which is followed, at least on its positive side, in Hos 14 3[180].

The relation of prophecy to cultic action needs to be set into a
broad context, for which only a few indications can here be given.
A form-critical analysis of ritual prescriptions shows that sacrifices
are as a rule not commanded but regulated in execution, often in the
form of private instructions to the priests; sacrifices were generally
not thought of as duties (except in the case of firstfruits) but as privi-

---

[175] עָצָב: Hos 4 17 8 4 13 2 14 9. פְּסִילִים: Hos 11 2. מַסֵּכָה: Hos 13 2.

[176] עָצָב (which simply means "image") is fairly neutral — though perhaps ironical —
in I Sam 31 9 and II Sam 5 21. פסל means "to hew;" נסך, "to pour." Judg 17f.
ridicules.

[177] Hos 2 10 8 4 13 2 14 4; K. Bernhardt, Gott und Bild, 1956, 93f. The defense in Exod 32
24 represents the calf as miraculously produced.

[178] E. g., ANET 417.

[179] Parke and Wormell op. cit. I 154. 378. 382f. For inscriptions at Delphi and at
other Greek temples, T. van Scheffer, Hellenistische Mysterien und Orakel, 1940,
155. 171. See also the oracles of the Pythia transmitted in the "Greek Anthology,"
XIV, 71 and 74 (ed. W. Paton, V 1918). Also in an international relation, ritual
recourse can be recognized as too weak (J. Harvey op. cit. 182).

[180] For details, see now H. Hermisson, Sprache und Ritus im altisraelitischen Kult,
1965.

leged actions with superior power. Furthermore, sacrifices, and especially images, have only a tenuous connection with a "high-god" figure; for instance, neither in the Near East nor elsewhere are images of the very supreme deity at all common. An outright opposition to sacrifices — as also to idolatry — is a feature of certain types of religious attitudes which are strongly negative in their orientation toward existing reality, whether in an otherworldly or in an eschatological manner. For sacrifice (with divine-human cooperation in bringing life out of death) is intended to heal gently, not to change radically, the present situation, so that it has a relatively undemanding and comfortable character, with little challenge for personal-moral involvement[181]. It has been said that the prophets oppose not cult as such but only the particular cult they observe[182]. It is indeed true that they borrow technical priestly terminology to indicate nonacceptance of sacrifices in a way that would be applicable to an individual situation[183]. But, at least in Hosea, the rejection is applied to the entire situation; it means a wholesale indictment of existence.

III. POSITIVE TERMS

A. Expectations or Hopes for Israel

Repeatedly in Hosea one finds the word "to turn" in a positive sense, usually in connection with the phrase, "to Yahweh, your God" or some variant of it[184]. The phrase, in fact, is a traditional one for a prophet's call in disaster[185]. In addition, like other prophets, Hosea laments the failure of Israel to turn to God even in distress[186].

---

[181] See M. Buss, JBR 32 (1964), 323f. On Zoroaster's opposition to sacrifice and festivals, G. Widengren, Stand und Aufgaben der iranischen Religionsgeschichte, 1955, 60, etc.

[182] E. g., F. Hesse, ZAW 68 (1956), 12.

[183] רצה: Hos 8 13. The verb חפץ belongs only indirectly to acceptance terminology, expressing an attitude to a person or process; with Hos 6 6, cf. Ps 40 7 51 18. See R. Rendtorff, TL 81 (1956), 342; E. Würthwein in: Weiser-Festschrift, 1963, 115—131; R. Rendtorff, Studien zur Geschichte des Opfers im Alten Israel, 1967, 253—260, identifying the two words too strongly and thus blunting the rejection.

[184] "Yahweh, your god": 14 2; "your god": 12 7; "Yahweh, their God": 7 10; "their God": 5 4. In 6 1, שוב is followed only by "to Yahweh;" in 11 5, it stands naked. For further analyses of the word, see W. Holladay, The Root Šubh, 1958; Fohrer, Studien, 225.

[185] Joel 2 13 I Kings 8 33. 48 Is 1 27 Jer 3 12. 14. 22 4 1 Mal 3 7 Job 22 23, etc.

[186] Hos 5 4 7 10 11 5 Am 4 6-11 Is 9 12 Jer 3 7 5 3 8 5 (the last two verses are similar to Hos 11 5) 15 7, etc. Cf. C. Westermann, Grundformen, 132.

To "seek" Yahweh appears to be a technical term for repentance in the situation of lament[187]. Seeking, however, also represents the wider range of every turning toward God[188].

An important word in Hosea is "knowledge[189]," already mentioned in connection with the theme of a *rib*. It has been suggested that "the knowledge of God" and "knowing Yahweh" carry different nuances[190]. It does indeed appear that two somewhat different motifs are involved, namely a quality of life and an identification with Yahweh[191]. The first may well have a base broader than Israelite religion, having its root in Near Eastern wisdom[192]. The second has a more specifically cultic meaning; it is probably associated somehow with priestly activity, as implied in Hos 4 6 Jer 2 8 and Mal 2 7. According to some theorists, "knowledge" means private information for the priests[193] or an emphasis on divine deeds[194], on the supposition that "knowledge" and *torā* in Hos 4 6 represent two divisions within priestly tradition. The term knowledge, however, is more or less parallel to *torā* and represents a teaching in which general ethics has fused with the more specific worship of the active Yahweh. Prophetic accusations, as in Hosea, relate themselves closely to it, continuing a critical aspect which shows itself in the fact that the term knowledge appears most frequently in negative constructions[195].

Similarly both cultic and moral is the concept of the "fear" of Yahweh; it is typical of wisdom literature, E, and Deuteronomy and is equivalent to an Akkadian term for honor paid to deity[196]. In Hos 10 3, it appears negatively in a predicted confession of failure.

The word "loving-kindness" (*hæsæd*) in Hosea is an unambiguously positive term. In three passages (4 1 6 6 12 7) it designates good behavior, with an implied, but not clearly stated, personal

---

[187] בקש: Hos 3 5 5 6. 15 7 10. Cf. II Sam 12 16 II Chr 20 4 Ps 27 8, etc. שחר: Hos 5 15. Cf. Ps 78 34.

[188] So especially דרש, as in Hos 10 12. On דרש: A. Kapelrud, Central Ideas in Amos, 1956, 36. On several words: C. Westermann, KuD 6 (1960), 2—30.

[189] Hos 2 10. 22 4 1. 6 5 4 6 3. 6 8 2 13 4.

[190] Especially by J. McKenzie, JBL 74 (1955), 22—27 (where also see earlier literature); cf. Gressmann 376.

[191] On the former, cf. Job 18 21 21 14 Prov 2 5 30 3 Jer 22 16. On the latter, cf. Ex 5 2 Judg 2 10 Ps 79 6.

[192] So, H. Gressmann, Israels Spruchweisheit, 1925, 54.

[193] So, again, following Begrich, R. Hentschke, Satzung und Setzender, 1963, 54. Not so, Mal 2 7!

[194] K. Marti, The Religion of the Old Testament, 1907, 158; H. Wolff, EvTh 12 (1952/53), 533—554; H. Stoebe, WuD NF 6 (1959), 180—194.

[195] Hos 4 1. 6 5 4, further by implication. See Wolff, EvTh 15 (1955), 429; W. Reiss, ZAW 58 (1940/41), 70—98; G. Fohrer, AfO 19 (1959/60), 91.

[196] J. Becker, Gottesfurcht im Alten Testament, 1965.

relation to Yahweh. All three occurrences stand in contexts suggesting a dependence on tradition. Its provenance is most likely a form of moral wisdom, which may even go back to Canaanite religion, as suggested by general formulations without specific references to Yahweh or Israel. Thus the famous passage of Mi 6 8 closely parallels Hos 12 7 in saying that "man" has been told what is good, namely "loving-kindness," "justice," and relying on "your God[197]." A psalmist also complains, like the prophet in Hos 4 1, that there are no longer any "loving ones" (ḥasîd) or any that speak "truth" among men (Ps 12 2).

Usually, ḥæsæd in a religious context means Yahweh's deed of "kindness." That probably is the primary denotation in the betrothal promise of Hos 2 21f., though this also involves human life drawn into the divine orbit. The joys involved in a close association with Yahweh are implied in Hos 10 12. In the Psalms, the ḥasîd are those who belong to Yahweh. The basic meaning of ḥæsæd is probably friendship and friendly concern[198], thus forming both in call and promise an antithetical category to that of enmity.

Loving-kindness is frequently joined with truthfulness or faithfulness (אֱמֶת, אֱמוּנָה) both as human and as divine characteristics. The combination is used for human behavior (negatively) in Hos 4 1, and for the divine betrothal gift in 2 22[199]. "Truthfulness" designates that solidity and "normality"[200] which is the opposite of the falsehood discussed earlier.

Joined with loving-kindness and truthfulness, as gifts in Hos 2 21, are "rightness" (צֶדֶק) and "judgment" (מִשְׁפָּט). The exhortation of 10 12 calls for "righteousness" (צְדָקָה) and "knowledge," with a promise of ḥæsæd and "rightness" from Yahweh[201]. Hos 12 7 parallels "judgment" with ḥæsæd as a characterization of the God-directed life. All these terms are positive ones, equivalent to divine order and ordering[202], which can be paralleled with שָׁלוֹם (harmony or fullness of being) or טוֹב (the good), as in Ps 85 11f. Forms of טוֹב occur in Hos 8 3 as something Israel rejects and in 3 5 and 14 3 as an object of hopeful seeking, contrasted with hostility or destruction.

---

[197] It seems that שׁוּב בְּ in Hos 12 7, means "to rest in," "be directed toward" (cf. R. Gordis, JBL 52 [1933], 153—162). The indicative verb form reflects a general transition from wisdom to apodictic law.

[198] E. g., II Sam 16 17; J. Montgomery, HTR 32 (1939), 101; G. Larue, Introduction to: N. Glueck, Ḥesed in the Bible, 1967.

[199] It is accidental that one word is used here for the human and another for the divine. (See F. Asensio, Misericordia et veritas, 1949, 309.)

[200] G. Quell, TWNT, I 233.

[201] Closely in line with the classical usage of צֶדֶק and צְדָקָה shown by A. Jepsen in: Hertzberg-Festschrift, 1965, 78—89.

[202] Cf. K. Koch, ZEE 5 (1961), 83—85.

The projected song of Hos 6 1-3 looks for healing and the reception of life and expects Yahweh's coming to be like that of the dawn or the rain. These motifs are familiar from other literature. Healing is sought and celebrated in psalms[203] and is promised or denied by prophets[204]. The giving of life is often requested in psalms, both in the Old Testament[205] and in other Near Eastern literature[206]. "On the third day" (6 2) probably indicates metaphorically a resurrection, which is traditionally expected then just before the soul leaves the vicinity of the body[207]. Three days were expected to elapse between the ritual identification of a sick person with Tammuz by means of a sacrificial kid and his recovery of health[208], so that the motif of healing is not separate from that of resurrection, which is of course not to be taken literally here[209].

Light and water are two important elements in cultic mythology and expectation[210]. Dawn, or morning, is a specially impressive form of the victory of light over darkness; dawn was personified in Ugaritic literature, while the theme of morning or light in general was often associated with the assertion of justice, as in Hos 6 5[211]. In Hos 10 12, Yahweh is expected to "rain righteousness." The "light" of Hos 6 5b (perhaps as a deliberate answer to the symbolism of v. 3) means the victorious presence of righteous assertion which cuts down evil. The theme of the "coming forth" of judgment, as in this verse, may belong to a larger cultic tradition[212]; it is probably secondary in its context, however, and perhaps post-Hoseanic.

In Hos 14 5f., Yahweh then promises to "heal" Israel's turning away and to be "as dew[213]." The result will be a sprouting like "Leb-

---

[203] Root רפא. Ps 6 3 30 3 41 5 107 20 147 3 Jer 15 18 17 14 Lam 2 13.

[204] Is 6 10 30 26 57 19 Jer 30 17 33 6.

[205] Ps 41 3 71 20 81 19 85 7 138 7 143 11, and often in Ps 119.

[206] E. g., Falkenstein-Soden 345.

[207] E. Freistedt, Altchristliche Totengedächtnistage, 1928, 53—118, etc. For general data, bibliography, and other possibilities, see Wolff 150; Fohrer, Studien, 227; E. Good, JBL 85 (1966), 273—286; S. Kramer, BASOR 183 (Oct. 1966), 31.

[208] E. Ebeling, Tod und Leben nach den Vorstellungen der Babylonier, 1931, 56.

[209] For its metaphorical use in politics, see J. Wijngaards, VT 17 (1967), 232—234.

[210] E. g., J. Obermann, Wind, Water, and Light in an Archaic Inscription from Shechem, JBL 57 (1938), 249f.

[211] E. g., Zeph 3 5. See S. Aalen, Die Begriffe "Licht" und "Finsternis," 1951; B. Meißner op. cit. 37, on Shamash; G. Roeder op. cit. 49, on the sun-god as judge; in the Koran, Surah 113.

[212] So, von Rad, Theology, I 1962, 380 (German 378). Seen by E. Sellin, Studien zur Entstehungsgeschichte der jüdischen Gemeinde, 1901, 83, with somewhat different material.

[213] On the dew in nature and symbolism, A. Gonzales Nuñez, Estudios Biblicos 22 (1963), 109—139.

anon," as repeatedly mentioned in the Psalms[214]. In v. 8 Israel's final state is identified with the Garden of Eden, with real "life." Fertility objects are at the same time love symbols, as employed in the Song of Songs; these include Lebanon (including its fragrance), the lily, wine, the flourishing vine, gardens, and fruit[215]. Closely related is the theme of dwelling in the lover's shadow (Hos 14 8 Cant 2 3).

The evidently technical term "restoration (or, change) of fortune" in 6 11 is comparable to an Akkadian expression for the change of fortune effected at the New Year festival and became widely used in later Israelite literature for a future restoration[216]; here in Hosea, an early Israelite usage with an intermediate meaning between these extremes is presupposed, but deliverance is declared by Yahweh to be morally impossible.

Natural peace and fertility are expected by the secondary passages of Hos 2 20. 23, in line with wide-spread hopes. Peace, as a positive concept with the absence of strife, disturbance, and enmity, is the very epitome of a good life[217]. Hos 2 20 ends with a favorite hope, "to dwell securely[218]." A messianic figure appears in 2 2 and 3 5, which are very close in wording to Jer 3 18 and 30 9 (both prose), and similar in content to Ez 37 22. In 3 5 it is not enough to delete the words "David, their king," as the parallel indicates, but some part of the verse may be genuine.

The supreme good comes in that Yahweh *loves* Israel even in its unfaithfulness (3 1), leading to a new betrothal after appropriate discipline (2 21). The word love has, of course, a definite sexual association[219]; in a slightly less colorful way a similar word had at this time a vogue in Egypt as a description of divine concern[220], while an Akkadian word for love expresses attachments within international

---

[214] Hos 14 6-8 (?) Ps 72 16 92 13 104 16.

[215] See Hos 14 6-9; Wolff 302, and add "fruit." These terms are especially heaped in Cant 4 5—5 1 (of North-Israelite provenance?). The beloved is related to a tree or a garden in Egyptian (H. Grapow, Vergleiche und andere bildliche Ausdrücke im Ägyptischen, 1920, 18) or to a vineyard in Ugaritic (77: 20—23). Cf. H. Wildberger, Jesaja, 1968, 169.

[216] In addition to other studies, see S. Mowinckel's comments, Psalmenstudien II, 75; He That Cometh, 1956, 147; TL 87 (1962), 36.

[217] F. Bammel, Die Religionen der Welt und Friede auf Erden, 1957; articles in Eranos-Jahrbuch, 1958; J. Stamm and H. Bietenhard, Der Weltfriede im Alten und Neuen Testament, 1959.

[218] Lev 25 19 26 5 Dtn 12 10 33 12. 28 Is 14 30 Jer 23 6 32 37 (exactly as in Hos 2 20) 33 16 Ez 34 25. 27 Zech 14 11. Cf. Ps 4 9 (similarly causative) 16 9, etc.

[219] G. Quell, TWNT, I 1933, 24.

[220] E. Drioton in: Pontificio Istituto Biblico, Oriens Antiquus (Analecta Biblica 12), 1959, 57—68, for the period of ca. 950—660 B. C.

covenants[221]. As is well known, the term came to play a considerable role in Deuteronomic tradition.

B. Recognitions of Yahweh

Positive sayings include statements concerning the past. Hosea speaks of Yahweh's leading Israel out of Egypt[222] and of his "finding" them in the "wilderness[223]." It is quite possible that two different motifs about the beginning of Israel are involved, perhaps corresponding to the Exodus and Sinai traditions, respectively. There is, however, no mention, and probably no knowledge, of a specific mountain on which law is given, or of a covenant concluded at such a place[224].

Some of the statements find close parallels in oracles addressed to kings by Mesopotamian deities. Ishtar says, "When you were small, I sustained you[225]," and (in the words of one translation) calls herself "your good nurse[226]." Adad speaks to Kallassu (at Mari) as one "whom I have held on my lap[227]." In the Ugaritic story of Keret, his son is promised breast-feeding by goddesses[228].

Closely connected is the self-introduction formula, "I am Yahweh." It appears in Hosea twice in the form, "I am Yahweh your God from the land of Egypt" (12 10 13 4). Repeatedly Yahweh is designated by an emphatic "I[229]." In the Old Testament and beyond the divine "I" or "I am" appears frequently in reference to both the past and the future[230].

Together with the self-introduction formula comes the assertion, "A god outside of me you do not known, and there is no savior beside me" (Hos 13 4). Similar declarations or ascriptions occur in I Sam 2 2 II Sam 7 22 Dtn 4 35. 39 32 39 Ps 18 32 Joel 2 27 Is 43 11 45 5. 21 64 3, in fairly standardized form, for instance with the word זוּלָה for "beside." The tendency to ascribe all of the functions and powers

---

[221] J. A. Thompson, Journal of Religious History 3 (1964), 19. A direct influence is unlikely.

[222] Hos 11 1 12 10 13 4.

[223] Hos 9 10, similarly 13 5.

[224] Ex 34 27 (J ?; cf. 19 19) describes one primarily between God and Moses; Ex 24 10 f. (E ?) is weak. Cf. M. Noth, Exodus; H. Gese, ZAW 79 (1967), 147—151.

[225] ANET 450. Cf. Hos 7 15 11 3.

[226] Langdon op. cit. (above, p. 80) 130. Cf. Hos 11 3f.

[227] A. Lods in: T. H. Robinson-Festschrift, 1950, 105.

[228] Text 128:II:26f. (Gordon); ANET 146.

[229] Hos 1 9 2 4. 10 4 6 5 2f. 12. 14 7 13 10 11 11 3. 9 13 5.

[230] See M. Buss, JBR 29 (1961), 106f.; also, C. Kayatz, Studien zu Proverbien 1—9, 1966, 87—91.

of divinity to one's own god — and indeed to call him the only one —
is a wide-spread phenomenon[231]; of the Creator Prajapati it is said
in the Rigveda (X, 121) that "he is the god of gods, and none beside
him." In Israel monolatry became sharply accentuated; Yahweh's
incomparability was often associated with the Exodus, as in Hosea.

One of the indications of the power of a deity is that it both smites
and heals, kills and brings to life, as implied in the prayer of Hos 6 1f.
Thus I Sam 2 6 Dtn 32 39 Is 19 22 and Job 5 18 make the same point —
with the accent usually on the positive activity. When Marduk
demonstrates that he can destroy and (re-)create, the gods acknowledge
that "Marduk is king," as recited at the Babylon New Year festival
(Enuma elish, IV, 18—26). Other parallels can be cited[232], including
the prayer of the Bhil in central India to their high-god, "You are the
one who smites and the one who heals[233]."

IV. OPEN OR AMBIGUOUS TERMS
FOR THE GOD-ISRAEL RELATIONSHIP AND ITS CULT

In personal terms, the God-Israel relation is presented as that
of husband to wife and of father to son. Images of deity as a husband
(to a goddess) or as a father (to another god, a king, or an individual)
are widespread in the Near East, though not in relation to a people[234].
The marriage figure, in an explicit positive form, is confined to Hos
1—3; references to whoredom (not explicitly adultery!) in chs. 4ff. are
only an imperfect allusion to this symbol. The antiquity of the father-
son image in Israel is uncertain[235]; it appears as the background of an
accusation in Dtn 32 5f. 18. A typical word for the concern of a parent
or of one member of a family for another is רחם, "care;" its negative
"not-care," "not-pity," is a terminus technicus for the cruel and
destructive attitude of enemies[236]. Hosea plays with this doubleedged
word in the name "Not-Pitied" (1 6 2 6, secondarily reversed 1 7 2 3. 25)
and in the betrothal gift "care" (2 21).

---

[231] In the first person, Osiris declares, "I am the Only One" (The Book of the Dead,
XVII, 5). For surveys, see M. Smith, JBL 71 (1952), 139f.; C. J. Labuschagne,
The Incomparability of Yahweh in the Old Testament, 1966.

[232] El-Amarna tablets 169, 7—10; 238, 31—33; a Tigrē inscription quoted by C. Brok-
kelmann, ZS 5 (1927), 6—38.

[233] W. Koppers, Der Urmensch und sein Weltbild, 1949, 126.

[234] G. Wright, JNES 1 (1942), 404—414; G. Östborn, Yahweh and Baal, 1956, 53. 80.

[235] Ex 4 22 is hardly earlier than Hosea.

[236] A. Jepsen, KuD 7 (1961), 261.

The vine, used as an image of Israel in Hos 9 10 and 10 1, is a traditional symbol of the nation[237]. The theme that Israel is planted in the mountain range of Palestine — an expression for the divinely appointed settlement[238] — is twisted to indicate that the ground is, underneath, a rock, according to a possible reading of Hos 9 13.

Another important image is that of Yahweh as a shepherd or tender of young cattle. Yahweh fed Israel in the wilderness (Hos 13 6), in line with a prominent theme in sacred history, probably implying the image of a tending of sheep[239]. He gave the nation a profitable and promising task of plowing — as a calf — in Palestine (10 11). But Israel plows badly (10 13); it is a "rebellious calf" (cf. Dtn 32 15), so that Yahweh — according to a possible interpretation — will need to take it back to sheep-status in the "broad place" (ironically) of the wilderness (4 16). The image of the shepherd is closely intertwined with that of the lover in the Song of Songs[240]. Unfortunately, Israel's shepherd turns into an attacking animal (Hos 13 7f.).

Bethel, the most important Northern sanctuary, was a center for cultic weeping, probably originally for a dying god. In its area, there were to be found the "Oak of Weeping," a locality Bochim ("Weeping"), and the spot Beth-awæn (Beth-'ôn?, "house of trouble"), perhaps all of them representing the town's sacred precinct. Rachel, whose tomb was nearby, is pictured as crying (Jer 31 15); she gives Benjamin the name Ben-'oni, "son of my sorrow" (Gen 35 18). Weeping occurs in Bethel, according to Judg 21 2[241]. Hos 12 5 associates weeping with Jacob's struggle with the angel and probably intends a pun in the word 'ôn-'awæn which means both "strength" (manhood) and "trouble." It is not clear whether the name Beth-awæn is intended by Hosea in a devaluative sense, but he was clearly skeptical of the ritual processes, even while accepting the locale as a place of revelation.

Hosea's intimate relation to the concrete cult — both Yahwist and Baalistic in character — has been pointed out in a number of studies, so that it need not be presented here in detail. S. Oettli already showed that Amos and Hosea together refer to most of the cult places, cult forms, cultic events and symbols, etc., to be found in the rest of the Old Testament[242]. Mauchline, in his introduction to

---

[237] Ps 80 9 Jer 2 21, etc. (ironically in Ez 15 ?). Cf. N. Snaith, Hymns of the Temple, 1951, 49, with reference to a golden vine in Herod's Temple.

[238] Similarly R. Bach in: von Rad-Festschrift, 1961, 13.

[239] On Israel as sheep, A. Wünsche, Die Bildersprache des Alten Testaments, 1906, 50—53.

[240] See data by A. Feuillet, BZ NF 8 (1964), 219—233.

[241] With F. Hvidberg, Weeping and Laughter in the Old Testament, 1962, 100f.

[242] Cremer-Festschrift, 1895, 1—34.

Hosea, has outlined the prophet's close relation to themes of the Israelite autumnal festival. Several studies have analyzed the prophet's relation to historical traditions, showing close relation to older strata, but also considerable (orally based?) independence in detail[243]. One final item, however, may be added. The sentence "I reject you from being a priest to me" (4 6) employs the same word (כהן, pi.) which is known in later literature as meaning "to serve as a priest." The priest, expected to dispence *torā*, has failed; thus God now removes him from his office.

V. CONCLUSION

In so far as the preceding discussion goes beyond the book of Hosea itself it can give only tentative indications. Yet it has become clear that Hosea is deeply dependent on tradition, that his terms are largely standardized. A final example may be given, which yields parallels to several aspects treated. It is a hymn to Shamash, from which another part has been quoted above; items paralleling Hosea are italicized.

> Spread is your wide *net*
>   ... over him,
> Who turned his eyes
>   *toward the wife of his companion.*
> On a *day* not meant for him (?)
>   ... he ...
> There is laid for him a horrible *snare*
>   ....
> When your weapon turns on him
>   he finds *no rescuer.*
> In his *controversy* there stands by him
>   not even his father.
> At the time of the *judge's word*
>   not even his brothers speak up.
> With a metal *bird-trap*
>   he is felled to the ground, unawares.
> Whoever does something *horrible*
>   his horn you *destroy.*
> For him who acts cunningly, full of *trickery*,
>   the ground is cut away[244].

---

[243] Probably best: J. Rieger, Die Bedeutung der Geschichte für die Verkündigung des Amos und Hosea, 1929. Hosea is repeatedly closer to J than to E (partly against O. Procksch, Geschichtsbetrachtung, 1902, 118—132).

[244] Falkenstein-Soden 243; ANET 388.

It has been shown, specifically, that Hosea is close to the Deuteronomic tradition in a broad sense of that word. Hosea's dependence on Deuteronomic terminology and motifs was recognized by E. Day[245]; as a result, he placed the writing into the Persian period. His procedure, however, led him inexorably to deny a pre-exilic date to any of the prophets whose writings are preserved[246], since it did not allow for an oral history of expressions and motifs or for writings now lost.

A striking phenomenon is the similarity between Hosea's terms and many that are used in the Psalms. Descriptions of enemies found in the Psalms revolve around the images of hunters, wild animals, and warriors[247], and include stylizations for moral qualities; all of these are employed by Hosea. This is not to say that psalm usage is the direct source of the prophet's terminology; for these conceptualizations have a fairly large range. Yet one can raise the question whether Hosea is violating the stylizations by pointing them in a new direction, namely against Israel[248]. In a sense, that is true; but even in traditions outside of the prophets, and beyond Israel, God's enemies are not thought to be always by definition equal to the people's or the individual's enemies, so that there is at least a theoretical distinction between one's opponents and "the wicked."

References to collective and individual sins are old and widespread in situations of difficulty; gods could be understood as opposing their own people in punishment for transgressions[249]. Long before Amos and Hosea, Israelite prophets engaged in criticism. The phenomenon of "opposition prophets" in Mari dispels any doubts about the antiquity of a critical tradition, even if not as profound or sharp as that of Hosea or of other Israelite prophets. Though most Near Eastern oracles are concerned with questions of success and advantage, a certain combination of prophecy with a moral emphasis had already taken place outside of Israel, especially in Mesopotamia. The sun-god Shamash was both the patron god of justice and the favorite deity of

---

[245] AJSL 26 (1909/10), 105—132.

[246] E. Day and W. Chapin, AJSL 18 (1901/02), 65—93.

[247] E. g., H. Kraus, Psalmen, 1959, 40. For neighboring data, G. Widengren, The Accadian and Hebrew Psalms of Lamentation, 1936, 122f., as also for other terms, such as "devise evil" (109). For the stylizations applied to death, see L. Wächter, Der Tod im Alten Testament, 1967.

[248] H. Birkeland, The Evildoers in the Book of Psalms, 1955, 27, holds that a similarity between prophetic accusations and psalm styles exemplifies the weakness of form-critical hypotheses; it does not, however, violate the form given to that approach in morphological analysis.

[249] J. Hempel, Die Mehrdeutigkeit der Geschichte, 1936, 29 (with references); W. Lambert op. cit. 60; W. Moran, CBQ 25 (1963), 83f.

seers. In Egypt, accusing and threatening moralists played a significant role well before Moses.

The existence of various motifs presupposed or employed by
Hosea shows that Israelite religion in his day already contained many
of the typical elements of its faith, unless the prophet himself authored
many major and minor patterns that eventually were accepted and
used in varying ways. For the present study, however, such historical
issues are subordinate to the literary issue of the meaning of the
stylized expressions. Most of the images and expressions used by
Hosea are not fresh creations but living symbols, even though they are
often given a new direction or application.

The symbols are related to the fundamental problems of the people,
revolving around the most basic fortunes of life[250]. They express
directly the emotional concerns of human existence, both of a positive
and a negative form[251]. A fundamental positive symbol is "Life" — if
one likes, "Being." When this includes a standard of evaluation to
which one is subject, it becomes "righteousness." Its opposite is death,
or non-Being, disorder, or "falsehood."

Emotive concerns are inherently relational[252]. A strongly negative
form is thus expressed in terms of enmity. Threatening evils are
regularly personified as one's enemies or opponents at a law-suit[253];
both physical and moral evils can be thought of as the enemies of
deity[254]. For Hosea, the nation itself is evil — at odds with its divine
lord.

---

[250] Similarly, the literary critic M. Bowra, The Prophetic Element, 1959, 13.

[251] M. Bodkin, Archetypal Patterns in Poetry, 1958, 35, speaks appropriately of
"emotional symbolism." F. Haeussermann, Wortempfang und Symbol, 1932, 30—32,
divides Old Testament symbols into those for evil, those for good, and those that
are ambivalent.

[252] The relational character of righteousness and evil has been emphasized by K. Fahlgren, Ṣedaḳa, 1932; E. Achtemeier, IDB, IV 80—85; Klopfenstein op. cit.

[253] So, often, in Mesopotamian incantations; further, Widengren, Psalms, 202—214;
M. Witzel, Tammuz-Liturgien, 1935, passim; for Egyptian, Zandee op. cit. 217.
259—263, etc.

[254] E. Podechard, Le Psautier, I 1949, 45; W. Lambert, AfO 19 (1960), 117; Zandee
op. cit. 217; J. Gonda, Die Religionen Indiens, I 42, etc.

Chapter VI: The Word as Message: Structure

I. THE FUNCTION OF PROPHECY IN ITS CONTEXT

Israelite culture distinguished between the priests, the prophets, and the wise. Wisdom was a strongly humanistic activity, representing what may be called the mastery relation of man. The ability to pursue wisdom was, it is true, considered to be a divine gift, but the pursuit itself laid emphasis on the exercise of intelligence. Priestly and prophetic word, on the other hand, were essentially thought of as receptive, though joined in part to reflection and observation. Priest and prophet thus present divine speech, which is absent from wisdom.

The categories of priestly and prophetic speech have their roots in religious structure as such. It is an essential feature of a culture that it define the basis and thus the norm of its existence. Commonly, this is done through creation narratives and various mythological traditions. It is also an inevitable characteristic of a group that it concern itself with that which lies ahead. Two main avenues of approach for the latter are possible. Either one can attempt to insure a good prospect by means of ritual — thought to be divinely given at the origin — or one can seek to pierce the developments of future events and attempt to adjust oneself to them by appropriate action or inaction. These two options provide a certain built-in tension between priest and prophet, but in theory and generally in practice their roles are complementary.

At any rate, it is the prophet's pre-eminent task to see ahead so that a catastrophe can be avoided and good fortunes maximized. The declarations of the future are not at all irrevocable; for if an oracle is unfavorable, the person involved will simply not proceed with his plans and thus prevent the prediction from being fulfilled[1]. The prophetic announcement does not possess an absolute character, at least in so far as it is rooted in a changeable human situation. It only clarifies the direction or trend of the individual moment, which one can then either accept or seek to change. Thereby the prophets are related to the process of decision[2].

---

[1] E. g., I Sam 23 12f., as generally in primitive and ancient life.

[2] In modern life, the maximizing of desired future effects is rationalized in what is known as "decision theory." See P. Wasserman and F. Silander, Decision-Making, An Annotated Bibliography, 1958, with Supplement, 1964.

The specialization of prophet and priest probably was not altogether mutually exclusive. In the surviving Israelite literature as presented in the canon, however, the separation of structures is rather pronounced. There are, indeed, almost no references to the historical "credo" in prophetic books; the few that do occur, as in Hosea, stand in the service of an accusation pointing out Israel's inadequate response[3]. Hosea, more than any other prophet, does refer positively to an ideal past; perhaps he stood personally, or as a member of the northern tradition, close to the priesthood. Yet even his employment of references to the ideal past is either one of parody or one of introducing an accusation, or both.

The relationship between the offices can be seen in the following manner[4]. While it is the task of the priest to remember and make effective the mythical time of an ideal past (more precisely, of an Origin), the prophet relates the individual moment of existence to the divinely given order and evaluates that moment accordingly. The prophet refers to the ordering system as one violated or fulfilled, in order to provide either guidance or curses and, sometimes, blessings.

Priestly declarations, like all norms, have a general application; prophetic speech, as evaluation, relates to a certain specific condition[5]. Therefore, the content of priestly knowledge needs to be given only once, to be applicable thereafter, while prophetic word requires constantly renewed insight. The priest's "knowledge" and *tôrā* does not rely on his own reception of new truth but harks back to a divine revelation in the past, given to a prophet such as Moses. Thus while the content of priestly speech is strongly revelatory — as in the laws of the Pentateuch — the priest himself as an individual is not a revelatory person. The new information applicable to each situation, how-

---

[3] Hos 11 1ff. 12 10. 14 13 4 f. Am 2 9ff. 3 1f. Mi 6 4 Ez 20 5ff. Cf. Westermann, Grundformen, 131.

[4] The concept "office" is to be understood in the broad sense applicable to the functional concept of an "institution" (above, p. 1). It designates roles expected by, and operative within, society. This analysis is not to be confused with what prophet and priest actually did with tradition, especially unconsciously. The past-orientation of the priest, however, naturally made him more conservative. Cf. Fohrer, Studien, 21—26.

[5] The direction of the prophet toward a particular situation has similarly been emphasized by O. Grether op. cit. 111—114; A. Gunneweg, Mündliche und schriftliche Tradition, 1959, 42; W. Beyerlin, Die Kulttraditionen Israels in der Verkündigung des Propheten Micha, 1959, 97; M. Newman in: Muilenburg-Festschrift, 1962, 93; L. Wood, The Relationship of the Priests and Prophets in Pre-exilic Israel, Diss. Michigan State Univ., 1963 (according to DA 24 [1963/64], 2601). Similarly, H. Reventlow, Wächter über Israel, 1962, 124, supposing, however, a personal identity between the law speaker and the prophet.

ever, requires fresh inspiration. Thus though the prophet's word is expected (in theory) to be subsidiary in content to the priest's tradition, as a person the prophet is thought more important than the other. One way in which this shows itself is that the prophet's name is carefully remembered — or else invented; anonymous oracles indeed would prove an embarrassment, since without their source they lack a legitimating point of reference[6]. Therefore, the name "Hosea" is placed carefully over the book under discussion — probably for the most part correctly — as the author of its message. Biographical and autobiographical narratives emphasize or reflect the peculiarly important role of a prophet's life.

Priests, too, could deliver oracles, but these were primarily based on mechanical means[7]. Such means have inherent drawbacks and did not harmonize well with the personal structure of Israelite religion; they are ridiculed in Hos 4 12. The mechanical oracle had as possibilities only a "yes" or "no" answer to a posed question; it was awkward to operate in determining the cause of evil, since successive lots would be required to narrow down the possibilities to be considered.

Like the priestly announcement, however, the prophetic prediction tends to limit itself in essence to a "yes" or "no" answer. For though the poetic descriptions of the future go on for some considerable length, they are so general and stylized that little is gained in the way of concrete insight into future happenings[8]. Such a specific insight, indeed, is quite unnecessary (even if it were possible), since it is the prophet's task not to satisfy curiosity but to either encourage or discourage a present or contemplated activity.

More important in the way of specific insight is the prophet's ability to pinpoint the cause of evil requiring correction; this is one of the most important functions of a diviner[9]. Though cultic accusations

---

[6] In Greece, "anonymous" oracles were attributed to the Sibyls, the Bakis, etc· (M. Nilsson, Cults, Myths, Oracles, and Politics in Ancient Greece, 1951, 124. 130). In the Old Testament, almost all oracles are placed under a name, even under such an artificial one as Malachi, and such names are not archetypal like Moses or Solomon for other traditions.

[7] A priestly oracle in poetry form is held, e. g., by G. Hylmö, Gamla Testamentets litteraturhistoria, 1938, 59—65, but even I Sam 1 17 (third-person jussive?) is not a very good example. Mechanical oracles appear in Josh 7 16-18 I Sam 14 36. 41f. 23 9-12. Egyptian priests freely used a mechanical process. The psalmists stood at least as close to the prophets as to the priests.

[8] So, also, E. Jenni, Die politischen Voraussagen der Propheten, 1956, for the original form of prophecies (sometimes secondarily concretized).

[9] E. g., E. E. Evans-Pritchard, Witchcraft, Oracles, and Magic Among the Azande, 1937; H. Hulbert, The Passing of Korea, 1906, 422; and Human Relations Area Files, category 787. See above, p. 90.

of sin are not very well attested in Israel, they must be assumed to have taken place, on the basis both of direct evidence elsewhere and of at least indirect indications within the Old Testament. What distinguished the great prophets of Israel from most of their contemporaries was not that they discovered evil which underlies an already present catastrophe — as in the pattern of Hos 4 1-3 — but that they saw present evil active in such a way that it culminates in doom still to come[10]; in other words, they see an operation of evil even without being required to do so by circumstances.

One can now ask how, or whether, prophetic literature should be divided into genres[11]. It has been shown (in Chapter IV) that in Hosea the forms of divine and human speech can be distinguished but cannot be separated as belonging to different oracles. It is even more fruitless to make boundaries between the future and the present, for these are interrelated both in form and meaning, as will be seen in some detail below.

More promising is a division according to the negative or positive character of a saying. Doom and hope are the two possible decisions which a prophet can render in regard to a specific situation. Whether a sharp line can be drawn between the two, or whether doom and hope may belong together, is still a difficult question; after all, a prophet may make a more complicated analysis than a simple yes or no and may combine the two. In any event, however, the positive and negative structures are the two alternatives inherent in the question of fate.

II. THE NEGATIVE STRUCTURE

The bulk of Hosea's prophecy is taken up by accusation and threat intimately related to each other. The manner of connection between the two elements can take various forms.

Very frequently the conjunction "for" (*kî*) introduces a reproach. Ordinarily the subordinate clause follows the main clause[12]. The re-

---

[10] So, rightly (even if an occasional exception should be found), A. Kapelrud, JBL 71 (1952), 38.

[11] The question of whether the genre is represented by an elementary motif or by a larger structure is also raised by K. von Rabenau, WZ Halle, G.-s. 5 (1955/56), 673, and is resolved by him, tentatively, in terms of the former. E. Scherer, Unpersönlich formulierte prophetische Orakel, Diss. Kirchliche Hochschule, Berlin, 1964, attempts to deal with non-divine indirect-address prophecies as a separate genre, derived from blessing and cursing.

[12] Hos 4 1. 10. 14 5 3f. 11 7 13 8 9 9 1. 17 10 3 11 5 14 1. Similarly *yă'ăn*, Hos 8 1. Beyond Hosea, cf. Wolff, ZAW 52 (1934), 8.

verse order, however, is followed in a group of statements, as discussed in Chapter IV, which relate threat to human sin as an appropriate result in a special form with prepositive *kî*. The reason for doom can be introduced by the prepositions עַל ("for the sake of," "because of")[13] and מִפְּנֵי (literally, "from")[14], which are felt synonymous[15]. The preposition מִן ("from")[16] is closely allied, though it carries with it the connotation of a fall from a proud position.

"Therefore" (*laken*), typical of introductions of prophetic threats, appears only in Hos 2 8. 11. 16[17]. In the third instance, the announcement eventually leads to a promise, but *laken* still fulfills the role of a transition from accusation to threat, namely that of being led into the wilderness.

At other times accusation is so closely interwoven with threat that the two cannot be separated. Declarations such as, "Now he will remember their guilt and visit their sins[18]," are an example. An accusation is implied in such threats as "He has rejected your calf"[19] and is expressly stated in "Destroyed will be the high places of Awen, the sin of Israel" (10 8). On the other hand, reproaches imply divine opposition, such as, "When I would heal Israel, there is revealed the iniquity of Ephraim[20]."

The Old Testament, indeed, does not distinguish sharply between the evil deed and its evil consequence. Such an outlook has been called a "synthetic view of life[21]." Certain Hebrew words indicate both sin and punishment[22]; occasionally it is hard to know which is meant. Typical of such an outlook is the expression, "You have stumbled in your iniquity[23]."

The punishment, as already noted in part, is characteristically expressed as an appropriate consequence of a sin. "Israel has rejected the good — the enemy will pursue him" (8 3). Israel's activity already carries within itself evil results. "A companion of idols is Ephraim — leave him!" (4 17). Yahweh will not punish the adultery of Israel's

---

[13] Hos 9 7. 15. For the form in Amos, Hylmö, Studier, 58f.

[14] Hos 10 15.

[15] Cf., e. g., Dtn 28 20 and Jer 4 4 with Hos 9 15.

[16] Hos 4 19 11 6. (Cf. above, Chapter V.)

[17] *Laken hinnē* . . . (Hos 2 8. 16) is a widespread construction.

[18] Hos 8 13 9 9. Similarly, 4 9 10 10 12 3. 15.

[19] Hos 8 5. Similarly, 10 2. 6.

[20] Hos 7 1. Similarly, 5 3 7 2.

[21] Fahlgren op. cit. 50ff.; similarly in Greece (S. Ranulf, The Jealousy of the Gods and Criminal Law in Athens, I 1932, 33).

[22] Attention has been drawn to the double meaning of רָע, פֶּשַׁע, עָוֹן, צְדָקָה, כָּשַׁל, and others (K. Koch, ZTK 52 [1955], 26—28). For אָשֵׁם in Hosea, see above, p. 92.

[23] Hos 14 2. Similarly, 5 5 14 10

women since cultic prostitution is practiced by the men (4 14). Punishment is geared to the crime. Israel's love for Baalistic rituals and fertility rites leads to a destruction of natural growth and a cessation of all cultic activity (9 1-6). Trust in worldly military power is answered by defeat in war (10 13f.). Generally speaking, accusations and threats both involve politics and cult.

Appropriateness can be indicated by verbal connections, as in Hos 4 6, with which may be compared the Egyptian word, "Amon knows who knows him and ignores who ignores him[24]." With bitter irony, Hosea exclaims, "He will return to the land of Egypt ..., for they have refused to (re)turn (to Yahweh)" (11 5). In a pun, he declares that the altars of Gilead and Gilgal will become *gallîm*, i. e., heaps of stones (12 12).

An action is so closely connected with its consequence that it can be said that evil is being sought by Israel. "Ephraim ... pursues the east wind" (12 2); it "has insisted on following after worthlessness" (5 11). "Their gold and their silver they turn into idols — to be destroyed" (8 4). In other words, Israel's direction is toward evil. That which lies ahead of the people, that toward which they move, is something that means annihilation and negation of human existence.

The prophet Hosea is fulfilling his expected function. Like other soothsayers who predict the future on the basis of omens observable in the present situation, he states the prospect lying ahead of Israel on the basis of present indications. Verbal connections and puns are an important stylistic part of this structure, in Israelite as well as in Arabic prophecy[25].

For this reason the very pointing out of wrongdoing implies already a threat, comparable to the diagnosis of a fatal disease by a physician. When Israel is said not merely to have "sinned" after the ordinary manner of a reasonably faithful people, but to be actually an enemy of Yahweh, its doom is sealed.

Even laments of the pitiable position of the nation form pronouncements of hopelessness. "A foolish people comes to fall with a whore" (4 14). "Crushed is Ephraim, broken in judgment" (5 11). "All their kings have fallen" (7 7). Ephraim is like an unturned or moldy cake (7 8f.). "They have become like a warped bow" (7 16). "Ephraim has become like a dove, silly and without sense" (7 11). Israel is now "like an undesirable vessel" (8 8). Ephraim's "root is dried up" (9 16); yes, he has "died" (13 1). Other examples of the form of lament, extremely common in Hosea, could be cited[26]. In a similar vein other Israelite

---

[24] J. Baillet, Introduction à l'étude des idées morales dans l'Égypte antique, 1912, 115.

[25] Guillaume op. cit. 117—128, on oracles of Bedouins; Am 8 1f. Jer 1 11f., etc.

[26] Hos 4 11. 14 5 11 8 8 9 11. 13. 16 11 7. All instances cited are non-divine words. The tone is lacking in ch. 2, where all negative speech is from Yahweh.

prophets, like singers the world over, have derided the inner weakness of enemies. At least one of the expressions cited ("an undesirable vessel") has elsewhere been used quite clearly as a pronouncement of doom (Jer 22 28 48 38).

Threat, accusation, lament — all three form aspects of the negative structure of prophecy, intertwined in such a way that it is often difficult to disentangle them from each other. They all lead toward the conclusion that Israel's direction and outlook is bad. Indeed, accusation and threat are present in every one of Hosea's negative oracles and lament occurs in most[27].

An essential evil castigated by Hosea is that of pride, self-sufficiency, and worldliness — in short, the failure to rely on, and to be oriented toward, Yahweh[28]. It is one of the characteristic motifs of Israelite prophecy that Yahweh destroys everything proud and lofty, that every human grandeur must fall. This motif is important in oracles against foreign nations; for the boasting of an enemy marks him for divine destruction[29]. Only the humble meet God's favor[30]. Punishment is thus not artificial but consists in the fall that follows pride. According to Hosea, the royal and cultic institutions are to disintegrate, and Israel's self-satisfaction in Canaan is to lead to a return to Egypt or to the Wilderness.

Though Hosea does describe specific evils, it is not at all certain that these form the fundamental basis of his prophecy. The existence of a tradition of opposition prophets, as well as Hosea's own stylizations, indicate that the thrust of denunciation and threat is more basic than the particular specifications drawn up against Israel. Nor can a sense of impending destruction by Assyria be the primary element of Hosea's prophecy, since it is hardly mentioned[31]. One may say only that certain definite actions of the nation and certain threats looming on the horizon entered into the picture even though they probably did not determine it. A central element is played by the confrontation of Israel by God. That the awareness of one's sinfulness is more basic than the recognition of certain offenses is a fairly general experience, especially for sensitive persons. Thus Hosea, "the watchman of Israel

---

[27] Jeremiah's oracles are similarly complex, as noted by Mowinckel, Edda 26 (1926), 272—274.

[28] Similarly, U. Türck, Die sittliche Forderung der israelitischen Propheten des 8. Jahrhunderts, 1935, 17.

[29] E. g., Is 14 13f. Ez 28 2.

[30] Humility toward God was stressed also by the Egyptians, Assyrians, and Babylonians (W. Albright, From the Stone Age to Christianity, 254).

[31] Hos 11 5. Assyrian domination seems to be vaguely indicated in 9 6; the reference to Assyria in 9 3 was probably added in the tradition. Elsewhere Assyria is mentioned in connection with Israel's sin in dealing with it (7 11 8 9 12 2).

with God" (9 8), declares the future of the basic movement of Israel's life, out of his special sensitivity to existence.

Joined to the personal confrontation with deity is a humanistic wisdom-like perspective, which is illustrated by the use of two proverbial-style sayings: "As they sow the wind, they will reap the whirlwind" (8 7) and "You have plowed wickedness, you will reap badness; you will eat the fruit of falsehood" (10 13)[32]. One of the central concepts of wisdom is that of "future" or "consequence," 'aḥarît[33]; it is the business of wisdom to declare the outcome or prospect of various general types of activity. That Israel is moving in a catastrophic direction is expressed in the prophet's own word, analyzed above as reflecting seer style; this style, together with its general tradition, has affinities with wisdom[34]. Yahweh's personal reaction is typically expressed in line with this as a judgment or as an enemy action in response to Israel's opposition to him.

The two aspects of inherent consequence and divine action are combined in the concept of Yahweh's "visiting" or "returning" Israel's ways upon it or of "abandoning" its bloodguilt to produce death[35]. Yahweh thus empowers and seals the destructive forces set in motion. Divine action furthermore is thought of as the basis of the order of events, as in the concept of a curse. Israel operated explicitly or implicitly on the theory of a covenant, i. e., a relationship originally entered voluntarily, but then supported by curses. The prophets, such as Hosea, can be understood as invoking curses — to call them "covenant curses" is almost redundant — which once uttered within sacred law by divine authority come into play almost by themselves[36].

---

[32] Similarly for sowing, plowing, and reaping: Prov 22 8 Job 4 8.

[33] For discussions, with literature, see H. Wildberger, VT 7 (1957), 72—77; G. Buchanan, JNES 20 (1961), 188—190. In wisdom, "end" denotes either the "result" of an evil act (Dtn 32 20. 29 Ps 73 17 Prov 5 4 14 12 [= 16 25] 20 21 23 32 25 8 29 21) or a "good prospect" available only to the righteous (Ps 37 37f. Prov 23 18 24 14. 20), as partly noted by Zimmerli, ZAW 51 (1933), 198.

[34] For such an affinity in Akkadian literature, see also Schmid op. cit. 127.

[35] Hos 2 15 4 9 8 13 9 9 12 3. 15. All of these end an oracle, except 12 3, which begins one.

[36] The role of sacred law in judgment is emphasized by H. Reventlow, VT 10 (1960), 316—319. D. Hillers, Treaty-Curses and the Old Testament Prophets, 1964, shows a number of similarities between prophetic announcements and Near Eastern curses, although his thesis that the curses were transmitted specifically by treaties is weak. The relation of prophetic word to curses has been noted by J. Hempel, Das Ethos des Alten Testaments, 1938, 94, and discussed in some detail by F. Fensham op. cit. 155—175. The most relevant parallels to Hoseanic expressions may be found in the following themes: Lack of progeny and infertility, drought, devouring animals, removal of joy, an incurable wound, and the category of "futility" curse which Hillers finds in Hos 4 10 5 6 8 7 9 12. 16.

It is necessary to adopt an appropriate concept of the "future." A long-standing discussion revolves around the question whether or not the prophet foresaw the future and then grounded its occurrence in the present situation[37]. It turns out that the problem, as thus stated, is a false one. The future of which wisdom and the seer speak is always thought of as a consequence or outcome of the present. A declaration of judgment represents a consequence of, or a reaction to, a present or accomplished deed. In both cases, the future is not simply an isolated happening unconnected with what precedes. Divination — as in Mesopotamia — observes the present state of the cosmos, in order to deduce from it a knowledge of the tendency of events[38]. The future *means* consequence, direction, response[39]. Hosea repeatedly expresses this future with the word עַתָּה, "now," which is related to the expression וְעַתָּה, "and now," used to express emotional decisions and judgments in response to a previous situation or disclosure[40].

There are, however, many ways in which the tendency of events can be understood. In Israelite religion, the tendency takes on what may be called a moral form, with a heavily personal element. The sinner — or the sinning nation — is charged with deviations not merely in circumspection but in will; he not merely commits an external oversight but is guilty of an action which contains his own soul. The divine

---

[37] The primacy of prediction over a moral emphasis has been emphasized by Wellhausen, e. g., Geschichte 110; W. R. Smith, The Old Testament in the Jewish Church, 1892, 286 f.; R. Smend, Lehrbuch der alttestamentlichen Religionsgeschichte, 1899², 187 f.; J. Kaplan, Psychology of Prophecy, 1908, 95; Gressmann, 1910, 322. 326; Duhm 13; Gunkel, Die Propheten, 29; Mowinckel, Edda 26 (1926), 259; Balla, Die Droh- und Scheltworte, 34; Hempel, Die althebräische Literatur, 66; Beyer op. cit. 39; Wolff, ZAW 52 (1934), 7. 17; Wildberger, Jahwewort, 104—125. Mowinckel, however, defines the future as including "what ought to be, but is not yet" (Prophecy and Tradition 55).

[38] A. Guillaume op. cit. 39 f. W. Howells, The Heathens, 1948, 67, entitles a chapter: "Divination: The Future in the Present." Similarly, E. König, Das Buch Jesaja, 1926, 13.

[39] The future as an outgrowth of the present has been emphasized by, among others, A. Kuenen, The Prophets and Prophecy in Israel, 1877, 350. 356; G. Smith 10; P. Volz, Die vorexilische Jahweprophetie und der Messias, 1897; B. Stade, Biblische Theologie Alten Testaments, I 1905, 214; E. Auerbach, Die Prophetie, 1920, 27. 64 f.; J. McIvor, The Literary Study of the Prophets, 1925, 248 f. 252; C. Kent, The Growth and Contents of the Old Testament, 1926, 99. 105; N. Micklem op. cit. 242; T. H. Robinson, ExpT 40 (1928/29), 298; H. Obbink, HUCA 14 (1939), 27; R. Scott, The Relevance of the Prophets, 1944, 10. 14; H. Rowley, HTR 38 (1945), 36; L. Longacre, The Old Testament, Its Form and Purpose, 1945, 112; R. Dunkerly, ExpT 61 (1949/50), 262; Fohrer, TR NF 19 (1951), 346; W. Williams, The Prophets, 1956, 50; J. Hyatt, Jeremiah, 1958, 20; Westermann, Grundformen.

[40] A. Laurentin, Biblica 45 (1964), 168—197.

reaction elicited has the character of a personal response[41] which in its inner character is an appropriate response. This rational-personal structure distinguishes Israelite prophecy from primitive forms of divination and gives it its own special attitude to the future. It is not the case that a grounding in the present has been added to a presentiment of the future (as though divination dealt only with the latter), but that the nature of the grounding has been transformed — from the observation of omens to a consideration of inner culpability.

Within the entire Old Testament there are virtually no ungrounded announcements of doom; for even the few that do not develop an accusation explicitly usually contain one implicitly[42]. Oracles against foreign nations have an inherent grounding in the opposition of the enemy to Yahweh and his people, while more specifically pride and other misdeeds are also attributed to them[43]. On the other hand, seemingly independent reproaches assume the form of a legal proceeding or of some other style (such as that of a "woe") which contains a threat implicitly[44]. Thus accusation and threat cannot be torn apart.

In their observation of the movement of life, the Old Testament prophets are not altogether isolated. As Demosthenes explicitly declared, the responsibility of the Greek political orator was to discern trends and tendencies and to warn and influence his people[45]; these same orators engaged in law suits which heavily involved invectives. Invectives and satire of course belong, as Aristotle pointed out, to that form of poetry which deals with the baser side of men[46]. The chief function of the ancient Arabic poet was to compose satires — as curses — against enemies[47]. Furthermore, a certain sense that death is the "destiny" of man was already current in the Near East, evidently including Syro-Palestinian literature[48].

As in Arabic poetry and in a considerable portion of popular Greek literature[49], a pronounced element of sharp irony makes itself felt in Hosea, for instance in the form of puns and parody. (E. g., "As Ephraim multiplied altars for sin-offerings — they became to him altars for sinning," 8 11.). Irony, indeed, is the main form of humor

---

[41] As emphasized by J. Plöger, Literarkritische, formgeschichtliche und stilkritische Untersuchungen zum Deuteronomium, 1967, 213.

[42] See examples of pure threats claimed by E. Balla, Die Droh- und Scheltworte des Amos, 6; K. Beyer op. cit. 30f.; A. Kapelrud, Central Ideas in Amos, 1956, 59. Some sayings are probably listed incorrectly as independent by these studies.

[43] Partially against C. Westermann, Grundformen, 18. 148.

[44] See Hylmö, Studier, 66ff. (even assuming that those listed are really independent).

[45] De Corona § 246; E. Strachey, Jewish History and Politics, 1874, 3, already referred to this. On him and Pericles, W. Caspari, Die israelitischen Propheten, 1914, 150.

[46] Poetics, ch. 4. On the role of lampoons in law-suits, e. g., S. Butcher, Demosthenes, 1882, 129f.

[47] E. g., R. Nicholson, A Literary History of the Arabs, 1956, 73.

[48] Cf. Ugaritic *uḥryt* in 2 Aqht VI:35 for "death" (elsewhere, "destiny" or "lot"); similarly *'aḥᵃrit*, Num 23 10. More important is the direct testimony of various well-known writings.

[49] H. Rose, A Handbook of Greek Literature, 1934, 344f.; Hvidberg op. cit. 151f. (on Arabic and Egyptian).

employed in the Old Testament[50]. It has recently been suggested — probably correctly — that its distinctive quality is "a will to righteousness," with an expression of the disparity between what is and what ought to be[51]. Similarly, satire and invective are connected with a moral will in the work of the seventh-century Greek Archilochus[52], arising from the form of curses in tragic mythology and from abusive invectives against evil forces in fertility rituals. Satire within a society, however, though overtly conservative — aiming ostensibly to protect the order that has become violated — can be recognized as anarchic and disruptive of ordinary social processes[53]. It will become apparent that a prophet like Hosea deeply shakes and opposes present reality; for he goes beyond practical programs of betterment (which generally avoid ironic satire) to a more absolute vision of existence.

The presence of irony illustrates the complexity of Hosea's speech. His negative structure may not be subdivided into separate genres, as though the component parts were independent of each other. Rather, the structure as a whole represents man and God in a relation of enmity, which is not altogether irrational[54] but is the end point of the human direction. This conflict spells fundamental disruption and death, even for a sacred people.

III. THE POSITIVE STRUCTURE

The positive form of Israelite prophecy does not ground its prediction in human activity. The prospect presented therein is not the future arising from man but an occurrence based in God. The movement of human life is toward doom, but the purpose of Yahweh is directed toward the good of his people. Most promises in Hosea lack any sort of grounding. One, however, gives a reason: "For I am God — and not man, the Holy One in your midst" (11 9). Hosea's pattern reflects the situation generally prevailing in Old Testament oracles of weal. Whatever grounding is given lies in the divine purpose[55].

---

[50] E. g., D. Lang, Judaism 11 (1962), 249—254. For an analysis, see now E. Good, Irony in the Old Testament, 1965 (with a good review of irony in general). Later Judaism practiced much self-irony (cf. Universal Jewish Encyclopedia, X 547, and M. Grotjahn, Beyond Laughter, 1957, 21—25).

[51] I. Knox, Judaism 12 (1963), 327—337 (e. g., 331).

[52] R. Elliott, The Power of Satire, 1960, 5—8. 58f.

[53] Ibid. 273f.

[54] Irrational non-moral enmity between man and God is described by G. van der Leeuw, Religion in Essence and Manifestation, 1938, 517f. — hardly appropriate to Judaism (except in Job ?).

[55] So, already, H. Hertzberg, NKZ 43 (1932), 513—534. For clear data, see Wolff, ZAW 52 (1934), 10. Cf. Beyer op. cit. 26—30. J. Hyatt, Prophetic Religion, 1947, 171f., refers to Is 43 25 ("for my own sake").

It is true that many Old Testament traditions promise reward for a faithful and good life, but almost nowhere does one find a word to the present generation which assures it a good future on the basis of its having achieved moral excellence[56]. A reward structure, it is true, is by no means irrelevant to prophecy; for, in its negative form, it is presupposed by the words of threat. But it belongs to general law, as it is pronounced and observed by priest and wise man[57]. God's goodness is said to exert itself in spite of Israel's activity. "Yahweh loves the children of Israel, though they turn to other gods and love raisin cakes" (Hos 3 1).

The question accordingly arises how positive statements are related to negative ones. Certain positive forms, namely those declaring God's goodness in the past, form the background for accusations. Israel's sin is viewed as one of false response to God. The nation has failed to acknowledge or remember his kindness (2 10 7 15 11 2f. 13 6) and has ignored his laws (4 6 8 12).

torā and exhortation perform a dual function. *torā* is quoted in order to illustrate the divine direction violated by the people (6 6 10 12 12 7). Other words point out the road now to be taken or to be avoided (4 15 14 2f.). The second meaning is to a certain extent implied by the first group of sayings.

Exhortations for the future are closely related to promises, often conditional, as already in Mari prophecy. Amos (5 14f.) exclaimed, "Seek good and not evil, so that you may live. . . . Perhaps Yahweh, the God of hosts, will have mercy on the remnant of Joseph." The word "perhaps" belongs in the context of attempts to avert the wrath of God[58]. For that which is to be done, or can be done, is not to build or earn a good future but to cast oneself on the mercy of God, seeking the substitution of a reality grounded in divine mercy for the one appropriately arising from man. Man thus seeks something beyond his control or determination. "I will love them of my own free will" (Hos 14 5) is Yahweh's reassuring promise. The people are encouraged to believe that his coming is "set" (ready) when there is openness to it (Hos 6 3).

The thrust of both *tôrā* and other calls indeed, is that Israel should seek and "wait for" Yahweh (12 7). Israel is to seek Yahweh "until he come and rain righteousness" on them (10 12). Negatively

---

[56] The closest approach to such a declaration is Is 51 7 addressing the righteous within Israel (cf. 50 10 51 1).

[57] Is 33 15f., the only definite occurrence of this structure in the prophets (see Wolff, ZAW 52 [1934], 10) is part of a "liturgy" and represents a cultic form similar to the wisdom psalms. Bentzen incorrectly regards priestly oracles as unconditional (op. cit. 187).

[58] So also Ex 32 30 Zeph 2 3. In Jon 3 9, "Who knows . . .".

this means that reliance on Assyria or on "horses" (14 4) is to be given up. The work of their own hands is not to be called "God" (14 4). Yahweh alone can grant a good future to Israel's existence. In the new situation, Israel will seek God and come trembling to his goodness (3 5) and will respond to him personally (2 17-22). In other words, the exhortation calls for an attitude of dependence on Yahweh instead of one of self-assertion. Even ethical action can be understood in this manner (6 6 10 12 12 7).

Hos 14 5ff. has usually been regarded as an answer to the prayer of 14 3f.[59], but that is probably incorrect. For the word uses third-person address, and it speaks of healing Israel's turning as does a similar exhortation in Jer 3 22. It is a divine promise that Yahweh will effect a change of life. Hos 14 2-4 and 5-9 are parallel to each other — one an exhortation, the other a supporting promise in part dependent on Israel's action. Somewhat analogously, the announcements of a saving process in 2 16 and 3 1 do not presuppose penitence, though the eventual salvation does; Yahweh is taking the first step to win over Israel by taking disciplinary measures.

The two structures of appropriate destruction and God-willed prosperity collided seriously in Old Testament prophecy and led to sharp controversies between prophets. Hope prophets naturally concluded from a knowledge of divine intent that Israel's future was bound to be good. Nevertheless the two seemingly opposing aspects could be combined by means of at least one of two views: Israel's sin is only of a relative sort; after judgment has run its course, salvation can again operate. Or, punishment has a chastening function; it leads the nation back to its lord[60]. The first of these possibilities is decisively rejected by Hosea, who thus sets himself apart from the typical viewpoint of his contemporaries. With his extremely negative attitudes, he also modifies the second possibility; for the seriousness of the situation requires not merely a normal discipline which one might bear repeatedly but a drastic destruction to be followed by a new situation altogether.

The fact that Hosea presents some promises should not lead one to believe that he has a perspective less harsh than that of Amos, who lacks them. On the contrary, it seems that Amos still entertained a hope — however slim — that doom might be averted; thus he did not make provision for what will happen if doom does come. For Amos, the possibility of an alternative still exists, calling for a decision[61]. For

---

[59] A notable exception is R. Hentschke, ZEE 4 (1960), 51, whose analysis shows that Hosea's pattern is by no means singular in the Old Testament.

[60] E. g., Job 5 17f. For a good survey, see J. Sanders, Suffering as Divine Discipline in the Old Testament and Post-Biblical Judaism, 1955, 80ff.

[61] Similarly, B. Napier, Songs of the Vineyard, 1962, 207f. The point of Amos' four visions (as a series) is not to pronounce inevitable doom, but to declare that pro-

Hosea, however, Israel's downfall is definitely sealed, so that it is appropriate for him to look beyond the impending disaster to a new order fulfilling the will of God. In other words, Hosea's words would be less drastic if they did not include a hope. The presence of the promise makes clear that — unlike that of most prophetic announcement — the content of the threats given by him is not avertable. W. Stinespring has correctly stated that we have in the book of Hosea "ten solid chapters of the most devastating denunciation in the Bible[62]." Precisely for this reason, however, an expectation of a new reality is appropriate.

If Hosea foresaw an inevitable doom, what was the aim of his proclamation? Is his message still related to the question of decision? It is possible to argue that Hosea's word was to accompany or execute judgment, that the power-laden word was to be a means in God's hand to destroy Israel. If Israel is an enemy of Yahweh's, such an outlook is easily understood, for oracles against enemies are not ordinarily designed to effect a change of attitude within the ones threatened. While this may be true, Hosea sees the judgment as having a disciplinary purpose. In order for this aim to be effective, it is necessary that the nation is persuaded to recognize its downfall for what it is, namely a divine judgment. Israel's disaster has to be accepted as deserved in order to make a new beginning possible: "Turn, Israel, to Yahweh your God, for you have stumbled in your iniquity" (14 2). The recognition of guilt forms part of the basis of a new life, as expressed in the request, "Take away all our iniquity" (14 3). Stated otherwise, self-judgment means the beginning step of self-transcendence.

Thus the negative structure of man's direction and the positive word of God's purpose are intimately connected with each other and are not to be considered as separate. The promises serve to underline the inescapability of the threats[63], while the threats lead on to a new situation.

IV. THE STRUCTURE OF ESCHATOLOGY

A. Hosea's Conceptual Pattern

The various elements and aspects of Hosea's message combine in what may be called his eschatological perspective. If the announcement of an imminent end and of a new perfect age is a criterion, Hosea

---

phetic intercession is no longer effective to have Yahweh "pass over," or ignore, the sins (Am 7 8 and 8 2; cf. Mi 7 18 and Prov 19 11, as pointed out by Harper).

[62] Crozer Quarterly 27 (1950), 204.

[63] Some Old Testament promises are barely veiled threats against the reigning king or established order, as pointed out already by Hempel, Die althebräische Literatur, 64. Cf. Jer 23 6.

may have been (perhaps alongside Zoroaster) the first "eschatological" prophet[64], so that his system may be of unusual general interest. But instead of adopting an *a priori* definition of eschatology, it is appropriate to examine the central features of Hosea's words, in order to gain an insight into the dynamics of the temporal order in which he lives.

For Hosea's view, one must distinguish several major periods or spheres of events. One period is represented by the time of Israel's beginning or "origin," when Yahweh led Israel out of Egypt or found it in the wilderness[65]. This is followed, or even accompanied, by a history of sin. This history, however, leads to destruction and is to be superseded by another ideal time, a final era. The second ideal time corresponds to the first, according to the well-known principle that end time mirrors original time[66]; it deals, namely, with the fulfillment of the basically intended order. Israel has to be returned to the wilderness, in order there to respond again in a true fashion (2 16. 17 b). Though a new Exodus is not specifically mentioned, it is announced that the nation will be turned back to Egypt, but fortunately not forever.

Egypt represents the ultimate chaos from which Israel was rescued in being created. For purposes of a technical terminology one can speak of such a chaos as Non-being, of the ideal order as Being, and of the deviation from the ideal as Existence. Being triumphs over Non-being but is modified in Existence; Existence tends again toward Non-being but is overcome at that point by a New Being[67]. Other possible terms for Non-being are death or hostility; for Being, life or righteousness or love; for New Being, salvation or reconciliation. In the Old Testament, as in primitive and other religions, true "life" is seen as coming from the divine and available only in a positive relation with deity[68]. Present reality is not equivalent to "life;" rather, it represents a structure based on life but tending toward death.

---

[64] So, once, J. Lindblom, Studia Theologica 6 (1952), 113, and, now, T. Vriezen, De godsdienst van Israël, 180, in wavering positions. The survey of H. Preuss, Jahweglaube und Zukunftserwartung, 1968, in contrast, is based on a concept of the future applicable everywhere.

[65] In the secondary 8 14, Yahweh is called Israel's "maker."

[66] For Old Testament prophecy, this was carefully shown by E. Dietrich, שוב שבות, 1925; M. Hoepers, Der neue Bund bei den Propheten, 1933; E. Rohland, Die Bedeutung der Erwählungstraditionen, Diss. Heidelberg, 1956.

[67] This terminology and conceptualization is similar to, but not identical with, that of P. Tillich, Systematic Theology, 1951—1963; cf. B. Childs, Myth and Reality in the Old Testament, 1960.

[68] See, e. g., J. Lindblom, Das ewige Leben, 1914, 2; R. Martin-Achard, From Death to Life, 1960, 18.

The time of Being, with its perfection, can be designated as a mythological category; the time of Existence, as the realm of imperfect human history[69]. Within such a conceptualization, Being is never strictly historical. That does not necessarily mean that the ideal state is non-worldly, if by world one means the order of bodily reality. Israelite religion has no opposition to the body; on the contrary, it takes the physical order for granted. Israel sees evil within man's voluntary actions rather than in his outside habitat. Thus Old Testament faith is not otherworldly in the sense that a presence on earth is rejected. But the rule of God is contrasted with the willful life of man.

Precisely because Israel sees evil as resting primarily in man himself, rather than in an outside material world, its faith has to oppose human history. The events of the Origin of the covenant grapple with the deviations of the human Past, in which historical figures play the role of chaos to be overcome. While the central interest of Hosea is the sacred community of Israel, he is also clearly aware that the world already had a history before the great saving events. Thus he refers to the Jacob tradition and speaks of God's "calling" Israel out of Egypt (11 1) and his "finding" it in the wilderness (9 10). He must have been at least partially conscious of a previous fall, to which God's work with Israel provided an answer, so that one can perhaps speak in his perspective of a second fall, as the divine covenant itself falls into disorder.

Israel's own rebellious existence involves forgetful satisfaction with Yahweh's feeding (13 6), probably already in the wilderness[70]. It shows itself in false worship as soon as the edge of the cultivated land is reached at Baal-Peor. Its evil is symbolically concentrated at Gilgal (9 15) — and at Adam (6 7) ? — where Israel crossed the Jordan[71]. Social corruption is archetypically represented by the atrocity at Gibea during the time of the Judges (9 9 10 9). The development of cultic constructions and of royalty with self-assertion form the quintessence of willful behavior; these two may be seen together, for royalty has connections with the cult places Gibea (Saul's home), Gilgal (where Saul was made king and where he also was rejected), and Bethel (the royal sanctuary).

---

[69] Similarly also M. Weber op. cit. 4. 69, and, in part, B. Anderson, Creation Versus Chaos, 1967, 164—169.

[70] An early tendency toward evil is rightly emphasized by Ward 69, though denied by G. Coats, Rebellion in the Wilderness, 1968, 206.

[71] See C. Simpson op. cit. 285. 316. 645, for a possible tradition of a crossing near Adam.

Hosea is not directly opposed to residence in Palestine, which he probably regarded as a promised land. But Israel's existence there is characterized by an ironical situation. As the original opposite side of the paradox of a "fortunate fall," Israel experiences an "unfortunate fulfilment." Divine feeding in the wilderness and the realization of promises in Palestine only produce pride (*hybris*) and deviation. "A luxuriant vine [as intended] is Israel, fruit he produces. According to the multitude of his fruit he multiples altars [wrongly]. According to the goodness of his earth [a gift!] he makes good his pillars" (10 1). The woman of Hos 2 credits the wrong persons with the gifts she has received. This inner paradox is a common one in religious traditions; for the creation of man as a being independent of God produces the possibility (indeed inevitability?) of rivalry and opposition. Hosea, who stands both on God's and on man's side, suffers acutely since he recognizes a terrible rift. Yet this rift is also, in a sense, a fortunate situation — in that it can lead to a final, surpassing Good[72].

It is not that the nomadic life of the desert is glorified by Hosea. The desert represents a Sheol in which the creative activity of Yahweh sets up the incipient nation. Israel is to be led again into the desert — either outside of Palestine or within it as a wasted land — in order to be re-created in that state of disorder[73]. Historically, Yahwism was as opposed to nomadic Bedouinism with its emphasis on self-reliance and honor as to Canaanite settled culture[74]. In Hosea, culture and success as such — even as a gift of God — is paradoxically a problem.

His message is thoroughly eschatological in the sense that it envisions a mythological order beyond statehood or human making[75]. The new life indeed will be collective and dedicated to natural welfare; but it will be one thoroughly dominated by Yahweh — just as the mythological order of paradise at creation is centered in the action of deity. The ordinary political function of the prophet is thus tran-

---

[72] One may compare the Hindu expectation that definitive deliverance (*moksha*) is possible only in the world of (evil) men, not in the state of the gods (R. Zaehner, Hinduism, 1962, 82). For Western religions, H. Weisinger, Tragedy and the Paradox of the Fortunate Fall, 1953.

[73] Cf., e. g., H. Ginsberg in: Yehezkel Kaufmann Jubilee Volume, 1960, 66ff.; P. Rieman, Desert and Return to Desert in the Pre-exilic Prophets, Diss. Harvard, 1963/64 (HTR 57 [1964], 391f.).

[74] S. Nyström, Beduinentum und Jahwismus, 1946.

[75] Similarly, G. von Rad, Das Gottesvolk im Deuteronomium, 1929, 83; K. Möbius, Die Aktualität der Eschatologie bei den alttestamentlichen Propheten, 1934, 357; H. Donner, Israel unter den Völkern, 1964, 175f., See Fohrer, Studien, 32—58, for a different terminology.

scended[76]. Not relative guidance within the imperfect historical order but a direction toward an ultimate reality is given. The fact that the new order is conceived in earthly terms should not hide the fact that its paradisiacal form goes beyond anything known to experience and points to a divine kingdom.

The question may be raised whether the promised redemption should not be interpreted literally as an absolutely final occurrence, but should be viewed as an ideological expression more or less deliberately exaggerated in content. That would be analogous to the court-style (*Hofstil*) of the Near East, according to which a king or founder of a dynasty can be spoken of as god or as the savior of mankind. A difference from court style, however, rests in the fact that Hosea's word is genuinely predictive, in the sense that it is not a vaticinium ex eventu which actually refers to the present even though laid on the lips of an earlier seer; its aim is not to praise the present, but to subject it to a divine victory. In any case, Hosea speaks *as if* a decisive End is to occur. It will be seen that such a perspective is intimately connected with his particular sense of life. To appreciate that situation, a theoretical and comparative analysis of eschatological expectations is in order.

B. The Dynamics of Eschatological Expectations

The discussion of Chapter V showed that individual terms were highly emotionally charged. Like all affective expressions, they tended to fall into a negative and a positive grouping. From this one can conclude that religious language is indeed — as has been suggested by some — a form of emotive language[77], and thus also allied to poetry. Emotive language falls into two major categories, norm (or imperative) and evaluation (or feeling for an object); both of these play an important role in faith[78]. It should be noted, however, that not all emotive categories are immediately religious. One must, for instance, make a fundamental distinction between such imperatives as are laid on the outside world for one's own benefit, i. e., in accordance with one's own free will, and such imperatives as are seen as directed

---

[76] For theories, see N. Gottwald, All the Kingdoms of the Earth, 1964. The revolutionary force of a "utopia", unrealized within a given social order, was well pointed out by K. Mannheim, Ideology and Utopia, 1936, 177. 179.

[77] For a cautious semi-objectivist (basically correct?) statement, see R. Hare in B. Mitchell (ed.), Faith and Logic, 1957, 176—193.

[78] See S. Pepper in V. Ferm (ed.), A History of Philosophical Systems, 1950, 493—503; R. Hartman in A. Maslow (ed.), New Knowledge in Human Values, 1959, 20; G. von Wright, The Logic of Preference, 1963, 7.

toward or against oneself; in other words, there are both assertive and receptive evaluations. Assertive statements deal with what some outside reality ought to be, for one's own sake; receptive statements declare what oneself ought to be, from the point of view of what is more absolute than oneself, commonly called the divine[79]. Hosea's emotive terms deal clearly not with an evaluation of extrahuman powers but with an evaluation of Israel — of oneself, if one is identified with it and accepts the message. In essence, then, Hosea's message is characterized by an emotive concern reflexively related to man.

As long as man still has a fundamentally outward concern and is largely at peace with himself as a part of the world, he can find comfort and satisfaction in rituals which provide for periodic renewals and in divinatory procedures which deal primarily with a self-projective future. It should be pointed out that at this stage self-assertion is still largely innocent and merges with the receptive order, since man operates as part of the cosmos and its divine principles[80]. Deliberate and haughty self-assertion is a later development, a thisworldly counterpart to a more transcendent faith. At any rate, in primitive and much of ancient religion ritual renewal, divination, and the integration of an individual life after death[81] form all that is necessary in the way of a religious direction toward the future; fears of a world-destruction or hopes for a possible return of a culture-hero appear only sporadically or remain quite vague[82].

More explicit myths of world destruction and of world renewal occur in societies which exist in a more complex stage. Such visions typically include descriptions of violent social evils which are similar to the wholesale denunciation of major Old Testament prophets. Thus Hindu theories of the last evil age in a cycle describe men as altogether full of lies, injustice, theft, adultery, low aim, as having an evil heart and lacking observance or proper inner attention to rituals[83]. In some Buddhist systems, a savior comes at the time when there is general moral and physical deterioration, with universal enmity[84]. The Nordic epic of an End predicts fighting among

---

[79] Very similarly, A. Koestler, The Act of Creation, 1964, 54. 273; in different terminology, E. Fromm, You Shall Be as Gods, A Radical Interpretation of the Old Testament, 1966, 59.

[80] Already G. Oehler, Über das Verhältnis der alttestamentlichen Prophetie zur heidnischen Mantik, 1861, emphasized the element of communion in manticism.

[81] The dead reappear at festivals, as reported by B. Malinowski, Baloma, Journal of the Royal Anthropological Institute 46 (1916), reprinted in Magic, Science and Religion and Other Essays, 1955.

[82] A. van Deursen, Der Heilbringer, 1931; C. Edsman, RGG³, II 650—655; M. Eliade, Myth and Reality, 1963, 54—60; F. Kamma, De Messiaanse Koreri-bewegingen, 1954, 41; W. Koppers, Saeculum 10 (1959), 43.

[83] E. g., E. Abegg, Der Messiasglaube in Indian und Iran, 1928, 28. 33.

[84] Ibid. 150. Similarly for the Near East, Reicke op. cit. 357—360 (above, p. 89).

brothers, adultery, and a generally evil world[85]. In the last age, according to Hesiod, fathers and children, guest and host, companions and brothers fight each other; oaths are not kept, might is right, envy rules[86]. Other examples of such expectations could be cited, for instance in Rome and in Persia. Hosea views such evils as currently present and sees himself as living just before the end of the historical era.

Egyptian tradition experienced severe social disorder toward the end of the third millenium B. C.; that situation led to denunciations, exhortations, and announcements, which seem to have influenced the form and content of Israelite prophecy, as noted for Hosea. The establishment of order thereafter in the Egyptian Middle Kingdom seems to have led to an experience of profound relief; the consequent motif of national salvation may also have left an eventual mark on Old Testament religion[87]. The Egyptian Book of the Dead (ch. 175) declares, in a rare approximation of a full-scale eschatology, that at the end the Creator Atum remains alone in the water as at the beginning. Mesopotamian texts feature descriptions of good and bad periods[88], which probably have left their imprint on Old Testament prophecy. One set of Akkadian apocalypses describes past good and bad reigns (the latter with strife, famine, destruction of sanctuaries, etc.) as though they are future and ends apparently in a somewhat vague future hope[89]. The Babylonian Erra Epic describes a universal catastrophe, to be followed by a world leadership by Babylon; but it has a ritual use for repeated application[90]. An unclear fragmentary text of doom describing moral evil with family strife and political dissensions may reflect a time when Babylonia was threatened by Assyria[91]. Despite certain inner tensions, Near Eastern society remained sufficiently secure in the hands of heroic or aristocratic figures, such as a king, to remain fundamentally thisworldly. A similar perspective pervaded Homeric religion and Brahmanism, at a comparable stage of culture.

A more shattering and transcending eschatological perspective comes somewhat later. Zoroastrianism made a human struggle between good and evil leading to an imminent End its central theme. Within Hinduism, the theory of *moksha* — free release from the cycle of life — developed to set forth a hope of transcending imperfect existence. Buddhism made such transcendence the central aim of its religious practices. Some Buddhists, especially Nichiren with a relatively pragmatic perspective, expected a speedy overthrow and redemption of the present evil reality[92]. Especially on a popular level, there are strong hopes for a future (Hindu) Krishna or Vishnu[93] or a coming Buddha; on central Asian mountains, "Come, Maitreya, come!" is inscribed[94]. In China, the idealistic lower-class Mo-tzŭ expected a future Golden Age

[85] E. Mudrak, Nordische Götter- und Helden-Sagen, 1961, 65.
[86] Works and Days, lines 180—200.
[87] See ANET 407—410. 441—446; G. Lanczkowski, Altägyptischer Prophetismus, 1960.
[88] E. g., H. Güterbock, ZA 42 (1934), 1—61.
[89] ANET 451f.; A. Grayson and W. Lambert, Journal of Cuneiform Studies 18 (1964), 7—30; W. Hallo, Israel Exploration Journal 16 (1966), 231—242.
[90] So, B. Meißner, Babylonien und Assyrien, II 1925, 186f.; Guillaume op. cit. 50—52.
[91] AOT 230f.; Gressmann, JTS 27 (1926), 250.
[92] E. g., J. Pratt, The Pilgrimage of Buddhism, 1928, 488f.; M. Anesaki, History of Japanese Religion, 1930, 201.
[93] A. Jeremias, Die außerbiblische Erlösererwartung, 1927, 252; Abegg op. cit. 144 (etc.).
[94] E. Conze, Buddhist Scriptures, 1959, 237.

contrasting sharply with present systems[95]. In short, decisive individual or collective eschatologies develop in connection with a sense of the problematics of the human situation. The more desperate and disturbed the human order appears — especially sharply felt in the more developed religions — the stronger is an expectation of an End[96].

A special test case is furnished by so-called "messianic movements" of recent times. In primitive societies threatened with ideological dissolution through contact with the modern world strong hopes for a decisive renewal and restoration have frequently arisen. Expectations usually involve a more or less passive — frequently an ecstatic — waiting for an imminent divine salvation. Not an achievement-oriented goal-directedness, but a receptive relation to the speedy coming of a paradisiacal good, characterizes their attitude, which can thus be properly termed an eschatological one[97]. There are indications that such a "foolish" approach — from a pragmatic standpoint — is closely related to a disorder in the society's value system and self-concept[98]. Generally speaking, it appears that pure physical hardship, unaccompanied by moral malaise, does not lead to a "messianic" movement; for it is spiritual or cultural disorder to which such eschatological hopes respond.

Chiliastic expectations have flourished among disadvantaged and confused groups within larger societies[99]. Both primitive and lowerclass movements are often led by a charismatic prophet who receives divine revelations about deliverance. Sometimes these groups expect to be able to hasten the End through a moral reformation of their own lives; their most powerful feeling, however, is one of violent opposition to an outgroup which is to be destroyed[100]. Therein they differ from Hosea, whose central point is repentance rather than miraculous self-justification.

In harmony, however, with this radical tradition, at the beginning of which he stands, Hosea announces an imminent End. Nearness expresses the intensity of the expectation; it thus is correlated with the depth of the disorder felt in the present situation[101]. Nearness is especially appropriate for a hope which deals with an element felt

---

[95] See, e. g., H. Rowley, Prophecy and Religion in Ancient Israel and China, 1956, 90f.

[96] H. Janke, Das Eschaton als Sinnverwirklichung, 1938; for the Hellenistic world, e. g., Nilsson op. cit. 142 (above, p. 118).

[97] See, e. g., W. Stanner, The South Seas in Transition, 1953, 67f.; K. Read, Southwestern Journal of Anthropology 14 (1958), 273f. On immobility caused in an organism by lack of confidence in its ability to accomplish something, see O. Mowrer, Learning Theory and Behavior, 1960, 197. 272. 458f.

[98] F. Voget, Man 59 (1959), 27; W. Mühlmann (ed.), Chiliasmus und Nativismus, 1961, 11f. 94. 205; F. Sierksma, Een Nieuwe Hemel en een Nieuwe Aarde, 1961, 257; S. Thrupp (ed.), Millenial Dreams in Action, 1962, 26. 214; V. Lanternari, The Religions of the Oppressed, 1963, 57. 308. Influence from "higher" religions is usually also present.

[99] E. g., A. Hübscher, Die Große Weissagung, 1952; N. Cohn, The Pursuit of the Millenium, 1957; A. Silver, A History of Messianic Speculation in Israel, 1927 (1959).

[100] E. g., B. Wilson, Sects and Society, 1961, 318f.

[101] On tension as a function of psychological nearness, D. Snygg and A. Combs, Individual Behavior, 1949, 109.

to be beyond one's own control, when there is no possibility of an emotional release in the process of working toward the desired end. A spiritual malaise is not only devastating in its effect but also not easily seen as amenable to remedial efforts; for how can one change one's own human reality? At any rate, in Hosea the rapidly approaching End is closely related to the moral and spiritual evil of which he accuses the nation. It is possible that some of the less well-known "hope-prophets" of Israel expected a distant ideal age, but Hosea differed sharply from such a comfortable view.

Eschatology can be described in terms of a solution of the contradiction between what is (history) and what ought to be (the mythological order)[102]. If the disorder is slight, periodic ritual regeneration is sufficient. A deepened sense of contradiction may underlie large-scale cyclical systems or views of long-range developments in history. A catastrophic anomie, however, expresses itself in the expectation of an impending overthrow. Just as a "goal-tension" in organismic and ordinary human life expresses the difference between desire and possession, so an "eschatological tension" describes symbolically the divergence between one's historical self-definition or humiliation and an ideal state.

It should be clear from earlier analysis that a severe tension is not simply the result of unfavorable external conditions, even though these may play a contributory role. Accordingly, End-expectations in Israel are not primarily the result of a political disappointment in the time of the Assyrian or Babylonian exile. They are more specifically a function of an extreme moral and religious sensitivity, connected with an overwhelming sense of the divine, evident in a prophet like Hosea. Although circumstantial factors undoubtedly contributed to the message, the word of the doom prophets represents an awakening of a more fully personal or self-conscious form of life, with a strong sense of responsibility[103]. Of course, even in his message, evil is seen not as lying within the prophetic speaker himself, but somewhat outside him in the community of Israel.

The expectation of Hosea is related to the patient waiting and hoping which is a central theme in the literature of wisdom and

---

[102] So, G. Oehler, Theology of the Old Testament, II 1875, 363—381; T. Manson, The Teaching of Jesus, 1931, 247; P. Volz, Der eschatologische Glaube im Alten Testament, 1935, 2; J. Moltmann, Theologie der Hoffnung, 1965, 243 (partly with E. Bloch, Das Prinzip Hoffnung, 1959, whose orientation, however, is more to the Future than to the End, even though the latter's role in religion is recognized).

[103] Political elements of disappointment are overemphasized by S. Mowinckel, Psalmenstudien II, 317; He That Cometh, 142; A. Bentzen, King and Messiah, 1955, 79.

psalmody[104]. In these traditions, however, waiting is for divine deliverance within the present order of reality and is closely related
to self-enhancement (with enemies lying on the outside); more precisely, in their structure the human and the divine projections do not
fall apart, but rather lie together fairly harmoniously. But Hosea's
orientation is one of overwhelming conflict between man and God.

The words of a man like Hosea were too sharp in their denunciation, and too radical in their announcement of an End, to be accepted fully by main-line Judaism which was centered in an on-going
religio-political community and which placed a certain emphasis on
human ethical achievement[105]. On the other hand, Hosea's message
is not equivalent to the Christian; his announcement is one of nearness
and not one of the presence of the End. He places greater demand on
human turning than does the Christian, for salvation is a promise
rather than a reality to be believed[106].

C. Future and End in Human Life and the Question of Love

End-expectations have clearly an important place in human life,
especially in so far as that is religious. It is important, then, to see
both the similarity and the distinction between this object of concern
and what may be called Future-directedness in a specific sense.
Future and End have this in common as categories, that they presuppose actuality and deal with its problems and lacks. In both of
them, in other words, positive or negative evils are an important
ground of operation. Both categories are an outgrowth of, or a response
to, the present situation, with a dynamism that depends on the present's instability and insufficiency. Both require human decision,
though in the End-expectation the choice means an acceptance of
Being rather than a provision for some possible form of imperfect
and ego-centric Existence. There is a difference in that Future-
directedness operates with exertion and foresight, with self-projection
and realization of possibility. The End, however, is approached with
openness to the divine, in which there is an eternal joy. In a loose

---

[104] C. Westermann, Theologia Viatorum 4 (1953), 19—70; J. van der Ploeg, RB 61
(1954), 481—507. Hos 12 7 probably is cultic wisdom of Bethel.

[105] The Talmud criticizes Isaiah for calling Israel an unclean people (Yebamoth 49b).
Y. Kaufmann, The Religion of Israel, 1960, 135. 430. 436, etc., quite properly
points out that some prophets exaggerate the sinfulness of their contemporaries.
That the prophets are simply too impractical for Existence is recognized by
I. Friedlaender, Past and Present, 1961, 69.

[106] Partly with M. Buber, The Prophetic Faith, 1949, 124, who, however, views the
prophets too much within the Israelite order.

manner of speaking, one may be able to continue to use the term "future" for both of these dimensions, in a sense continuing the original general meaning of "arrival" for French *avenir* and German *Zukunft*, but such a use has an archaic ring.

Like the category of Beginning or Origin, the Eschaton is an ultimate structure containing infinity — especially an infinity of value, that is, a state of perfection. While the Origin contains the basic power and norm of the ultimate good, the End wrestles with the evil of Existence and overcomes it as a supreme reaction to it[107]. To be in touch with infinity, one must necessarily relate oneself to it receptively[108]. The style of divine speech is a fitting symbol to embody both an imperative laid upon one and a divine victory over the self.

Future-directedness seeks a continuation and enhancement of finite reality. It thus leads ultimately to death, as reflective thinkers in general, from Near Eastern wisdom to modern philosophy, have recognized. In Hosea's style, Israel's directionality toward destruction is appropriately expressed in non-divine speech. That same form also concretizes Hosea's hope into a semipolitical expectation (2 1-3 3 4f. 11 10f.), toward what may be called a social future.

The phenomenon of selfhood in this regard is a complex one, for the object of an action or word is to be distinguished from its subject. Self-projection has the ego for its subject, not for its object of concern; it looks outward onto the world to be conquered rather than inward to the self to be changed. In contrast to this, eschatological salvation, which is centered in the divine, relates to a self which is questioned[109]; it seeks what one can "be" rather than what one can "have[110]." A. Heschel thus designated divine speech, because of its object, by the term "anthropopathy," i. e., feeling for man[111]. Indeed, selfhood finds a fulfillment in self-transcendence within the divine or the eternal, as

---

[107] Similarly, T. Cossmann, Die Entwicklung des Gerichtsgedankens bei den alttestamentlichen Propheten, 1915, 1. In the conceptualization of P. Althaus, Die letzten Dinge, 1926³, 15. 20, "axiological" eschatology plays the role of Origin, while "teleological" eschatology is closer to Future than to End.

[108] A. Maslow has properly noted that "Being-cognition" (an experience of creative fullness) is receptive and ego-transcending in character (Journal of Genetic Psychology 94 [1959], 43—66; Toward a Psychology of Being, 1962, 74. 81); the contrasting "Deficiency-cognition" is closely related to the category of the Future. Similarly, O. Bollnow, Das Wesen der Stimmungen, 1943², 158. Also the Buddha opposed self-salvation through asceticism, according to F. Manthey, Das Problem der Erlösung in den Religionen der Menschheit, 1964, 224f.

[109] J. Wach, Der Erlösungsgedanke und seine Deutung, 1922, 12.

[110] In the terminology of H. Jonas, Augustin und das paulinische Freiheitsproblem, 1930, 63f. Cf. S. Freud, Group Psychology, Ch. VII (Standard Edition, XVIII 1935, 106).   [111] The Prophets 268.

often expressed in great literature[112]. The concept of the self, it must be emphasized, is not an individualistic but rather a social one; for reflexivity is possible only in a context of reciprocity between persons; it is here even applied to the community as a whole.

While Future and End can be distinguished as different movements of human life, they must in some way be related to each other. At one point, in fact, the distinction between them commonly breaks down, namely in the experience of sexuality. Abandonment in love contains an element of timelessness, even while it involves an object-love related to biological self-projection. Such love relations form a natural focus for religious structures in which man and God are felt as reasonably harmonious, as in Canaanite Baalism. Israelite religion, with a strongly personal-moral structure containing considerable elements of guilt, did not recognize a continuing harmony between man, nature, and God. Erotic rituals are therefore condemned as harlotry, especially so by Hosea. Israelite faith instead emphasizes divine speech which embodies, in psychological terms, a father figure or Super-ego, providing both a law and a salvation to be humbly received. An overwhelming eschatology has often been skeptical of sexuality, as a possible diversion from a serious view of reality[113], except as the eschaton is concretized into the present.

In Hosea, Future and End are related to each other ironically, for the directionality toward death leads into redemption, not automatically but by a divine doing accepted by man. A complex approach is revealed in his extensive and varied use of sexual emotion and terminology[114]. A negative side of such an emotion is felt in the declaration of enmity between man and God. But positive love then triumphs mysteriously. For Hosea deity is like an ancient husband at once master and lover, so that punishment leads on to tender healing.

Hosea's prophetic word points to a reconciliation which incorporates, but goes beyond, a consciousness of personal reality with a sense of responsibility and alienation. In dialectical terminology, it is a negation of the negation. It does not ignore a condition of tension, but having pictured reality in the blackest terms possible, it goes on to announce a victory beyond. It offers an ecstasy of joy beyond anguish, challenging the hearer to an openness toward love.

---

[112] See, e. g., W. Lynch, Christ and Apollo, 1960, 34f.; M. Buss, Journal of Religion 45 (1965), 46—53.

[113] For an effort to deal with this, see W. Schubert, Religion und Eros, 1944.

[114] The word "love" both positively and derogatively is quite common in Hosea, with a more or less sexual overtone (3 1 4 18 9 1. 15 11 1 12 8 14 5, as discussed by C. Wiener, Recherches sur l'amour pour Dieu dans l'Ancien Testament, 1957, 26—30). Allwohn op. cit. 75 has seen that Hosea synthesizes Baalistic pleasure with Yahwist rigour.

Index

A. *Index of Selected Exegetical Discussions*

B. *Index of Deviations from the Form of Closely Knit Quatrains*

C. Index of Selected Hebrew Words

Beihefte
zur Zeitschrift für die alttestamentliche Wissenschaft

Herausgegeben von Georg Fohrer

Zuletzt erschienen:

Studien zur alttestamentlichen Prophetie (1949—1965). Von G. Fohrer. XII, 303 Seiten. 1967. Ganzleinen DM 60,— (Heft 99)

Jüdische Lehre und Frömmigkeit in den paralipomena Jeremiae. Von G. Delling. VIII, 77 Seiten. 1967. Ganzleinen DM 24,— (Heft 100)

Wesen und Geschichte der Weisheit. Eine Untersuchung zur altorientalischen und israelitischen Weisheitsliteratur. Von H.-H. Schmid. XIV, 250 Seiten. 1966. Ganzleinen DM 52,— (Heft 101)

Nehemia. Quellen, Überlieferung und Geschichte. Von U. Kellermann. XII, 227 Seiten. 1967. Ganzleinen DM 50,— (Heft 102)

In Memoriam Paul Kahle. Herausgegeben von M. Black und G. Fohrer. VIII, 253 Seiten. Mit 1 Titelbild und 20 Tafeln. 1968. Ganzleinen DM 86,— (Heft 103)

Das Königtum in Israel. Ursprünge, Spannungen, Entwicklung. Von J. A. Soggin. X, 167 Seiten. 1967. Ganzleinen DM 36,— (Heft 104)

Das ferne und nahe Wort. Festschrift Leonhard Rost zur Vollendung seines 70. Lebensjahres am 30. XI. 1966 gewidmet. Im Auftrag der Mitarbeiter herausgegeben von F. Maass. Mit 1 Frontispiz. VIII, 275 Seiten. 1967. Ganzleinen DM 62,— (Heft 105)

Yariḫ und Nikkal und der Preis der Kuṯarāt-Göttinnen. Ein kultisch-magischer Text aus Ras Schamra. Von W. Herrmann. X, 48 Seiten. Mit 1 Tafel. 1968. DM 18,— (Heft 106)

The Samaritan Chronicle II or: Sepher Ha-Yamim from Joshua to Nebuchadnezzar. Edited and translated by J. Macdonald. Etwa 320 Seiten. 1969. Etwa DM 70,—. Im Druck (Heft 107)

The Problem of Etiological Narrative in the Old Testament. By B. O. Long. VIII, 94 Seiten. 1968. Ganzleinen DM 24,— (Heft 108)

Ursprünge und Strukturen alttestamentlicher Eschatologie. Von H.-P. Müller. XII, 232 Seiten. 1969. Ganzleinen DM 46,— (Heft 109)

Mose. Überlieferung und Geschichte. Von H. Schmid. VIII, 113 Seiten. 1968. Ganzleinen DM 32,— (Heft 110)

Text und Textform im hebräischen Sirach. Untersuchungen zur Textgeschichte und Textkritik der hebräischen Sirachfragmente aus der Kairoer Geniza. Von H. P. Rüger. Etwa 144 Seiten. 1969. Ganzleinen etwa DM 46,—. In Vorbereitung (Heft 112)

Die Wurzel שלם im Alten Testament. Von W. Eisenbeis. Etwa 416 Seiten. In Vorbereitung (Heft 113)

Das Todesrecht im Alten Testament. Von H. Schulz. Etwa 232 Seiten. Ganzleinen etwa DM 56,—. In Vorbereitung (Heft 114)

Studien zur alttestamentlichen Theologie und Geschichte (1949—1966). Von G. Fohrer. Etwa 320 Seiten. 1969. Ganzleinen etwa DM 76,—. In Vorbereitung (Heft 115)

Lieferungsmöglichkeiten und Preise der früheren Hefte auf Anfrage

---

Verlag Alfred Töpelmann · Berlin 30

Julius Wellhausen

Die kleinen Propheten

Übersetzt und erklärt
4., unveränderte Auflage. Oktav. VIII, 222 Seiten. 1963.
Ganzleinen DM 28,—

Julius Wellhausen

Israelitische und Jüdische Geschichte

9. Auflage. Oktav. VIII, 371 Seiten. 1958.
Ganzleinen DM 19,80

Abraham Schalit

König Herodes

Der Mann und sein Werk

Die deutsche Ausgabe ist eine vom Verfasser überarbeitete und bedeutend erweiterte Fassung
des 1960 im Bialik-Institut, Jerusalem, erschienenen hebräischen Originals. Die Übersetzung
der hebräischen Originalfassung wurde von Jehoshua Amir besorgt.

Groß-Oktav. XVI, 890 Seiten. Mit 1 Frontispiz, 8 Bildtafeln, 4 Karten und 1 Stammtafel.
1969. Ganzleinen DM 148,—
(Studia Judaica Band 4)

Arnold M. Goldberg

Untersuchungen über die Vorstellung von der Schekhinah in der frühen rabbinischen Literatur

Groß-Oktav. XII, 564 Seiten. 1969. Ganzleinen DM 72,—
(Studia Judaica Band 5)

Johannes Hempel

Die althebräische Literatur und ihr hellenistisch-jüdisches Nachleben

Quart. 203 Seiten mit Abbildungen und Tafeln. 1930
Nachdruck 1968. Ganzleinen DM 36,—
(Mit Genehmigung des Athenaion-Verlages)

Walter de Gruyter & Co · Berlin 30